Beyond the Pampas

Beyond the Pampas

In Search of Patagonia

Imogen Rhia Herrad

SEREN

Seren is the book imprint of
Poetry Wales Press Ltd
Nolton Street, Bridgend, Wales

www.serenbooks.com
facebook.com/SerenBooks
Twitter: @SerenBooks

ISBN 978-1-85411-591-1
E-pub 978-1-85411-609-3
Kindle 978-1-78172-012-7

A CIP record for this title is available from
the British Library

The publisher works with the financial assistance
of the Welsh Books Council

Printed by Short Run Press, Exeter

Beyond the Pampas

In Search of Patagonia

Prelude

IT REVEALS ITSELF SLOWLY. At first there is just the land, flat as a plate under the huge blue sky. The earth is a bare, dusty brown. Not much grows here except for scrubby greygreen bushes.

Rocky hills appear on the horizon, brown and copper and gold. Slowly they close in on both sides until they hold me as if in cupped hands. The sunlight is hot and piercing, the air dry and clear. There is no sound except for occasional bird calls; the rustling of the wind in the long, dry grass stalks; my footsteps. Then, slowly, the rush and whisper of water: I'm near the river now. Trees appear: poplars and willows. The dry air turns softer and cooler and smells of water. There is uneven grassland with rocky outcrops in brown and gold.

This is where the first canal branches off from the River Chubut. They dug it without the help of machines.

The water rushes before me, blue and foaming white. I try to imagine what it would have been like here more than a hundred years ago. The valley would have looked much the same: half-wild, greygreen and brown and copper red. From where I stand – where they once stood with their picks and shovels – it is more than forty miles to their farms, to the first Welsh settlement on the coast by the mouth of the river. The nearest town was four hundred miles to the north. There were no roads. Wales, on the other side of the Atlantic Ocean, might as well have been on the moon.

What was it like back then for James Davies, Anne Freeman, Joseph Jones, Gwenllian Thomas, Mary Evans, Griffith Griffiths, John Morgan, in this huge empty land where everything looked different, sounded different, smelt different? They worked the land, made bricks out of clay, built houses, traded with the Indians, held *nosau lawen*, baked bread, gave birth, buried their dead, wrote infrequent letters home. They dug miles of canals by hand. Irrigated with water channelled from the river, the dry crumbly soil of the valley proved fruitful beyond anybody's wildest hopes.

What was it like back then, in this not-so-empty land, for Chikichan and Sayhueke, for Foyel, Agar, Francisco, Inakayal: the

Tehuelche, Mapuche and Pampas Indians who had lived here for millennia? What did they think when the pale strangers appeared and built houses and showed every sign of settling down?

The success of the settlement of Patagonia started here, at the end of the wide river valley, where first the rocky hills and then the desert takes over: miles and miles and miles of dry brown land, stark and beautiful and empty of everything but dust and brush-wood and the cool whistling wind that never, ever stops.

Before

1

THE FIRST TIME I WENT to Patagonia, I didn't know a soul there. I only meant to go once, just for a couple of weeks, to look at the place. I didn't know that it would work its way under my skin until I would always be homesick for it, always come back to it. I didn't know that it was going to change me, draw me out of myself and out of my orbit. I had fallen in love with Patagonia from afar: with the story of the people who had left Wales a century and a half ago to follow a dream and live in this place on the other side of the earth.

I had thought of the place only as *Y Wladfa*: the place of the Welsh settlement. Over time, I came to know its other inhabitants, those who had been there before the Welsh, and who are still there today: the indigenous Tehuelche and Mapuche nations. Entirely unprepared, I stumbled upon their history, a seldom-told story of genocide five generations ago. I met freedom fighters and trauma-tised survivors of ethnic cleansing; men and women determined that their culture should not die, whatever the odds.

I could not have foreseen where this journey would eventually take me as I travelled ever further into Patagonia: to a night by an open fire under the stars, deep in the foothills of the Andes.

All of this began in the late 1980s in Aberystwyth, where I had gone to live for a year.

I'm German. I was born and grew up in Germany, and like a lot of my compatriots have a fascination for things Celtic. As a child I read Irish fairy tales and Celtic legends, and dreamed of fair maidens, green hills, fierce witches, noble warriors.

So when the time came to choose my subjects at university, and there was the option to take Celtic Studies as a minor subject, I went for it straight away. What Celtic Studies might be, I couldn't have said. I vaguely imagined in-depth readings of more Celtic tales, more maidens, witches, warriors etc.

What I got instead was a branch of comparative linguistics. It was a tiny department, made up of some ten students and one and a half lecturers. The half lecturer travelled from a neighbouring university city for two days a week. Sometimes he brought his wife's small, fluffy shi-tzu dog, which would sit on the table in front of him and regard us all gravely. Most of the other students had Early and Pre-History as their major subject. They played the fiddle or the flute in their spare time and sported beards and long hair. Nobody displayed any practical bent whatsoever. We studied aspects of contemporary and mediaeval Welsh and Irish. Unexpectedly, I found that I enjoyed etymology, grammar and general linguistic hairsplitting very much.

A couple of years later I got the chance to spend a year in Britain as a Foreign Language Assistant. I didn't, like everybody else, choose London. I plumped for rural Wales, because I'd been there on holiday the year before, and had, in the space of less than a week, fallen utterly in love with the place. There was something about the grandiose beauty of the mountains that sent shivers up my spine. It was a totally new and unfamiliar landscape, and at the same time one I felt instantly at home in.

I was fascinated by the weirdly spelled place-names on bilingual signposts. Could there really be a place called Llwchwr? These names seemed to betoken the presence of not just another language, but a whole other layer of reality. Who, after all, spoke Welsh? But in shops and pubs in Wales, I heard people converse in Welsh, over their groceries or a pint. Nobody had told me that the language was still alive today. The Celtic Studies people had only mentioned Gaelic in Ireland. There seemed to be a mystery about Welsh somehow. In this small land beyond England, beyond the mountains, they had kept a language for the initiated.

I discovered that it was possible to join the initiated. A two-month, intensive Welsh course ran every summer. I decided to go on the course, then spend a year teaching German in the schools of the coastal town of Aberystwyth. It would be a splendidly eccentric thing to do. Also, perhaps the language would come in handy in the classroom.

It did. There I was, in my first week in the Welsh-language comprehensive, in my classroom with five fourth-formers earnestly practising reflexive German verbs, while outside raged what appeared to be a tornado. The first-form teacher had not yet arrived to unlock his classroom, and the corridor was awash with small children making a hell of a racket. I marched to the door, flung it open, stuck my head out and shouted, '*Beth sy'n bod te?*' What's going on here?

The effect was most gratifying: total, stunned silence. Then a shocked little voice said: 'She speaks *Welsh*!'

It was in Aberystwyth that I first heard of Patagonia.

'*Bydd rhywun yn siarad am Batagonia yn y coleg heno!*' my flatmate told me, excitedly, one evening. There'll be somebody in the college giving a talk about Patagonia tonight.

I gave her a blank look. Patagonia, what was that? Could you eat it? Read it? Could you wear it?

'Patagonia! In Argentina,' she explained impatiently. 'Right at the southern end of South America. There's Welsh people living there. Welsh speakers.'

I was doing something else that night, so I didn't go to the talk, but from then on, the Welsh speakers at the very end of the South American continent stayed in my mind, for years. I thought of them as a mythical people on an old map, living in a place that nobody had ever come back from.

It was on that day in Aberystwyth that I began to dream of going to Patagonia. Just to see what it was like.

East

2

MORE THAN A DECADE LATER, I walk up the steps to a jumbo jet bound for Buenos Aires. I am as nervous as hell. I can't believe that my dream is finally coming true. We fly through the night and I am so excited I can't sleep for most of it. Morning comes just as the plane begins its descent to Buenos Aires. The city lies beneath us in the early morning dark, streetlights glittering like a huge golden cobweb. A glowing streak of red in the sky shows where the sun is beginning to rise.

I am to meet a Patagonian in Buenos Aires. Someone in Wales has given me the email address of somebody in Patagonia, who has given me the phone number of Lisa James, a native Welsh speaker from Patagonia who has been living in Buenos Aires for many years. Somehow, she has already heard about me when I ring her from London, and she says she'll be delighted to meet me and show me the city.

I only have one day in Buenos Aires. Tomorrow morning, I'm off again on a plane down south. I'm not interested in Buenos Aires. Or Argentina, for that matter. Not yet. I am single-mindedly obsessed with the Welsh of Patagonia. I have learnt only a handful of Spanish words. To communicate, I will have to get by in Welsh.

There she is: a small, grey-haired, energetic woman.

'*Croeso i Buenos Aires!*'

I get a kiss on the cheek and we're off. I am jet-lagged and tired. I feel as though there is a duvet wrapped round my head. Buenos Aires passes by in a blur of palm trees and hot sunshine, beautiful nineteenth century buildings, tree-lined avenues, thin women, screeching green parakeets in a park, cafés where they serve the most wonderful coffee: hot, sweet, bitter.

There is a red pillar box. I rub my eyes.

'Lisa... tell me I'm not seeing a British post box.'

'It's an Argentinian post box,' Lisa says kindly. 'Look, it says *Correo Argentino* on the side.'

For a moment, I am disappointed in Buenos Aires. I have come all the way to the other side of the world, and they have the same post boxes as in Britain.

Next morning, I'm in the air again, flying south: to Patagonia, at last.

We come in to land in the little airport of Trelew. And then I stand in the hot sunshine on the dry, dusty airfield, craning my neck to see beyond the fence, to get my first real glimpse of the arid brown Patagonian steppe. The air is cooler and drier here than in Buenos Aires. It smells not of car exhaust and people, but of large open spaces: of the desert.

I have arrived.

Gaiman, the main Welsh town in the region, seems to be hiding behind large hoardings erected by the roadside, ready to spring on unsuspecting visitors. All of the hoardings advertise the presence of tea shops. There are five of them, and they all have Welsh names: *Tŷ Cymraeg* (Welsh House), *Casa de Té Gaiman* (Gaiman Tea Shop), *Plas y Coed* (Wood Court), *Tŷ Nain* (Grandma's House), *Tŷ Té Caerdydd* (The Cardiff Tea Shop). 'Lady Diana Spencer took tea here!', the last proclaims proudly.

I see them from Jorge's car. Jorge Oliveira is married to Natalia Evans who runs *Ar Lan yr Afon* (Riverside), the Welsh-speaking B&B where I'll be staying in Gaiman. He has given me a lift from the airport. Jorge originally comes from the far north of Argentina, but he has begun to learn the strange tongue his wife's folk speak. Natalia Evans is a native of Gaiman and bilingual, which comes in handy for running the B&B. They get a lot of Welsh visitors.

Gaiman's main street is about four lanes wide and almost empty. There are dusty pick-up trucks, kids on bicycles, dogs dozing in the shade, shop fronts and flowering shrubs and single-storey brick houses. Everything is covered with a thin film of whitish dust. The dry air smells of it. Between the houses I glimpse a line of tall poplars. Sunlight glints on water where the river winds its way through the town. There is a profusion of flowers on the *plaza* – the main square – and behind it, a beautiful little Spanish-style church.

Away from *la plaza*, everything looks slightly U.S. American to me, like a scene from a road movie: the wide, empty street, the big cars; the big, *big*, flat landscape. The road out of Gaiman leads long and straight all the way to the horizon. I feel as though I've landed in Marlboro country, only the cowboys are missing.

It's the siesta hour, hot and quiet, and virtually the whole town is indoors, resting. So should I be, but only a locked door would keep me inside. It took me more than a decade to get to Patagonia and I want to go out and look at it.

Dogs sleep in the shade. I'm the only person abroad on the wide empty *avenida* (the high street). Nobody stirs in the narrower – but still wide – side streets with their single-storey houses, their gardens colourful with flowers. The shops on the high street are all closed: the supermarket, the two greengrocers, three bakeries, the pharmacy, the clothes shop; even the petrol station. I feel as though I'm wandering through Sleeping Beauty's castle.

Beautiful old red-brick houses line *la avenida*, their front windows coyly draped by snow-white net curtains. Low trees line the side streets. The dark green of their leaves and the pastel red of the weathered brick make refreshing splashes of colour in the grey and brown expanse of the autumnal steppe.

When the town comes back to life, I go for a cup of tea. I want to see one of those much-advertised Patagonian tea shops for myself. My Welsh-language guide book recommends *Casa de Té Tŷ Nain*, where – it says – Welsh is spoken, and there is a small exhibition about the first Welsh settlers. *Casa de Té* is Spanish for tea shop; *Tŷ Nain* Welsh for 'Grandma's House'.

The door is locked, but a faded hand-written sign says – I think – 'Please ring bell' in Spanish. I ring. Nothing happens. Maybe I have misunderstood the sign? Finally I can hear footsteps, and then the door is opened by a woman with black and white hair, an apron and a slow smile.

'*Buenas tardes.*' Good afternoon.

I use for the first time what will be my standard Spanish-language sentence here: '*Por favor, ¿habla usted galés?*' Do you speak Welsh please?

'*O... typyn bach,*' she says. A little bit.

I explain that I'm interested in the history of the Welsh settlers. And in a cup of tea.

'Of course!' she says. 'Come in!'

She bustles off, and I can hear banging and rattling of crockery in what is presumably the kitchen. Two grandfather clocks tick loudly. Then the loudspeakers crackle and a Welsh choir bursts into song.

It is comparatively cool indoors after the heat outside. The air smells cosily of dust; domestic dust, not the scent of the wide open spaces that reigns outside. I'm reminded of a second-hand bookshop. The walls are covered with old photographs, assorted tools, two ancient telephones: the first of their kind in Patagonia, the sign next to them proclaims proudly. By the front door hangs, ceremonially behind glass, a complicated family tree that traces its roots back all the way to the proprietors' Welsh forefathers and foremothers – including the places they came from. The names of new arrivals in the family, born after the family tree was framed, have been written on pieces of paper stuck on the glass.

The woman comes back, bearing a large teapot in a red, hand-crocheted tea-cosy. She is followed by her husband. They introduce themselves as Mirna Jones de Ferrari and Rubén Ferrari. Rubén doesn't speak much Welsh, Mirna explains, but knows a lot about the history of the Welsh in Argentina. She bustles off and returns with a tray full of cakes, bread-and-butter and cheese.

'This is *teisen du, torta negra*: black cake, a fruit cake with raisins soaked in brandy. Very nice.' I believe her at once. 'That's a cream cake with chocolate – the Welsh like sweet things, you know. Then there's apple pie, lemon cake and scones. And bread-and-butter.'

I have never seen a tea like it in Wales. I've never had a tea like this in my life, anywhere in the world. The bread is home-made and wonderful. The cream cake tastes of paradise. (Later, I see the recipe: one pint of cream, three ounces of sugar, four egg yolks, vanilla essence. It's cholesterol central. No wonder it tastes so good.) The *torta negra* reminds me a little bit of *bara brith*, but it is heavier, moister, richer. The raisins drowned in brandy explode on my tongue in a burst of spirit fumes.

We talk about the Welsh in Gaiman. I speak Welsh with Mirna who translates for Rubén. Occasionally, I venture into tentative Spanish, which for some reason she translates as well. Rubén speaks sometimes in Spanish, sometimes in Welsh or a mixture of both, sometimes in gestures.

'My mother used to speak Welsh,' Rubén tells me in Welsh. 'But I... no.' He switches into Spanish. 'When Mirna here went to primary school as a little child...'

'...I didn't speak a word of Spanish!' Mirna says. In Spanish. 'I was six years old, and I could only speak Welsh!'

'*Todo Cymraeg!*' Rubén confirms.

'But you were born here?' I ask, confused.

'Oh yes,' she says. 'I grew up on my parents' farm. We only

spoke Welsh there. I didn't learn Spanish till I went to school.'

'My great-grandfather,' Rubén says, not wanting to be left out; 'came from *Ynys Môn*, Anglesey. John Thomas Evans was his name.'

'He came over in 1874, nine years after the very first settlers,' Mirna adds.

'I have family in Anglesey still.' Rubén again. 'Although my uncle John Lasarus Williams died recently. He was a learned man – a teacher, a nationalist and an M.P. He would send us short letters in Welsh. I don't really speak Welsh. But I sing in Welsh! The Welsh have got such beautiful, lively songs!'

'Please, sing one!'

'Oh no. I can't really sing...'

'Please...'

He gives in. 'But don't tell anybody in the town!'

I later find out that there are *four* choirs in Gaiman. Is he afraid that he will be press-ganged into one of them if people know that he can sing? I promise not to tell, and he bursts into a Welsh drinking song in a beautiful baritone.

Somewhat dazed by this display of Welshness, I ask the two if they feel themselves to be Welsh or Argentinian.

'We're Argentinians!' Rubén says strongly. 'We were born here. Our children, our grandchildren were born here. *Somos argentinos*. We're Argentinians. But we're well aware of the history of our forebears. We know what life was like for them in Wales. We even have some Welsh customs here that have long died out in Wales. That makes us Argentinians of Welsh extraction. We don't forget that – it's something we're proud of. Argentina is an immigrant country that hasn't found its own identity yet. There's no such thing as "the typical Argentinian". We have instead our history: the wonderful history of the Welsh colony. *A beautiful history!*' he exclaims, suddenly in English.

'*Cymry yn y galon,*' says Mirna. We're Welsh in our hearts.

'*¡En la sangre!*' Rubén proclaims passionately. In our blood! Mirna nods. 'It's in our blood, yes.'

3

WE HAVE ANOTHER CUP of tea, then I'm shown round the exhibition by Mirna. She points out the mantelpiece that her great-grandmother had sent over from Wales.

'She didn't bring this over on the *Mimosa*?' I ask, incredulous. The *Mimosa* is the Patagonian *Mayflower*, the ship on which the first group of Welsh immigrants arrived in 1865.

'No, no!' Mirna laughs. 'Later, a trading company was formed, the *Compañía Mercantil*, and they shipped things between Wales and Argentina. These came over on the *Mimosa* though.'

'These' are a pair of china dogs.

'They were a wedding present. My husband's great-grand-mother brought them over.'

I try to imagine that. The first settlers who came over into the unknown, into a vast region many times the size of Britain, a region where no other Europeans lived, would have left Wales for good. Their only connection to all they had left behind – country, family, friends, sights and sounds and smells and tastes – would for many years be occasional letters, nothing else. It must have helped the young bride to take these two fragile reminders of home with her into the untamed, unknown wilderness.

'I've seen those dogs somewhere before, I'm sure,' I say and ponder. 'Oh, I know: In Bruce Chatwin's Patagonia book.'

'Yes, that's possible,' agrees Mirna. 'Bruce Chatwin. Yes, could be. But you know, you mustn't believe everything in that book. *Nofel ydy o!* It's a novel.'

Several hours have passed when I finally get up to leave. Mirna steadfastly refuses to accept any money for cakes and tea.

'No, no, no,' she says. 'We had such a lovely afternoon! You'll pay next time. When you come back next year!'

We spend half an hour standing in the doorway, saying good-bye. Finally I'm outside on the road again, in the dust, mosquitoes, shrill unknown bird calls, dogs barking and the drone and buzz of the cars and motorbikes of Gaiman.

I arrived in Patagonia only a few hours ago, alone and rather lost in the unknown. Now, after just a few hours of conversation, I feel anchored; as if I had already spent days, weeks here. John Lasarus Williams on Anglesey; the ancestor John Thomas Evans, Caernarfon – they are from a world I know, stepping stones, links between there and here, then and now: and through these reference points I find that Gaiman, part Welsh and wholly Argentinian, is still just as strange, but suddenly not as foreign as before.

I walk slowly back to my B&B, tired from exploring and speaking in tongues, and all those cakes.

But my day is not yet over. In B&B *Ar Lan yr Afon* a party is just beginning. I enter the house through the back door, hoping to make it unobserved to my room, and bed, and a long rest.

'Perfect timing!' Jorge exclaims merrily as I tiptoe past the kitchen. He works as an IT consultant but sometimes helps out in the B&B as well. Just now, he is pouring wine into a trayful of glasses. 'We're just about to start. Come on through.'

Oh, heck, I think. Not now. I'm tired and dusty and sunburnt and half eaten by mosquitoes. I've had a lovely afternoon, but I only arrived this morning. I'm jet-lagged and tired and cranky. I don't want to meet more people. I'm not a people person.

I wouldn't admit it, but I'm a bit freaked out by being here. *South America*. Argentina. I'm much, much further away from home than I've ever been in my life. What I really want to do is crawl into bed and pull the covers over my head.

I open my mouth to tell Jorge that I have jet lag and a headache. Not now, I will say. Another day perhaps. *Nos da*. Good night.

Then I change my mind. I've travelled all the way to South America in pursuit of a dream, and I'm damned if I am now going to hide behind my usual wall of shyness. I decide to give this party, and anything else that is new and alarming and unfamiliar, the benefit of the doubt.

You might like this, I tell my unconvinced self, and follow Jorge and the wine glasses into the big living room.

The first thing that strikes me is that I can understand what people are saying. That's because everybody is speaking Welsh. A whole group of Welsh people have come to Gaiman for a wedding between a boy from Carmarthen and a Patagonian girl. Some of them have been staying in *Ar Lan yr Afon*, and tomorrow they are going to go back home to Wales. Hence the party. Hence the fact that they fan out across the living room, arrange themselves in formation, draw a collective deep breath and begin to sing. In harmony.

First, a song about the wedding and the hospitality of the people of Gaiman at *priodas Morgan ni*, our Morgan's wedding. Then some hymns and folk songs. And finally, as though all of that wasn't enough, the Welsh national anthem: *Hen Wlad fy Nhadau*, Land of my Fathers.

The singing gives way to chatter. The Argentinian wine isn't bad at all. In fact, it's downright good. I hadn't known that I like red wine. I have another glass and some nibbles.

When everybody goes out for a meal at eleven o'clock I don't join them; I go to bed instead. But I am a lot more cheerful, and I sleep well with the murmurings of the river in my ears all night. Next morning I wake up to the sun streaming in through the window, and birds calling and trilling and screeching in the big blue sky, and I feel no longer lost as I go out to explore Patagonia.

4

LET ME TAKE YOU ON A detour for a moment. Back to the old country. Wales.

Mountains and disused coal mines, sheep and slate and chapels. It has no great monuments apart from neolithic chambered cairns and mediaeval castles, no famous paintings, no outstanding architecture. The Welsh seem to have poured all their energies into three things: faith, language and music. The place is thick with saints and chapels. There is a huge body of mediaeval literature in Welsh. The earliest mentions of King Arthur occur in Welsh tales. The biggest festival in the country, the National Eisteddfod, is built around the celebration of song and poetry and poets in the Welsh language.

These days, Welsh is a minority language, with some 500,000 native speakers. But once, an early form of it was spoken in the whole island of Britain. It's a Celtic language, no more similar to English than Russian or Spanish. Welsh is related to Scottish and Irish Gaelic, to Breton, and to the almost extinct Celtic tongues Cornish and Manx, and, further back in time, Gaulish. At the time of the Roman conquest, almost two millennia ago, the Celtic tribes of Britain spoke a language that was the direct ancestor of the Welsh language of today. And unlike their Celtic brethren on the continent, the British held on to their language. (French, Spanish and Portuguese have developed from Latin while the Celtic languages once spoken in Gaul and Iberia died out.)

When the Romans left in the fifth century and pagan, Germanic barbarians began to raid Britain, the Romano-Britons defended their island, their newly acquired Christian faith and their old tongue. As wave after wave of Angles, Saxons and Jutes arrived in Britain, the Celts withdrew into the mountainous, the more easily defensible regions of Britain, into the North (Scotland) and the West (Wales and Cornwall). Over time, their kingdoms and their language melted away, until the only place where it was still spoken were two rocky peninsulas to the west of a bulwark which had been built by one of the new Anglo-Saxon rulers: Offa's Dyke. Wales.

All of this is ancient history, literally; but it's very alive still in Wales. The Welsh language is as much an identity as a language: it's a whole country in words. In the Middle Ages, King Edward I besieged Wales with a choking chain of castles; a few centuries later Henry VIII merged Wales with England in the Act of Union in

1536 in which he stated his intention 'utterly to extirp all and singular the sinister Usages and Customs'[1] of Wales. The language was pretty much all that people had to hold on to. And they held on to it with stubborn determination through the centuries.

The Industrial Revolution, a couple of centuries after the Welsh Bible, cut great inroads of English into Wales. From then on, there were fewer speakers every year.

The 1860s were not good years in Wales. Workers were being laid off in the slate mines in the North, the coal mines in the valleys of the south. Rain had caused bad harvests for the small tenant hill farmers, but the rents of the farms still had to be paid. The big landowners – English or Anglicised – could (and did) evict tenants with ease. They could dictate the way their tenants voted, worshipped, even what language they spoke. Or what language they were not allowed to speak. In their own country, Welsh people were forbidden to speak Welsh anywhere except at home. Emigration seemed a reasonable way out of hereditary poverty and bondage. Almost the only chance a tenant farmer had ever to be his own master and work his own land was to seek it somewhere far away across the ocean, in America or Australia.

Ever since the 1846 report of the Royal Commission on the State of Education in Wales (today known throughout Wales as *Brad y Llyfrau Gleision*, 'The Treason of the Blue Books'), a lot of English and some Welsh people had been calling for more 'enlightenment' to be brought to the Principality. As *The Times* put it in 1865, 'The Welsh language is the curse of Wales.'[2] English education and Anglicanism, it was widely felt – especially in England – would be the salvation of the backward Welsh. A movement had sprung up in the Principality to defend the Welsh way of things, but most people's energy was poured into religious channels, the Chapels and the Nonconformist movements, not into direct politics.

There were exceptions. Whilst *The Times* did the Welsh language down, in Bala the Reverend Michael D. Jones thundered: 'The Welsh are a conquered people in their own country!'[3]

But even he didn't see much hope for a revolution in Wales. Instead, he proposed a New Wales somewhere else, a fresh start far away from England. This had been tried before, in several parts of the United States and once in Brazil, but both times without success.[4] The Rev. Michael D. Jones thought he knew why: those other ventures had been founded on ideas of economic independence alone. What they lacked was soul, a moral dimension. He dreamed of a place where Welsh judges would administer Welsh law, where Welsh men and women could take pride in the Welsh language, in Welsh history and literature and Nonconformist Christianity.

'There will be a chapel,' he wrote, 'a school and an assembly, and the Old Tongue will be the medium of worship, commerce, science, education and government. We will make a strong and self-sustaining nation grow within a Welsh colony.'[5] What he really wanted was a free Welsh state, but all the available land on the globe had already been claimed by other countries. However, far-away Patagonia was not yet settled.

There were people living there, of course, the nomadic *Aoniken* (Tehuelche) in the deep south, *Günün A Künna* (Pampas Indians) and Mapuche in the green plains south of Buenos Aires and further west in the fertile foothills of the Andes. But in European eyes, they did not own their own land. So the Rev. Jones' searching gaze fell upon 'empty' Patagonia. 'The land... is not owned by anybody except by some Indians,' he wrote in 1856 when he first started considering Patagonia.[6]

Now there was a reason why the 'far south' of the South American continent had not yet been settled. Most of Patagonia is desert and entirely unsuitable for agriculture. But perhaps that was just an added bonus for the Rev. M.D. Jones. It will not have escaped him how Biblical the whole thing was: the exodus of the oppressed Welsh led by a bearded patriarch (Lewis Jones) into the promised land of *Y Wladfa* (The Colony): a desert and a wilderness.

The Argentine government in Buenos Aires was perplexed as to why anybody would wish to settle Patagonia, but the then Minister of the Interior, Dr Guillermo Rawson, fell in readily enough with the plans of Messrs. Jones and Jones. Argentina, just fifty years old as a nation, claimed all land south of Buenos Aires and east of the Andes mountain range as its own territory, but did not have much in the way of population to back this claim up. (Chile, on the other side of the Andes mountain range, claimed the same land as Chilean, with just the same lack of actual citizens on the ground.)

A deal was made: the Welsh would be given land in the inhospitable south. They could administer their colony, if not as a state, as an autonomous province where they could govern themselves, teach whatever subjects in whichever language they pleased and worship in their own way. In return, they would declare the land Argentinian.

It was a mad scheme, but the Rev. Jones was a convincing orator, and there were enough dreamers in Wales to fill a boat, several even. The first ship bound for Patagonia, the *Mimosa*, left Liverpool on 28 May 1865 with 153 Welsh men, women and children on board.

Two months to the day after leaving Liverpool, the *Mimosa* dropped anchor in the New Bay.

'There was the desolate and sandy beach,' wrote in his memoir William Hughes. His boat arrived in Patagonia in 1881, sixteen years after the *Mimosa*, but the first view must have been much the same as it had been for those first settlers. 'It was truly a pleasure to put my feet on the ground once more, be it on this sand or any other solid ground. There were no houses there in those days, only sand dunes and some clumps of tussock grass, whose bushy heads barely broke up the monotony of the sandy land.'

The settlers on the *Mimosa* had arrived at the end of July, in the middle of the Patagonian winter. They disembarked by means of a rowing boat, in small groups, and stood shivering on the sands, looking around them at the land that was to be their new home. There was the beach and the dunes beyond it, and beyond them endless plains of greyish scrubland. In the cold mist, it would have looked like the moors they knew in Britain.

'A strange sentiment took hold of us,' Thomas Jones, one of the first settlers, wrote in his diary; 'when the ship left us there like pilgrims on the deserted shores of Patagonia, without knowing what awaited us.'

They looked out over the sea, and there was nothing but ten thousand miles of ocean between them and Wales.

But there wouldn't have been much time to think about that, and probably just as well. A child was born, right there in a crude little shelter on the beach of the New Bay, and its bawling must have made a cheerful sound, reminding all that life went on, regardless.

5

EVERYBODY IN GAIMAN has been telling me about Eirlys Griffiths, founder and curator of *Amgueddfa Gaiman*, the local museum, and resident historian of *Y Wladfa*. Her museum is open every day except Sundays from 4pm to 8pm. It is housed in the old railway station. There's no mistaking it: the building looks, bizarrely, like any small rural railway station in Britain, down to the lacy ornamental roof edge. *Siaredur Cymraeg yma*, a sticker in the window proclaims and *Se habla galés*. Welsh is spoken here.

A little bell rings when I open the old-fashioned door to what must once have been the waiting room, and is now the entrance hall of the museum. The air is wonderfully cool after the dusty heat outside. Out of the dark interior appears a young man with a beard and glasses and a friendly smile.

'*P'nawn da*,' I say in Welsh. My Welsh, somewhat rusty at first, has been improving. It feels very strange to be in a place where I *have* to speak *Cymraeg* to make myself understood. In Wales, I speak it for political reasons and out of respect for the *Cymry Cymraeg*, the native Welsh speakers; secure in the knowledge that, when the going gets tough, I can always switch to English. Here, there is no such safety-net, it's Welsh or nothing (or Spanish, which for me amounts to much the same thing). With that motivation, my Welsh has come on beautifully.

I ask for Eirlys Griffiths. The young man looks crestfallen.

'She's not around, she's gone to a tea in Trelew. Do you want to come back tomorrow? I don't know anything, myself,' he admits with engaging candour. 'I only mind the place while she's away.'

'Yes,' I say, 'no problem, I'll come back tomorrow.' And then I end up staying anyway, for more than an hour. We talk about *Y Wladfa* – of course – and about languages. It turns out that as well as excellent Welsh, the young man – Miguel – also speaks excellent English, much to my delight.

'So what do you do when you're not minding the museum?'

'Nothing. I learn things.'

'You're a student.'

'No. I don't study, I learn. I learn about things that I find interesting.'

I feel a trifle envious, and I'd like to know what he lives on. I wouldn't mind spending my time learning about interesting things.

Miguel, like me, learnt his Welsh on the Ulpan course in Lampeter.

'I like speaking Welsh, but I also like speaking English. That Welsh-only mania some people have in Wales... I don't get it. Not everyone in the world speaks Welsh. Why should they? Welsh people come here and speak Welsh with us but they don't speak the language of my country, Spanish. *Norteamericanos* come to visit the museum who speak neither Welsh nor Spanish. How should we communicate with them if we don't use English? And anyway,' he grins, 'Spanish is really easy. You just speak English with a Spanish accent.' He points to a large old-fashioned gun displayed on one of the museum walls. 'What do you call that?'

'Um... a gun?'

'A rifle. In Spanish: *rifle*.' He pronounces it *reefla*. 'And this?'

'A computer.'

'*Computadora*.'

'This?'

'A plate.'

'*Un plato*. And that one?'

'A bottle.'

'*Una botella*. You see?' He beams. 'It's the same language really.'

I like Miguel's Spanish lessons; and I like, too, the way he stresses similarities over differences.

'So what are you doing later on?' he wants to know. 'Any plans?'

Why, does he want to ask me out?

'It's choir practice tonight.'

Ah.

'The mixed choir. There's also a male-voice choir and a women's choir, and a children's. You should come – it'll be fun.'

Choir practice. I should have expected it really. This place was, after all, founded by Welsh people.

'I'm sure you'd enjoy it. I'm a member, too,' he adds modestly.

6

AT A QUARTER PAST NINE I'm on my way to choir practice. Past the pharmacy, the agricultural co-op, the newspaper stall (now closed), houses, bakery, petrol station, the other bakery, green-grocer, 'Blue Moon' *taverna*. A group of people stand waiting by a house with a large porch.

'*Por favor, ¿habla usted galés?*' Regretful shaking of heads. They don't speak Welsh.

I clear my throat again, try to think of Spanish words. I haven't been here long, but already my exceedingly sketchy beginner's Spanish is expanding, taking in new words. 'Er... *yo busco el coro galés.*'

'*¡Sí, sí! Acá.*' They nod vigorously. I have come to the right place. Ten minutes later some cars pull up, a group of women get out. Somebody nudges me in the direction of one of them.

'*Ella habla galés.*' She speaks Welsh.

'*¡Muchas gracias!*' I say thankfully and address myself to the woman, explaining that I am a visitor from Germany – with some Welsh – and that I would like to sit in at choir practice tonight. Will they mind?

'No, of course not. Come in.'

The door is unlocked, a rectangle of light illuminates the dusty pavement. A large group of people pours into the room. There must be at least thirty of them; all ages, both sexes, though there are more women than men. There is a very respectable number of boys and young men, Miguel among them, who gives me a cheery wave.

I sit down between two middle-aged ladies, both Welsh speakers. Somebody hands me a sheet of music. And they're off. I close my eyes and feast my ears.

I imagined that all the songs were going to be in Welsh, but the first one is in Spanish, the second something by Händel and the third, to my utter surprise, in German. It is one of Johannes Brahms' *lieder*.

One of my seated neighbours has caught hold of the fact that I am German. She leans across and whispers.

'You speak German?'

I admit that I do.

'Couldn't you translate this for us?'

'This' are the words to the Brahms *lied*. Good grief. I do speak some Welsh, but nowhere near enough to translate poetry! I nearly eat an entire pencil in linguistic anguish. How do you say 'the bitter pain of loneliness' in Welsh?

Finally I'm done. In the next break between songs, I hand the sheet to the lady, who reads it and nods.

'*Gracias*,' she says and smiles and repeats her thanks in Welsh. '*Diolch yn fawr.*'

While the next piece is being rehearsed – something spirited in Spanish – I amuse myself by looking about me and trying to guess from people's faces which are of Welsh descent and which are not. Some of the old ladies seem very Welsh to me – it's their colouring, and something about their faces that looks familiar. With everyone else, I am reduced to guessing. Almost everybody in the room is deeply tanned, and a lot of people have dark hair. Then again, quite a few Welsh people in Wales have dark hair and eyes. I give up on the guessing and just people-watch.

In the front row sits a young woman of no more than twenty-five, clad in tight jeans and a short jumper that shows off her midriff. I am envious; it is a very lovely midriff. She looks downright cool – certainly not like somebody from the provinces. I hadn't thought of the choir as being cool.

Patagonia is rearranging and prodding some of my assumptions. I like that. I will go home and be changed through having been here. I will wash the dust from the desert off my clothes and my tan will fade over time; but Patagonia will stay with me.

A little boy and girl, neither more than four years old, are playing while the choir rehearses. They draw with coloured chalk on a blackboard, and then the little girl amuses herself by wiping the board methodically while the boy is still drawing. An argument erupts. The members of the choir take this entirely in their stride. The young woman jumps up and arbitrates in whispers; the rest go on singing, with only the occasional look and smile in the direction of the children. Nobody shushes disapprovingly.

After the rehearsal has ended, some people rush straight out into the night with only a brief good-bye. Others stay a while for a chat. Outside in the dark, crickets are rasping, every now and then a car passes, a dog barks, people walk past, chatting and laughing.

I talk to Clara Roberts, the choir mistress. Her Welsh is quick and businesslike and comfortable, she speaks it as well as Spanish, in an accent that is pure south Walian. It's only now that I notice that most of the people of Gaiman with whom I've spoken so far use the Welsh of the north. They said *rŵan*, not *nawr*, for now; *hogyn* for boy instead of *bachgen*; *efo*, not *gyda*, for with; not *mam-gu* but *nain* for grandmother.

'Yes – my great-grandparents came from Aberdare,' says Clara when I ask about her accent. 'Edward Morgan and Ann Philips. They got married when they were very young and came out to live in Patagonia. They never went back to Wales.'

Clara tells me about occasions when the choir travelled to Wales, to compete at the International Music Eisteddfod in Llangollen, or at the National Eisteddfod.

'Every time we go, I want us to visit new places, to see where our great-grandmothers and great-grandfathers came from. Some of the members of the choir have relatives in Wales who work in a coal-mine. So once, some of us went down the mine.' She shakes her head. 'Edward Morgan, my great-grandfather, came from a family of miners. I never imagined how hard the work was. Seeing it made me understand why people wanted to leave and have a better life. They went to a place so far away, so dry, so *different* when everywhere in Wales is so green. But at least they had freedom here, and the language, and the chapels.'

'And you?' I want to know, although I suspect I know the answer. 'How do you feel, Welsh or Argentinian?'

'Argentinian,' Clara replies promptly. 'But, you know... I'm very grateful to my parents that they taught me to speak Welsh. I didn't speak any Spanish at all when I started school at five. But then I married a *Spaenwr*, a Spanish speaker, so the language of the house is Spanish. But he's learning Welsh now, in the evening classes at the college, you know. And the girls, our daughters, they sing in Welsh, they both sing in the choir.'

'The choir is fantastic,' I tell her. 'This really isn't my kind of thing usually, but I did enjoy all the different songs tonight. And the range of people!'

She laughs. 'All our visitors from Wales say that. They're always surprised that we've got old people, young people – everybody in the choir. Our oldest gentleman is seventy-one, and the youngest boy fifteen. I started the mixed choir in 1989. Last year we went up to Buenos Aires and sang for parliament there. We try to get around, you know.'

I walk back to *Ar Lan yr Afon* through the cooling night air.

Gaiman is quiet at this hour, but by no means asleep: the crickets are still singing, and there are cars abroad, and from a garden somewhere I hear the voices of children. It's past midnight, but children are still up and playing in the middle of the night. I walk through the dusty darkness, smiling.

7

ONE DAY IN MY LAST WEEK in Patagonia, Natalia puts her head round the door to announce that a couple of other guests are going an excursion to the penguin colony at Punta Tombo. There's a spare seat. Do I want to come? I didn't know there *was* a penguin colony near Gaiman. I have never really thought about penguins. I'm here for the Welsh flavour, not the wildlife. But I'm in Patagonia, where I have decided to see new things and to try out the new and the unexpected. So why not penguins?

The tour guide arrives in a beautiful new 4x4. Meinir and Jayne, two Welsh travellers, and I make up the entire group. That makes it nice and cosy, except that Guillermo, the guide, has no English or Welsh whatever, and neither Jayne nor Meinir speak a word of Spanish.

How can those two travel to another country without speaking its language? I'd have expected better of *Cymry Cymraeg*. They always complain – quite rightly, too – about English people coming to Wales in utter ignorance of the Welsh language.

'You speak Spanish, don't you?' Jayne says blithely and clambers into the back seat next to Meinir. That leaves the front seat for me. I have picked up a bit of Spanish by now, so that I can just about communicate in a me-Tarzan-you-Jane kind of way what I want to say. But when Guillermo answers my halting questions in rapid-fire Spanish, I am utterly lost. I have to ask him to repeat most things two or three times before I get them. It's great practice, but I can feel steam beginning to pour from my ears with the effort.

We travel along the main road for a while, past the city of Trelew, then turn onto a gravel road. Only the main roads in Patagonia are tarmacked, most side roads (even those fairly frequently used) are somewhat bumpy dirt-and-gravel affairs. Stones fly up and smack into the underside of the car. I had wondered why every single vehicle I have so far seen in Patagonia (with the exception of Guillermo's, which is obviously brand new) has at least one crack in the windscreen.

It takes two hours to reach the penguins. I have already learned that this is not a long distance in South America. But the sheer size of the land continues to astonish me. There is so much of it. The few people who live here are simply swallowed up by the vastness.

While we're on this road the only living beings we see are a few dusty horses and some birds. Then, in the middle of nowhere, a gate, a gift shop, a café. We stop at the gate to buy our tickets, then bump slowly along a pot-holed track. We are now inside the nature reserve of Punta Tombo: the home of the largest colony of Magellanic penguins in the world, according to a sign by the entrance. In front of us, framed left and right by cliffs as red as a landscape on Mars, lies the sea: blue and green and sparkling in the sun. All three of us sit glued to the car windows, eyes peeled for penguins, cameras at the ready.

'There!' we shout as one woman. 'Stop the car! A penguin!'

Guillermo grins and stops for a minute so we can take our photos, then goes slowly on round the next bend.

'Another one!' we yell. 'And there.... and there....'

We're round the next bend, and we're speechless.

Then: *'Mae nhw ym mhobman,'* Jayne says in a small voice. They're everywhere.

The place is black and white with penguins. Penguins are sitting under shrubs; in shallow holes in the ground; smack bang in the middle of the track. Some lie flat on their fronts, and for a second I am afraid they might be dead, perhaps having succumbed to heat stroke in the sun. I associate penguins with ice and Antarctica and freezing temperatures. The dry heat of the Patagonian autumn seems not quite the right environment.

One of the 'corpses' lifts its head, lets its gaze sweep briefly over the car, closes its eyes again. *Tourists*, the look says.

Guillermo laughs. 'They're just asleep,' he says, lets the clutch in and drives on, careful not to run over any penguins.

Penguins waddle across the track, penguins lie and stand every-where on the dusty, stony ground; by the roadside, not giving a hoot about us. I become aware of the fact that I am pressing my nose flat against the window and making little ecstatic noises in my throat.

Guillermo parks the car and pulls the key from the ignition.

'¿Bueno?' he asks and smiles. He's probably used to seeing awestruck first-time visitors. We clamber out of the car, looking everywhere at once.

Penguins stand about like garden gnomes, faces turned towards the sun, eyes half closed, not moving a muscle. Others waddle about solemnly. I know it's a cliché, but they really do look as though they're wearing miniature frock coats. I walk slowly, wanting to take in as much as possible.

I never knew penguins made sounds, but these most certainly do. Every now and again, one of the dozing ones will wake up, blink, look around. Then it tilts its head back, opens its beak and produces the most astonishing sounds. They start as a series of small hoots until the penguin has built up a head of steam. Then it lets fly with a big, noisy, braying honk. The penguins are fairly small, maybe knee high, with as much mass as a small cat. The amount of noise they produce is out of all proportion. They sound like small elephants, or like donkeys: hooting and shrilling and trumpeting. (Which is, as I learn later, why in English they're called Jackass Penguins.)

I wander among penguins, speechless with delight. The sea before me shimmers and rolls in the breeze, its water jade green. The rocks that surround it are an unlikely brick red. Penguins waddle past, adding patterns of black and white to the red rocks, the green sea. Mosquitoes buzz, penguins bray. Minute downy feathers drift on the breeze like snowflakes.

One hour doesn't seem nearly enough. All too quickly it is over. I tear myself away from the penguins and return, reluctantly, to the car where Guillermo and Meinir and Jayne are already waiting.

I have fallen deeply and irrevocably in love with penguins. What I would really like to do is stay here and spend the night. One day, I promise myself, I will return with a sleeping bag, and wake up by the sea to the trumpeting of the *pingüinos* of Punta Tombo.

Exhausted with speaking Spanish and the wonder of penguins, I fall asleep and don't wake up until we're back by the roundabout just outside Gaiman in the early evening. Guillermo makes to turn onto the main road, then half swivels towards me.

'Have you seen the tunnel yet? The railway tunnel?'

I did notice it on a picture postcard of Gaiman and wondered why it was considered a tourist attraction. Jayne and Meinir didn't even know Gaiman had a tunnel. Guillermo takes pity on our ignorance and turns the car towards the old railway station where the museum is now housed. A rocky hill rears up a little further on, and in it, sure enough, a tunnel opening. I expect Guillermo to stop the car so we can admire the tunnel, and then to turn around and drive back. Instead, he drives straight at it.

The opening in the hillside is narrow and the car rather wide. I wait to hear the wing mirrors scrape along the tunnel sides. The tunnel is long and dark and dusty, as though no air had stirred in it for many decades. It makes me think of ghost trains in the Wild West, of train robbers and desperadoes and Butch Cassidy and the Sundance Kid. We go slowly. The beams of our headlights travel along greyish, slightly curving brick walls. There is no trace of tracks on the ground, just sand and more dust.

Once upon a time, a railway line connected the Welsh settlements in the lower Chubut valley with the sea port of Puerto Madryn fifty miles to the east of Gaiman. The last trains ran in the 1960s, and all that remains of the railway today are the station buildings in Puerto Madryn, Trelew and Gaiman – and the tunnel. With very few exceptions,s eastern Patagonia is as flat as a board. The railway tunnel is both a feat of engineering and an exotic occurrence, something Gaiman is proud of.

8

THE FIRST YEARS WERE desperately hard for the colonists. They had come to live off the land, but only a few knew anything about farming. The majority had been coal miners from the south Wales valleys or slate miners from the north, with some assorted craftsmen thrown in. Only a handful of them were farmers. Among the first contingent on the *Mimosa* had also arrived three ministers of religion and a doctor of medicine. This latter, Dr. Thomas Green, accompanied Lewis Jones to Buenos Aires to see the Argentine government, and never returned to Patagonia.[7] Instead, he kept going north until he reached the United States, where he settled. Nobody knows why he deserted the colony. Perhaps in the bustle of Buenos Aires he found that he just couldn't face a return to the isolation, the loneliness, the monotony and the endless hard work that was *Y Wladfa*. His chest of medicines was still in Patagonia. He never went back for it. When people fell ill, they had to sort through the Latin labels of the drugs, making sense of them as much as they could. It must have been a desperate choice sometimes: not to treat an illness or to take a drug without quite knowing what effect it would have.

The settlers did their best with their limited knowledge of farming and almost complete ignorance as to the local soil and weather conditions. In hindsight, it is not surprising that the first harvests failed, but at the time, the settlers must have been increasingly worried. Here they were, having left everything at home for this promised land, and all it gave them were stones and thorns. Twice they had to ask for more supplies of foodstuffs from the Argentine government simply to have enough to eat.

And that is much, much easier for me to write today than it was for them to do in 1866. How do you ask the government for help when the government is eight hundred miles away and there is no phone, no telegraph or postal service, no pony express even, no roads for carts? How long *would* a cart have taken to Buenos Aires and back? Eight hundred miles. That's as long as the entire island of Britain from John O'Groats to Land's End.

What they did have was a small ship. (The *Mimosa,* in which they had arrived, had only been hired for the journey, so the colonists decided to buy a small vessel for transport). And so a letter was written and Lewis Jones got himself elected to be the messenger to take it all the way to Buenos Aires. There was much sense in his election. He was an educated man, he had negotiated with the government before, he spoke good Spanish: He would be able to make their case as eloquently and convincingly as possible.

Meanwhile, the settlers were stuck in the valley with dwindling supplies. They waited. It was now 1866. They had been here for over a year and were beginning to understand the land a little better. They had learnt, though trial and error, I imagine, which of the local plants were edible and which were not. They dug up roots, used edible leaves, collected berries.

A report from those early years recounts that a group of Welsh men out exploring in the valley ran out of water. So thirsty were they in the end, with no hope of finding liquid any time soon, that they shot down a hawk and drank its blood.[8] They must have felt very, very far away from civilisation as they looked at each other with their red-smeared mouths. Did they worry? Did they ask themselves what had become of them, of their high-flying dreams of life according to their own faith and their own Welsh laws in a new land? Or did they laugh it off, think of it as a story to tell their grandchildren, later, when there would be not only grandchildren, but hearths and armchairs and pipes and china cups of tea, and nobody would be able to imagine how they had once lived?

When Lewis Jones finally returned from Buenos Aires, he brought with him sheep, potatoes, wheat, sugar, tea and other staples. The ghost of starvation was banished for the time being.

Things began to look up. The year after, the settlers finally worked out how to farm the land efficiently. Methods that had worked in Wales were not suited to the dry climate and the sandy soil of the Chubut valley. Here, you couldn't just sow your wheat and wait for it to grow. Annual rainfall in the region is only about a third of what it is in Wales, and what little there is usually falls in winter, while the summers are long and warm and dry. (Occasionally, it rains *a lot* and then the river would burst its banks and flood the entire valley. But, perhaps luckily, they didn't know that yet.) Precious little rain fell in spring and summer and the young wheat plants shrivelled and died through lack of water. So the new farmers carried water from the river in pails and buckets. It was slow, back-breaking work; and they just could not carry enough water to save the first couple of harvests.

It was Rachel Jenkins, a coal-miner's wife from Mountain Ash in the south Wales valleys, who first raised the idea of digging irrigation channels to bring water from the river directly to the fields. The other farmers listened but shook their heads doubtfully: thinking of how much more work her plan would entail, of how doubtful the results would be. But Rachel's husband Aaron was prepared to give it a try. Their plot of land was near the river, so it wasn't too much work for him to dig a channel to his wheat, just a few inches deep and a few inches wide. And while everybody else's fields dried up once more that summer, Aaron and Rachel's wheat thrived and grew. (All the history books written until just a few years ago credited Aaron Jenkins with suggesting the irrigation canals, not Rachel.)

So now they knew how to do it. The 1867 harvest wasn't enough to feed everybody, and certainly not enough to feed everybody *and* keep wheat to use for seed the following year. Lewis Jones had to board the *Denby* and sail up the coast to Buenos Aires once more and grovel to the Argentine government, and once more he was successful and they gave him supplies.

Now the digging started. With the few implements they had – shovels, pickaxes, harrows and rakes – with boards and stones and even bare hands the men went and dug. The owners of neighbouring farms clubbed together and dug one main channel which would then branch off into smaller ones, leading to each field. Altogether, the colonists would dig a network of irrigation channels of almost 200 miles in length.

It was a gargantuan undertaking. Fifteen years later, in 1881 when William Hughes arrived in the colony, it was still not finished. (In his autobiographical account the reason he gives for going to *Y Wladfa* was his delicate health. His doctor had strongly advised him to seek a dryer climate in which to recuperate. Either the climate restored him to health instantaneously, or else the life he had led in Wales had been even more strenuous.) Hughes recalled,

> Thither I went, carrying on my shoulder my new pick-axe and spade, and in my heart the determination to work and thus open up the land. It was then the beginning of July, the middle of winter; and what a cold and hard winter it was... There were severe frosts every night, and in the shade the frost stayed during the days as well. We walked, a number of us, against the cutting, icy wind from the west, two miles every morning to

where the ditch was being dug; and upon arriving, found the earth frozen solid, so that it proved impossible to dig up. It was therefore necessary to collect firewood, heap it all together and light a fire to thaw the ground before any work could commence. The ditch we dug was one yard wide and between three and five feet deep. It was hard work to cut between ten and twelve cubic yards per day, although some achieved even more than this.[9]

The heavy work paid off. The harvest of 1868 exceeded their wildest expectations. *Now* they had truly arrived. The had unlocked the puzzle of the land. During the harvest festival in the communal barn that still served as storehouse and meeting house and law court and chapel, Abraham Matthews preached a sermon on 'Israel in the Wilderness'.

A year later, they were back in the wilderness. After the first staggeringly abundant crop of wheat, the harvest failed once more in 1869. Argentina was under a new leadership, that of liberal president Domingo Sarmiento. He and his government were much less interested in the success of the Welsh colony; indeed, they were convinced that the venture had been doomed from the start. They refused to invest any more money in it and instead offered to resettle the Welsh elsewhere in Argentina.

By then, however, the Welsh did not want to be resettled. With all the difficulties and hardship of the last five years – perhaps in part precisely because of them – the Chubut Valley, *Dyffryn Camwy*, had become their home. They were used to its moods, to the light, the murmur of the river, the dry cool air that always smelt, ever so slightly, of the clean dust of the desert. Lack of furniture, implements, clothes, medical care and luxuries of every description notwithstanding: they had fought for their existence here and won the land over. It belonged to them and they to it. Their children were growing up on it. Many of them had never known anything else.

Also, apart from those times when famine threatened, they liked being so far away from the government. They had drawn up a constitution for themselves. Every adult voted on every decision taken – and that, very unusually for the times, really did mean every adult: all women and men over eighteen; half a century before women got the vote in Britain.[10]

School was in Welsh. Chapel was in Welsh. Life was pretty much as grassroots-democratic as it could get. It must have been not unlike an alternative community of the 1960s or '70s: no worldly goods and lots of spiritual fervour; children and beards and long, patched skirts; although there were no mind-altering substances and no free love, only a hell of a lot of hard work.

Every one of those not-very-well-washed, weather-beaten, lean-faced men and women in threadbare and patchy clothes had been and was and would be instrumental in shaping their own lives, their own futures. They were free and independent and in charge, and they liked it.

To be quite honest: Not all of them *did* like it. A handful of them liked it not at all and in fact signed a petition to ask the governor of the Falkland Islands – the nearest British official – to take them away from Patagonia where they would all starve. The families of Cadfan Hughes, Edward Price, William Davies, Thomas Davies and Gruffydd Hughes[11] (nobody bothered to name their womenfolk in the accounts) were in due course picked up from the beach of the New Bay – today Puerto Madryn – by a British ship. Some settled in Carmen de Patagones, some in the – much more clement – north of Argentina and a couple of families went all the way to Canada. None returned to Wales. All the rest, three quarters of the settlers, remained; although some of them took some persuading. But in the end they stayed.[12]

9

A YEAR AND A HALF after my first visit, I am back in Argentina.

This time, I have a couple of days in Buenos Aires before heading south. My Patagonian friend Lisa James is already in Gaiman for the summer, but she has arranged for me to stay with an acquaintance of hers. Marcela Valetti is an Argentinian of Italian extraction, with no Welsh roots. Her son lives in the United States, and she will be happy to have me to practice English with, she told me in the couple of emails we have exchanged prior to my arrival.

Now it's early evening and I have just arrived on a sixteen-hour flight from London. I can't quite believe that I'm back in Buenos Aires. Even in the airport, everything is simultaneously strange and familiar: the corridors, the signs; the faint, enticing smell of coffee and cigarettes; the quick rhythm of *Castellano*, Argentine Spanish. *I'm back!*, I say to the arrivals hall, and to Argentina in general.

Arrivals. Baggage reclaim. Except there's nothing for me to reclaim, because my very large, very purple, very easy-to-spot suitcase isn't there to be spotted. I wait until everybody else has triumphantly snatched up their bags and left, but it's still not there.

Damn. I make my way to the lost-and-found counter and wait for what seems like a very long time while other people queue-jump. Did I not notice, in my befuddled post-flight state, that they had already been there before me? Or are they doing what I think they're doing – *viz*. sneak in front of me and get served first? I'm rather annoyed as well as tired, jet-lagged and unwashed. Finally, my turn has come to make my missing baggage claim. Happily, the lost-and-found lady speaks English. I'm not up to speaking Spanish just now. Not with all my things missing. I feel as though my brain is in my case.

The lost-and-found lady regrets that she cannot say where my bag might be at this moment. Its label might have come off and it might be here, or it might have been temporarily left behind on the other side of the Atlantic. She will investigate. Meanwhile, she takes my details and Marcela's address and phone number, and assures me with fake, professional cheerfulness that I will have my bag back in no time.

It's ridiculous how rumpled and unwashed I feel just because I know that I can't have a change of clothes just now. This isn't helped by meeting Marcela, who is very beautiful and poised and rather on the glamorous side. She's a cosmetic surgeon: clearly a walking advertisement for her profession.

Buenos Aires is among the cities in the world with the highest per-capita numbers of both cosmetic surgeons and psychoanalysts. It's a fact I read somewhere and remembered for its oddity, but it never seemed to describe the place I had experienced. Now I get a glimpse of how the other half live.

Marcela's apartment is on the tenth floor of a modern apartment block in the posh *barrio* (neighbourhood) of Palermo. When I first heard the name, it conjured up visions of espresso bars in Sicily, fishing boats and rural poverty and the Mafia. Nothing could be further from the Palermo of Buenos Aires. This one is made up of sleek apartment blocks, well-groomed parks and swish boutiques, all of which flash by the windows of Marcela's car.

Her apartment takes up the entire floor, and comes complete with round-the-clock doorman, plush lift and not one but two balconies (one of them runs the entire length of the building) and I don't know how many rooms. We sit in what in Argentinian Spanish is known as *el living* (pronounced *leeving*): the living room. It's marginally smaller than a tennis court and boasts a spectacular view. Outside in the dark, hundreds of lighted windows are shimmering, seemingly heaped in large, upright rectangular shapes. They belong to the luxury apartment blocks – similar to Marcela's – across the park. The park itself is visible too, palm trees and blossoms brightly lit by streetlamps.

Early next morning, I tiptoe into the kitchen for coffee. Marcela is still asleep. The kitchen is equipped with every appliance one could possibly desire. The fridge is a gleaming white monster, half the size of an igloo.

Coffee in hand, I wander around, exploring. At one end, the kitchen gives on a family dining room, a comfortable space, much less grand and imposing than *el living*. At the other end of the kitchen, a door leads out to a sort of utility balcony with a washing machine and a clothes line. Behind the balcony, running parallel to the kitchen, lies a narrow, dark space that I take for a store room, or perhaps more utility space. There is a sink and toilet at the front, then a doorway with empty hinges, and beyond it, a small, dark, windowless room with a narrow bed. Perhaps the guest bedroom for less favoured visitors.

I need to make a phone call to the airport to enquire about my missing bag. I've had a shower, and a change of underwear from my hand luggage, but apart from that, I'm wearing yesterday's clothes – jeans and a sweatshirt. Good clothes for October in Britain. Not so good in Buenos Aires where October is early summer: the temperature is set to reach twenty-five degrees today.

I ask Marcela if she can call my airline and find out the whereabouts of my luggage. I speak more Spanish now, but I still dread talking on the phone.

She agrees at once, and is magnificent: she rings up the airport under my name.

'Listen,' she says, drawing herself up to her full height at her desk, 'I am a prize-winning author!' (I have told her that one of my short stories has been shortlisted in a literary competition back in Britain.) 'I'm writing a book about Patagonia, I am going there tomorrow and I need my luggage! What do you think I will wear in Patagonia?! Get me my luggage!'

But to no avail. The airline is inconsolable. They regret infinitely that they cannot say what has happened to my suitcase. It is not to be found. But they will have news, they promise. Soon.

Marcela snorts. 'They're useless!' she says and slams the phone down. 'I used the same airline once to fly to Europe, and they lost my case and it didn't turn up for six weeks.'

I feel myself blench. 'Six *weeks*?'

But in fact, by noon that same day, the doorman rings Marcela's flat and says that he is sending something up in the lift.

And there, as the doors ping open in *el living*, as large as life, violently purple, is my suitcase.

I think of myself, by and large, as someone not unduly attached to material objects, to *things*. People, yes; animals, places: yes. Things, no. But of course, I usually have my things around me, I take them for granted. Here in Buenos Aires, I am without them, in a foreign land, with a foreign language, in only the clothes I'm wearing and one small rucksack. It's as though I have no personal space here. No way to tell other people about me, my personality, my likes, my character.

I feel much more solid now that I have my case back. I croon over my treasures: my own clothes, my shoes, my socks, my books, my odds, my ends!

10

AFTER I HAVE CHANGED – into wondrously clean, summery clothes – Marcela whisks me off for a day's sight-seeing in Buenos Aires. Her idea of the city's must-sees are different to Lisa's. She takes me, first, to MALBA, the museum of modern Latin American art, the largest of its kind, she tells me, on the entire continent. It is a bright, modern building, all glass and white-painted steel and concrete. Its mix of paintings and sculptures is eclectic. My favourite is the 'Fossil Machine' by Jorge Michel, a contemporary Argentinian sculptor. It has been made of one entire, highly polished tree-trunk which splits into asymmetrical, spherical and oval limbs. The effect is very beautiful.

The small (and, to be honest, not terribly good) Frida Kahlo is the only work by a Latin American artist whose name I recognise. Marcela appears startled by this fact. She knows a lot about modern and contemporary art (indeed, if her living room is anything to go by, she's something of a collector herself). So it is only natural that she would know more about it than me. But some of those artists are household names in Latin America, as well-known as Matisse and Rodin are in Europe. Except that Matisse and Rodin are just as well-known here; and Marcela by her own admission travels to the US or Europe at least twice a year, to see her son, yes, but also to visit museums and galleries.

I've never consciously thought about modern South American art before. I need to widen my outlook. The world to me looks upside-down from here, so far south. So far away from everywhere else. Although that, of course, depends on how one defines *everywhere*.

That evening, Marcela cooks in my honour: *ñoquis*. Which is gnocchi in Spanish spelling. More than a third of the immigrants who flocked to Argentina in the late nineteenth and early twentieth centuries were Italian, and they have left an enduring legacy in Argentine cuisine. Of course, the most typically Argentine dish is steak, but I am vegetarian and steak isn't an option. So Marcela has made gnocchi, or rather *ñoquis,* with a herby tomato sauce and grated parmesan cheese.

After dinner, we sit out on the balcony with our coffee, and Marcela bums a cigarette off me ('I don't *really* smoke') and we talk about ice cream. She tells me enthusiastically of the new development of Puerto Madero: the old docks of Buenos Aires which have been redeveloped much like Cardiff Bay, and turned into a glitzy new shopping and eating district. The absolute best ice cream parlour of the city has just opened a branch there. It is run, of course, by Italians.

By which Argentines mean Argentinians of Italian extraction.

'Do you like ice cream?' Marcela asks me.

'*Síííííííí,*' I say. I'm beginning to pick up the Argentine habit of extending vowels almost indefinitely. It's fun.

'Would you like one?'

What, now?

'Let's go out for an ice cream!' Marcela declares. It is almost eleven o'clock on a Monday evening.

We go down in the lift to the residents' garage in the basement, and back up to street level, *inside* the car, in another lift. A car-sized lift! Marcela laughs at my amazement.

Then we're on the street with the roof open and the windows down and the warm wind in our hair, and Marcela is driving like a madwoman. But so is everybody else. Cars weave in and out of lanes, across lanes, overtake other drivers on the left and the right, screech to a halt in front of red lights as though on a sudden whim.

I have fastened my seat belt (Marcela hasn't. Very likely nobody else has, either. But it makes me feel a little bit safer) and hold on to the edge of my seat until Marcela comes in to land and park the car at Puerto Madero. I half expected to see the buildings lying still and dark, the lights off, the people all gone home.

But of course, this is Buenos Aires. You can go out for a meal long after midnight, an amused Marcela explains to me. Lots of cafés are open all night. You can go for a coffee or a pizza at three in the morning, should you so desire. At a club, you shouldn't even bother turning up before one o'clock. When I tell her that in London, many clubs open around ten and close at two or three in the morning, she laughs.

The bricked pavement along the water's edge is alive with people and lights. Tango music and the smell of roast meat drift from the restaurants. Well-dressed couples and families stroll slowly along, chatting and laughing. It looks like an ad from the Argentine Tourist Board.

There is the ice cream parlour. Marcela ushers me inside, and we go abruptly from twenty-odd degrees outside into what feels like an ice cave. Ugh. Air conditioning.

'What would you like?'

'Holy cow!'

All along one wall behind the glass counter runs a double row of plastic containers, each the size of a bucket, each containing a different flavour of ice cream. There must be about thirty in all. Forty? There are at least half a dozen different flavours of chocolate alone: ordinary, dark, with almonds, with nuts, Swiss chocolate, white chocolate.... There is banana split, Irish cream, American cream (which appears to be blue), fruits of the forest, mascarpone, melon, strawberry, vanilla, mint, lemon. And a whole bank of flavours headed *dulce de leche*, an Argentine specialty: caramel creme.

We take our cones outside, strolling along the brightly lit basins of Puerto Madero in the warm, sticky night air. Almost midnight, and I'm in fashionable Buenos Aires eating ice cream.

Life is mad, and good.

We talk about houses, and living space, about house prices in the U.K. and the U.S.A. and Argentina, and I remember that small room in her apartment, behind the kitchen. The guest room, I call it.

But no. That's not what it is.

'It's for my *empleada*,' Marcela explains.

'Your employee?' That doesn't seem to make sense.

'The girl who works for me. You know, she does the dishes, the cleaning, the grocery shopping, some of the cooking. She's off at the moment because my daughter is away on holidays, but normally she lives with us, and these are her quarters.'

I don't know what to say. Marcela has a *maid*? A maid who lives in a windowless room at the back of the kitchen.

11

Retiro, the central coach station in Buenos Aires, is large and noisy and busy. I have decided to take the scenic route south this time: I will go to Patagonia, not on the plane, but by road. Trelew lies over eight hundred miles south of the capital: a twenty-one hour coach trip.

People hurry through corridors, tugging large suitcases and small children behind them. Some have a mountain of luggage that consists simply of their possessions bundled into shiny black bin liners. Everywhere is noise and hubbub and hurry. Cafés offer last-minute coffees and sandwiches, shops sell suitcases and clothes and souvenirs from all over Argentina. Outside, coaches stand lined up or leave in clouds of exhaust fumes. They are big beasts, double-deckers, with large comfortable reclining seats.

We start at noon. Tomorrow morning, I will be in Patagonia.

We leave the city behind, drive slowly through tattered suburbs with pot-holed roads, stop on the very outskirts of the Buenos Aires sprawl. Sellers of sandwiches, sweetmeats and newspapers cluster around the doors of the coach, singing out their wares. My fellow passengers scramble out to stock up as though this were the last outpost of civilisation. Then the doors hiss shut once more, and we're on our way. The houses thin out, disappear altogether.

The road stretches ahead, as straight as an arrow. The land to both sides is lush; green, flat fields stretch all the way to the horizon. This is the *pampa húmeda*, the fertile pampas where millions of cattle graze. It goes on for hour after hour, unchanging.

Birds resembling snow-white herons stand unmoving in small ponds; others, small and tan, perch on the backs of grazing cows. Larger birds sport a lovely pattern of browns and cream, and fly away with indignant squawks as soon as the coach approaches. I recognise their calls. I have heard those before in Patagonia, last time. They are *teros*, named after their piercing cries of 'Tero – tero – tero!'

There is a swamp every now and then by the side of the road, ominously bright green or turquoise water fringed by spiky rushes. Occasionally, we pass a crossroads or a turn-off from the main road, but at times an hour goes by without any change at all, just the road dead straight ahead and the unending green outside the windows.

Road signs flash by: Bahía Blanca 427 km, Puerto Madryn 1469 km, Ushuaia 2918 km. I've never seen a four-figure distances on a road sign before.

Green fields. Cattle. The odd homestead on the horizon. Some reddish rocky hills outside the small settlement of Azul, a welcome change and very beautiful after all the green flatness. Every now and again the tattered remains of blown-out tyres lie by the roadside. I try not to think about those.

It starts to rain and the sky becomes dull and grey. Dusk falls, and the landscape is swallowed up by darkness.

On and on we go.

I fall asleep, and am jerked awake again when the bus bumps over a ramp, into a large, brightly lit space. It's 9 pm, and we have arrived at Bahía Blanca. Forty minutes' break for supper. After the meal – which is included in the price of the ticket – I stretch my stiff legs and walk outside the coach station, curious about Bahía Blanca. The town isn't very much to look at, especially in the dark. There are very few streetlights along dusty, pot-holed roads and dusty, uneven pavements. Small houses and lit windows, dogs and cars on the roads. I wander about its few streets for a while, and I feel like a stranger in a strange place; alone and far away in the darkness, in a land that isn't mine.

After Bahía Blanca the road follows the line of the coast. Orange chains of streetlights are visible in the distance, the lights of other places, mirrored in the sea. I wonder whether it has really been a good idea to come back. Perhaps I should have gone on dreaming of Patagonia without exposing myself to the reality of it again.

Visions of multi-coloured lights on the road appear to swim towards us: squares or triangles winking orange, green, yellow, red. Am I seeing UFOs? As they come closer, they turn out to belong to the long-distance lorries that travel between the port of Buenos Aires and the far south of the world, Patagonia and Tierra del Fuego. Colourful bulbs are strung around the drivers' cabs and sometimes all along the length of the vehicle.

I follow them with my eyes until they're lost from sight. I'd love to travel to the end of the continent, by car or in the cab of such a lorry. As a teenager, I used to dream of being a long-distance truck driver one day: tough and calm, with a long plait of red hair and a cool gaze and a swagger.

On and on. Night. Darkness. Sleep. Somebody snores.

I wake up around 5.30am to a bright sky and clouds. Brownish scrubland stretches to the left and right of the road. It is a sunny spring day in early November. My uneasiness evaporates. This isn't the unknown. We're in Patagonia, and everything looks familiar.

As I get off the big coach in Trelew and board a local bus to Gaiman, I feel as though I've come home, and sternly admonish myself not to get carried away. I may be filled with memories of places and people, but that doesn't mean that anybody else will have remembered me. Visitors from Europe are not exactly a rarity in Patagonia. I expect to spend some quiet weeks in Gaiman; sightseeing, going on excursions to beauty spots and into the desert, perhaps visiting the penguins again; sitting by the canal reading about the Welsh settlers, going for long walks in the valley. Nothing more.

Instead, I keep bumping into people who remember me from last time. They stop me in the street or the shop, ask me how I am. Annegret John in the health food shop is delighted when I remember her name. Clara Roberts, the choir mistress, gives me a hug in the street and tells me to come round and see her in the music school to tell her how I've been. The man at the supermarket check-out looks at me for a long moment, then breaks into a smile and says, 'You're the German writer, aren't you?'

It is strange and wonderful and I'm not quite sure what to make of it. Everybody is so *nice*. I still don't entirely understand why I have fallen so much in love with Patagonia, but this is surely one of the main reasons: the people. They are open and spontaneous, warm and friendly.

Like sunlight after a long, hard winter.

12

I GREW UP IN A PLACE much like Gaiman, small and rural and far away from everywhere, a farming village in central Germany. My parents had moved there when I was a year old. We were incomers; I grew up there but I always knew I wasn't *from* there.

Everybody in the village knew everybody else and their business. Everybody knew that the owner of the largest farm also had the biggest financial problems because he went out every weekend and spent a fortune in the bars and brothel of the market town, while his wife worked sixteen hours a day to keep the farm going. Nobody suggested she divorce him. You didn't do things like that in the village. It wouldn't have been considered right.

Everybody knew that my father was beating me whenever he felt like it and that my mother saw no reason to stop him. Walls didn't have ears but neighbours did, they heard thumps and cries. I went to some of them for help, asking them to stop what was happening to me, but they just shrugged and told me that life was like that. Nobody called in the social workers. You just didn't. It wouldn't have been considered right.

So as soon as I could, I left. There was nothing holding me in the area. I had no other family, neither brothers nor sisters, and life had taught me that I was better off without my parents. I missed the house and the farmyard sometimes, the stream and the wooded hills and the warm, dusty straw smell of harvest time, but for years I wouldn't have admitted it. I was too glad to have got away, too afraid that the past would catch up with me. I gave villages and small towns a wide berth. They reminded me, brought back old fears and the feeling of being trapped with no escape. I preferred to live and work in large cities. The year I had spent in Aberystwyth as a student had shown me that I could live by myself. I spent seven years in Berlin, then moved to Britain. I made some friends, slowly, but avoided people on the whole. After my childhood, I tended not to trust the human race very much.

And then Gaiman, small and provincial and far away from the rest of the world, where everybody knew everybody else and their business. The first time I went there, I came as an obvious stranger. I didn't know anybody and just drifted around the place for a while and then went back to where I'd come from.

On my return, Gaiman looks familiar. I remember the way the light changes on the long white hill across the valley; the dip in the road just before the turn into the main street towards the *plaza*. I recognise the dry, dusty scent of the air and the bird calls that are no longer foreign. I know people's faces, the names of streets and houses, I have memories on almost every street corner.

People remember me. I walk down the high street exchanging greetings and stopping to chat. I am most definitely not a stranger. I am somebody who has come back. It is wonderful and moving and I love it, but it scares me too. I am in a place where everybody knows everybody. I suddenly feel nine years old and back in the past. I feel trapped. I almost wish I was back in Britain. I do wish I was back in Buenos Aires, drinking coffee and smoking a cigarette in a street café, watching the endless stream of cars go by on the busy roads. I catch myself thinking that returning to Gaiman has been a mistake.

I walk past the greengrocer's, and Dudú Hughes waves at me through the window. We had laborious conversations over a pound of apples or half a dozen tomatoes the last time I was here, me in my limited Spanish and she in her limited Welsh. We stumbled over words, got caught by grammatical snares and came up against the boundaries of our knowledge. But somehow, it didn't matter. We talked anyway, mixing Welsh and Spanish regardless, waving our arms and contorting our faces to mime words we didn't know. Despite the difficulties in communicating, I got to like her very much. I go into the shop to say hello.

'You're back!' They kiss your cheek in Argentina, not the air two inches away. I feel warmed and welcome, and at the same time wary. I feel that I ought to remember what small-town people are really like, the lessons the past has taught me: not to trust them, because although they might know, they don't care. They won't help. I try to remind myself that in the years since I left the village, I have found that not everybody is untrustworthy.

I stand by the counter, feeling embarrassed and nervous and pleased to see Dudú again.

She is talking with two other women customers who have finished their shopping and now stand by the counter, gossiping. They all keep a watch on the high street out of the large front window.

'Look at her,' one of the women says, nodding at a passing car.

'New hairstyle *again*. And whose car is that she's in anyway?' She doesn't sound hostile, just curious, as though it is her right to know these things.

'Eva hasn't been to choir practice this week for the third week running,' the other contributes. 'Wonder what she's doing with her Wednesday evenings?'

'Have you heard? Elena's youngest is expecting.'

'How have you been?' Dudú asks me. 'She's from Germany, and she speaks Welsh!' she tells the two women proudly, introducing me.

I tell her that I am very well, glad to be back. I have learned more Spanish in the intervening time, so that I can now communicate with relative ease. I speak about my work, a short story that has been published in Wales, another that has won a small prize in a writing competition. She is delighted for me, asks more questions, but just then, more customers come into the shop.

'Are you doing anything tomorrow morning?' she asks. 'It's my day off. If you like, you could come to my house to drink *maté*. Then we can catch up.'

I take a long walk that evening, along the road and over the creaking footbridge that crosses the River Chubut, into the relative dark and quiet of the south side of the town. The wind whispers in the poplars that grow along the river near the old chapel, some distance back from the road and invisible now in the dark.

I feel disoriented. This is as far away from home as I have been, and here of all places I feel reminded of the village where I grew up, the village I left as soon as I could. And instead of fighting the feeling that I have returned to somewhere like my childhood home, I am welcoming it. That frightens me. I half expect a trap-door to open in the pavement, swallow me and spit me out *bang!* thirty years back in the past. I think about the things that go on behind the closed doors of Gaiman and wonder who would care enough to listen and to know. I am afraid that if I lower my guard just a little, I will lose my judgement and not be able to tell friend from foe.

I feel naked; not exposed but unprotected, reduced to my bare essentials. In the clear air of Patagonia, I'm forced to look at myself without distractions. I've never admitted before that I missed the village. Or my parents. They had been bad for me, had harmed and damaged me in ways I am still finding out about more than a decade and a half after I left them for good.

As a child, I built myself a mental shelter in which I could survive. It was founded on the firm belief that I was, in every way that counted, utterly unlike my parents. I had nothing to do with them. I would never be like them. I long ago stopped loving them. Even now it seems to me insane and dangerous to miss them when they did me so much harm, but here under the dark, brilliant night sky of Gaiman, I can admit for the first time that I do.

I look up at the unfamiliar stars of the southern hemisphere, and imagine that I am on another planet. I can *feel* how far away I am; just me, memories and fears and dreams and hopes, ten thousand miles away from home. Just me and my life and the stars in the huge, velvety Patagonian night.

13

NEXT MORNING, I TAKE THE back way to Dudú's house, turning off the main road and on to a promising footpath that dips and winds around a hillside, in and out of thorny shrubs. Every now and again I slide down in a mini landslide of gravel and dust and clamber back up onto the path, negotiating the thorns as best I can. A sudden rustling noise makes me jump: a large hare runs from the shelter of the bushes across the path and disappears again behind a rock on the other side.

The path seems to mark the boundary between Gaiman and the wilderness. To my left are houses and back gardens with clothes-lines, toys, flowers, to my right only dust and thorn bushes and wild hares.

I emerge abruptly onto a road, firmly back in civilisation with no idea where I am in relation to Dudú's house. I have to ask a woman who is passing me in the otherwise empty street. She knows Dudú, nods and pours forth a stream of rapid Spanish. I am pleased and surprised to find that I understand her. A few minutes later, I find myself outside Dudú's house.

'So there you are,' she says with her slow, warm smile when I knock on her door. 'Come in, come in, I've just put the kettle on. Do you drink *maté*?'

'Why not,' I say. 'I'd like to give it a go.'

She looks doubtful. 'Are you sure? I can make you a cup of tea if you like.'

Maté is the Argentinian national drink, made by pouring not-quite-boiling water over the leaves of the *yerba* bush. I took some back with me from my last visit and tried to brew a cup of *maté* at home, but I don't think I did it right. The result tasted horrible.

'I'll try *maté*,' I say firmly.

Maté is drunk out of a gourd and through the *bombilla*, a kind of metal straw with a little sieve at the lower end to keep the *yerba* leaves out of your mouth. When you drink *maté* with someone, you share cup and *bombilla*. It's a companionable kind of drink. Bitter, admittedly, but Dudú has added camomile blossoms and plenty of sugar. She laughs when I say that I sort of like it.

We talk about money, and life, and work. When I tell her what I earn per hour in the temping jobs I sometimes do, she gasps.

'I make less than that in a day!'

The Argentinian currency crashed disastrously some years ago and lost three quarters of its value. But even before, my earnings would clearly have been way above hers. I feel very rich and first-world, and not entirely comfortable with it.

'Do you have a flat or a house?' Dudú asks me.

I make a face. 'Neither. I rent a room in a house-share, that's all I can afford.'

'Oh,' Dudú says and looks around herself. 'This is my house, I finally paid the mortgage off.'

Before coming here, I worried that our meeting would be strained and awkward. Our backgrounds are so different, my Spanish is still quite basic, and we don't really know each other at all. But it isn't awkward, and it turns out that we aren't all that different.

Dudú asks about my parents. I never quite know how to answer that one, so I cautiously say that I'm not in touch with them.

'Oh?' she says, and I tell her a bit more.

'They mistreated me when I was little.'

People have all sorts of different ways of reacting to this state-ment. Some look uncomfortable, pretend they haven't heard and go on to talk about the weather. Others get almost aggressive in defence of The Family, tell me that I ought to forgive and forget and extend the hand of friendship. Most avoid actually talking about what happened.

There is a brief silence.

'They hit you?' asks Dudú.

'Yes,' I say and let out a long breath. I am relieved and nervous, all at once.

She nods slowly. 'And so you left? How old were you when you left?'

'Twenty-two,' I say.

'Oh?' she says again, maybe because it seems to her quite old to leave a bad home.

'I was afraid of them, afraid to leave,' I try to explain. 'I wasn't sure I knew how to live on my own.' She nods again, accepting what I have said. We sit in silence for a while, but it is a comfort-able silence. I light a cigarette, Dudú opens the front door to let the smoke out. Sunlight and bird calls drift in, the occasional noise of a car driving by. Dudú refills the *maté* gourd with hot water, adds a couple of sugars and pushes it across the table to me. The taste is just as strong and bitter as I remember it, with added sweetness. Then she tells me about herself. She comes from a small place in the Andes, where she lived with her husband and four children. But the husband treated her badly, and so in the end she took the children and left him. She stayed with her parents first, but that was in the same small town, still too close to the home she had left. She left and came to Gaiman, several hundred miles away. Here, she found herself a flat.

'Eventually,' she says emphatically and takes a long sip of *maté*, hot, sweet, bitter, comforting. People saw her arrive, a single woman with four children. The place she had left was far away, but news travelled fast. Like a lot of the people of Gaiman, Dudú is of Welsh extraction, and inevitably related to a lot of them, albeit distantly. Soon everybody knew that she had left her husband. There was a lot of gossip. Everybody had a firm opinion of Dudú: she had broken up the family. She was a bad woman. She should not have left him. When she was finally given a council flat, people said that the council shouldn't have given her the place – that it was a flat for a family, not for a single woman.

I stare at Dudú incredulously when she tells me that bit. 'You weren't a single woman, you had four kids to look after!'

'But I didn't have a husband,' she explains patiently. She seems amused by my indignation, and at the same time angry in a distant way. 'While we waited for the council flat, we lived for three years in a house without running water and electricity. With four small children, can you imagine?'

I can't.

I admire Dudú's courage, her determination, her lack of bitterness.

'He didn't let me live,' Dudú says, talking about the man she left. 'I didn't want to leave him, but there wasn't any other way. He would wash *at least* twice a day and change all his clothes. I had to wash them, iron them. Everything had to be in its place, always, the way he liked it. Always. And when it wasn't...'

She shakes her head, her eyes turned inwards.

'Did he ever get violent?' I ask.

'Sometimes,' she says, matter-of-factly, 'you couldn't talk to him. Everything had to be exactly how he wanted. He wouldn't allow me to go out, to go to work, to read even! I couldn't have any sort of life at all. So in the end, I took the children and left.'

I hadn't wanted to leave my parents, hadn't wanted to give up hope that one day, things would change. I'd been afraid to leave, unsure what they might do; I'd doubted my ability to earn a living, run my own life. My belief in myself had been badly undermined. But I did want to have my own life. So, like Dudú, I eventually decided to leave so I could live and be myself.

'It was the right thing to do,' I say, to myself as much as to her.

She smiles, sighs. 'It was. But it was hard. I didn't have any money. I had to look for a job and everything. I put all four kids through school, but there wasn't enough money for all of them to go to university.'

She gets up. 'Let's have another *maté*. Or perhaps a cup of tea for you?'

I had tried not to grimace at the bitterness of the *maté*, but she must have noticed my less than enthusiastic response to it.

'Yes, please. *Panad o de i fi*. I'll have a cuppa.'

I feel shaky and alarmed and comforted as I walk away from Dudú's house. We spent nearly three hours talking over *maté* and tea. I can't remember when I last told a virtual stranger so much about myself, so many personal things that I usually keep hidden. But it isn't just that. I feel again as I did the night before when I was out walking under the stars: stripped of my everyday masks, down to the bare bones of who I really am. I am a battered child, a grown-up woman and a writer, all at once. I didn't give up on the humanity in me and in others, despite everything. And in Patagonia, of all places, I have met a kindred soul.

I clamber up the hill. From up here, I can see all of Gaiman laid out beneath my feet, the valley gathered up in folds and hills along both sides. Bryngwyn (the white hill) across the valley lies smooth and golden in the sunlight. The river sparkles like a silver snake. It's quiet, so quiet. The only noise comes from bird calls, the buzzing of insects and the occasional drone of a plane high overhead.

14

John Morgan James was born in 1870, the youngest of a family of twelve. He grew up on a 200-acre sheep farm in Ponterwyd in mid Wales. By the time he was in his teens, he could see that his chances of ever inheriting anything worth farming were slim. He would have known other people who left Wales in search of land and a better life; older siblings and cousins and friends who'd gone to Wisconsin or New South Wales to make a fresh start. He would have seen envelopes arrive, covered with writing in a familiar hand and strange, unknown stamps; bringing news from distant places. The New World was far away, but it contained people he knew. So he, too, decided to take the big step into the unknown. In 1886, when he was just sixteen, he left the farm, and Wales and Britain, and everything familiar, and went across the ocean to Patagonia where they were looking for settlers. He may have reasoned that the small colony in the Chubut valley was at least self-contained, Welsh-speaking and chapel-going, a village on the other side of the world that was perhaps not so different from Ponterwyd. He arrived just in time for someone to put a shovel into his hand and tell him to help dig the new irrigation canal. Not, perhaps, the welcome he had envisaged.

But when the canal had been finished, he was given a hundred acres of land in the valley, and in time he built himself a house and got married. He and his wife had twelve children and innumerable grandchildren. One of his granddaughters is named Lisa: the very Lisa James who gave me that memorable Welsh-language tour of Buenos Aires.

'*¿Hola, Lisa? Imogen ydw i,*' I say, clutching the phone. My Spanish has improved so much that when I try to speak in Welsh, my sentences come out in a wild jumble of Welsh and Spanish. Somehow, it's even worse when I talk on the phone. 'I'm back in the valley, and I'd love to meet up. Do you have time?'

'*Wrth gwrs!*' she replies in Welsh. Of course. We arrange to meet for a cup of tea, and over the apple pie she announces that if I like, she is going to give me a tour of the *chacras* – the farms – in the valley, and show me where she grew up. She never sold the farm house that John Morgan James built with his own hands more than a hundred years ago.

We set out next afternoon. The sky is its customary blue. The wind rustles the leaves of the poplar trees by the river as we cross the bridge. A couple of kilometres on, Lisa turns off the main road. Now we are travelling on a gravel track, the Patagonian B road. Occasionally, another vehicle comes towards us. Every time one of them passes us in the road, Lisa puts the back of her hand against the windscreen and turns her head away, in case a stone should hit the glass. All the roads are straight, crossing each other at regular intervals. You can tell that they were mapped out on a drawing board before they were built.

We drive past fields, cows, sheep, wheat and the occasional row of high, slender trees. In this land where the wind is never silent, the fast-growing poplars make a good wind break. Lisa turns off the gravel road onto a grass track and stops the car. In a field in front of us stands a red-brick building.

'*Capel Bethesda*,' Lisa says. We speak Welsh (mostly), and every now and again she slips in a sentence in Spanish. 'This is where I went to Chapel and Sunday School as a child. I even taught here myself, briefly, after I'd been to university and become a teacher. I was so nervous! I was only twenty years old, and I still felt like a child, being back in my old school, you know.'

We get out and walk around. There stands a Welsh chapel – sheltered porch, red-brick walls, elongated pointed windows and all – in the middle of the flat Patagonian landscape. On the façade is engraved, 'Bethesda 1904'.

John Morgan James would have been thirty-four the year this chapel was built. He had become a successful farmer with a growing family. The first settlers, the adults of that small group of 153 that had come over on the *Mimosa* nearly forty years earlier, were old people by then, some of them dead and laid to rest in the earth they had chosen over that of their homeland. Their children had been born here or had made the crossing as infants, too young to remember anything but this dusty landscape of brown and gold, the white hill across the valley, the huge horizon, the endless skies. This was their home. Did they think of themselves as Welsh or Argentinian, or both? Were they secretly wishing for a ship that would take them back to the land of their fathers and mothers?

I try to imagine them, and find that I can't think of them in any other way but as people who loved the land, this land: the wind whispering in the poplar trees, the dry air scented with the clean smell of dust, the murmuring river, the wide open sky and the roads that go on forever, into the unknown, towards the Andes mountain range hundreds of miles to the west. Some of them might have longed for life in a large city, a variety of people, no minister to tell them what to do, not to swear and not to sin. They might have felt constricted by a life of work and morality and not much else. Some no doubt left. But perhaps even they, like Lisa (like me) would come back from time to time, would not want to cut themselves off completely from the land. They would miss the city when they were here, and the open land, the sky and the stars, when they were back in the city.

The word *chacra* comes from Quetchua, the Inca language that is still spoken today by millions of people in Bolivia, Peru, Ecuador and the north-western parts of Argentina. *Chacra* in Quetchua means land, plains, field. In Argentinian Spanish the word has come to mean a smallish farm.

'And now I'll show you where I grew up,' says Lisa as we get back into the car to drive on.

It isn't far from the chapel, another kilometre or so. To our left is a field full of cows, ahead another row of green poplars swaying in the wind. We turn left into a short driveway and Lisa stops the car.

'*Treborth*,' she says, introducing the house. It is a compact, good-sized building, made of red brick with a tiled roof and a sturdy wooden front door. A wonderful smell of woodsmoke scents the air. Across the road lies the entrance to another farmyard.

'My neighbours,' Lisa says. 'They're keeping an eye on the place for me when I'm not here. We'll go and say hello presently, I want to have a look at the house first. Oh, I hope everything will be all right! I haven't been here for months and months, and we've had such storms and rain! I hope it hasn't been burgled, it is so isolated out here...'

We go round the house first. The large round metal water tank on the roof appears undamaged. The window panes are hung with cobwebs and blind with dust, but they are whole. The chimney still stands where it should. In the shrubs that divide the garden from the field beyond, a white turkey scratches in the soil and seems to watch us out of the corner of its eye.

To the side of the house, a stack of metal pipes lie in the long, unkempt grass. Lisa nudges them with a foot.

'For water,' she says, annoyed. 'We don't get piped water out here. Recently, the council finally decided to connect us to the water grid. We had to pay for the pipes, and *they*'re supposed to put them in the ground and do the plumbing work. Half a year ago I bought those pipes, and nothing at all has happened.'

She sighs.

'Let's go inside,' she says and walks to the front door. 'Oh, Imogen, I hope everything will be all right inside!'

The front door is stuck. Lisa stands for a moment, perhaps entertaining visions of fallen masonry blocking it from the inside. Then she takes a deep breath and applies her shoulder. The door opens with a screech of wood scraping on stone and a creak of unoiled hinges, and we are inside. The light is dim, all the curtains are drawn. There is a strong smell of mothballs, dust and enclosed air.

The house feels like a place that has not been lived in for a long time. Everything in it looks old-fashioned and unused.

Lisa goes from room to room, exclaiming with relief that things are just as she left them. In the *parlwr* (the parlour), stern, high-backed wooden chairs are assembled around a long, dark table. An old wooden chest covered with a white cloth looks like a coffin. At the head of the table, over the fireplace, hangs a Bible text done in cross-stitch in a large, gilded frame.

The only furniture in the master bedroom are two ornate iron bedsteads, side by side but separated from each other by a decorous distance.

Lisa nods at the furniture. 'All this was brought over from Wales.'

Across the corridor lies the nursery for Lisa and her sister. Somebody has scratched LISA in large, inch-high letters on the brick mantelpiece.

'I did that when I was little!' Lisa says. 'Look at it, isn't it terrible?!'

I have to smile. 'No, it's not.'

But Lisa is still shaking her head. She has become rather respectable. What would the child Lisa think if she could see herself now?

The floorboards creak under our feet. I try to imagine Lisa and her sister Bethan living here as children, surrounded by solid

Victorian furniture that had come all the way from Wales, straight-backed chairs and Bible verses on the wall, and the Bible-black cast-iron stove that lives in a small room off the parlour. The stove is a proper work of art. Except for the top, every square inch of it is covered in ornate swirls and scrollwork. It crouches in a corner like a prehistoric beast, aware that its time has passed but refusing to die.

'My mother used that for cooking and baking,' Lisa says.

There are electric sockets in the walls, switches by the doors and light bulbs under the shades that hang from the ceiling. Everything seems to be the latest technology, *circa* 1930. I'm not entirely sure that the twenty-first century has arrived inside the house. Gaiman may be small and provincial, but it lives in the present: it has *two* internet cafés, bars with pinball machines, a health food shop. Out here in Treborth, the past has massed like clouds. Every room is thick with days long gone.

'Let's have a cup of tea!' Lisa says.

I follow her to the kitchen, glad to have my train of thought interrupted. But she isn't in the kitchen, she has gone out to the car and is now wrestling a large water canister through the front door.

'No piped water out here,' she says somewhat out of breath, and sets the canister down with a thump on the table. 'That water tank on the roof is only for washing and for flushing the toilet, you can't drink the stuff. We have to bring our own.'

She rattles about in the cupboard and extracts a kettle, opens the gas supply and lights one ring. I am glad to see the modern white gas cooker. For a moment I was afraid that we'd have to boil our water on the cast-iron beast.

We drink our tea in the *parlwr* at the long table. Sunlight comes in through the opened curtains and the front door that Lisa has left open. We can hear the sighing of the wind in the trees from outside, the fluttering of their leaves, bird voices and an occasional moo from the cows.

Slowly, the house is drawing breath and reviving, filling with fresh air and light.

15

AFTER TEA, LISA AND I put the shroud back over table and chairs and go outside. We stow the canister in the car, then cross the track and walk towards the source of the wonderful smell of woodsmoke, the neighbouring *chacra*.

They are having an *asado* over there, an Argentinian barbecue: half a cow or sheep or goat on iron skewers over a large open fire. The smell is delicious, even to a vegetarian.

A bow-legged man, his face brown and wrinkly like a walnut under the broad brim of his black hat, comes out to meet us.

'*¡Hola!*' says Lisa to him, and to me, 'This is David Evans – *Cymro ydy o!* He's Welsh.'

This last seemed hard to believe. But the improbably named David Evans nods vigorously.

'*Mi abuelo era galés*,' he says in Spanish. Grandfather was Welsh.

He himself doesn't speak the language any more. 'But I've got the blood,' he says proudly.

He and Lisa chat in rapid Spanish, about Treborth and the water pipes – the council haven't got round to connecting the Evans farm to the water supply either – and the weather. We are invited to the *asado*, but Lisa declines. We're off again.

'I'm going to show you my sister's farm,' she explains in the car.

We drive along another gravel track past cows, sheep, tall green poplars swaying in the wind, pastures, wheat, more sheep. Lisa stops the car by a little stream.

I can make out the faint outlines of a house through a thick screen of tall bushes. We hop across the stream. A large, black-and-white border collie comes running, barking energetically. I can guess without being told that its ancestors, too, came over from Wales. Lisa laughs and greets the dog by name. It stops barking and wags its tail. The kitchen door opens and a woman comes out.

I haven't met Bethan yet, I only know her from imagining her childhood with Lisa in Treborth. I don't realise that I am thinking of her as a little girl until I see a woman of sixty-odd with her hair in a grey bun walk towards us from the house, and hear Lisa greet her, in Welsh, as Bethan. Behind her comes a younger woman with straight black hair and Asian features.

Lisa performs the introductions. 'Bethan, Nasako, this is

Imogen. She is from Germany and she speaks Welsh and Spanish. *Es un bicho raro, ¿no?'* (She is a rare beast.)

Everybody laughs.

'This is my sister Bethan, and this is Nasako, Jaime's wife. Jaime is my nephew, Bethan's son.' She turns to Bethan. 'I suppose he's still out on the *camp*, or is he here?'

(*Camp* comes from Spanish *campo*, meaning the countryside.)

'No, he's in the kitchen,' Bethan says. 'There's cake.'

I learn belatedly that today is Mothering Sunday in Argentina, a very important holiday. That's why Bethan – who usually lives in Trelew – is out here on the farm that is now being run by Jaime and Nasako, having cake with her family. Lisa has skipped a similar celebration with her own son and his wife in Gaiman, in order to show me the *chacras*. I feel honoured, and touched.

'Nasako is Japanese,' Lisa continues. 'As you can see.'

'Japanese, or Japanese-Argentinian?' I ask.

'I was born here, in Argentina. Buenos Aires,' Nasako explains. There is a very slight Japanese accent to her Spanish. 'My parents came from Japan. I spent half a year there, studying; but I did the rest of my degree in Buenos Aires, like Jaime. That's where we met. We're both agricultural engineers.'

'The children,' Lisa adds as we go into the house, 'are trilingual: they speak Japanese, Spanish – and Welsh, of course!'

Of course.

The kitchen is a wonderfully warm, welcoming, lived-in, cluttered space, and looks like farm-house kitchens everywhere in the world. On the tiled floor are cats and an elderly dog and pot plants and drying rubber boots. On the table books, newspapers, fruit, toys, a teapot and various cakes jostle for space.

Chairs scrape as Jaime and his father get up to greet us ladies.

'Do have some cake!' Nasako says hospitably.

I exchange smiles with her eldest daughter, a girl of thirteen or so who sits on a bench with a cat on her lap. We sit down and have more tea and cake. For a moment or two I'm not quite sure where I am, Argentina, Wales, Germany even. I feel at home and welcome. Somehow, I don't get round to feeling shy or nervous.

Lisa and Bethan and Jaime have a chat about the farm while I talk to Bethan's husband Gwylim. He speaks wonderful Welsh, round and fluent and full of flourishes. Many of the younger generation – that is, fifty and under – in Patagonia speak the language well enough, but a lot of them have a distinct Spanish accent on it, and they often leave out mutations and the more complicated and obscure grammatical rules. Gwylim Jones doesn't, and although I find him harder to understand because of it, I bask in the beauty of his language.

16

IN THE MID NINETEENTH CENTURY, Captain George Chaworth Musters wanted to travel to the ends of the earth: somewhere wild, uncivilised, unexplored; to a grand wild empty country. So he went to Patagonia.

He arrived in 1869 and spent the best part of one year not – as one might expect from a British gentleman explorer – hunting, shooting and fishing with fellow officers. He went to live with the indigenous Patagonians, the *Aoniken* or Tehuelche, travelling with them through the desert and the tablelands. (He did manage to get quite a lot of hunting and shooting in, though.) His account, *At Home with the Patagonians*, makes a refreshing change from the travel writing perpetrated by many of his Victorian contemporaries. He displays great liking and respect for the Tehuelche and takes them pretty much as equals. He describes them as an independent, hospitable people, at ease with themselves and not overly curious about the outside world; and not at all worried – not yet – that people were coming to settle on their land.

The Patagonians spent their winters on the coast where the cold was less severe. In spring and summer, they followed and hunted the guanaco across the steppe to the foothills of the Andes. They covered vast distances, ranging all the way to the Strait of Magellan, 800 miles to the south. They lived in *toldos*, large tents made of guanaco hides strung over wooden poles, 'strongly resembling those of our gipsies,' Musters wrote. 'The furniture of the toldos consists of one or two bolsters and a horse hide or two to each sleeping compartment, one to act as a curtain and the other as bedding.... As a rule all the inmates of the toldo sit upon Nature's carpet, which has the advantage of being easily cleaned, for the Tehuelches are very particular about the cleanliness of the interior of their dwellings.'[13]

They fashioned intricate silver ornaments – belt buckles, earrings, spurs, necklaces – from silver dollars; squabbled amongst themselves like all small communities do; stole horses for a laugh and to show off their skill. Tehuelche ideas of personal property were different from European ones. 'They believe that when they find something belonging to another person,' William Hughes wrote in his memoir; 'or when the rightful owner had not looked after it properly, he loses all right to it, and they appropriate the item with the greatest naturalness. They also believe that if a person has more possessions than he needs, he ought to share his belongings with those who own less. If that opinion is not favourably received by the proprietor, one who owns less will take it upon himself to redistribute the said belongings by abstracting the necessary – or frequently more than necessary, especially in the case of "Cristianos", Christians, as they call all Spaniards.'[14]

George Musters had a somewhat different take on the Tehuelche character. 'Their natural bias is towards independence, and they have rather insubordinate ideas of "one man being as good as another". Cuastro's dying words, "I die as I have lived – no *cacique* (chief) orders me," aptly express the prevalent feelings on this subject.'[15]

A number of different indigenous peoples once lived in the vast territory of Patagonia, of which the Chubut valley is only one small part. The three main groups were the *Günün A Künna* (the Pampas Indians), the Tehuelche (*Aoniken* in their own language), and Mapuche. They each spoke a different language, lived in different – but overlapping – territories and differed somewhat in their culture. But it would be wrong to imagine the three peoples as modern nation-states, keeping to themselves within their respective borders. Probably no more than 100,000 people shared that vast territory. (Even today, with 1.9 million people living in an area five times the size of Great Britain, Patagonia is extremely thinly populated.) They would have gone for months without meeting anyone. But when they did meet, they did not just pass as ships in the night. Every meeting was like a funfair, a marriage market, a party. There were squabbles, raids, battles and fights, trading, frequent intermarriages and cultural crossovers.

The Tehuelche, George Musters' Patagonians, are generally described as gentle giants, tall and peaceful. (Charles Darwin in 1834, in the diary he kept during the voyage of the *Beagle*, found them 'thoroughly good-humoured & unsuspecting'.)[16]

The hunting grounds of the Pampas Indians lay to the north of the river Chubut and stretched into the green and fruitful prairies of the pampas, where they lived by hunting and cattle-raiding. They were generally described as more mobile and more warlike than the Tehuelche. To the best of my knowledge, there are no Pampas Indians left today.

The last – and the biggest – major group are the Mapuche (the *Araucanos* or *Chilenos* of nineteenth-century accounts). They are described as short of stature and fiery of temperament; a proud, warrior people. Mapuche have been living on both sides of the Andes for almost a millennium[17]; originating, probably, on the western side of the mountains, the area they call *Gülü Mapu*, the Western Earth: today the country of Chile.

Mapuche make their first appearance in the accounts of Inca historians in the fifteenth century. The expansionist Inca had sent an army down the spine of the South American continent all the way to Patagonia, to incorporate its fertile valleys into *Tawantinsuyu*, the Land of Four Corners, their Empire: at the time the largest in the world. But they met with unexpected resistance. The Mapuche fought back and in the end the Inca army – although superior in numbers and technology – was forced to retreat. It was a story that would repeat itself when Mapuche armies resisted the Spanish, too, fiercely and successfully for several centuries. They fought off armies equipped with firearms and forced Spain to acknowledge in a binding treaty the sovereignty of the Mapuche Nation: a unique case in the history of South America.[18] When the newly established Republic of Chile attained independence early in the nineteenth century, it inherited the treaty. And broke it a few decades later by sending more armies south. By the end of the century, the firepower of modern guns finally forced the Mapuche to give up armed struggle.

The situation was somewhat different in Argentine Patagonia. The Chilean Mapuche lived in rich, lush valleys attractive for agriculture. But the travellers to the Argentinian south had unanimously reported everlasting, flat, dry, horrible and empty desert. If the Indians wanted to live there, they were welcome to it. So they were left in peace.

17

BEFORE THEY SET OUT from Liverpool, the Welsh pioneers had been told that the native Patagonians were peaceful, and that they were happy to trade. Even so, the settlers still worried. Patagonia did not have the best of reputations. When Lady Florence Dixie, desirous of adventure and novelty, planned a trip there in 1879, her friends were aghast: 'Who would ever think of going to such a place? Why, you will be eaten up by cannibals!'[19] Welsh papers like the *Herald Gymreig* had predicted a bloody end to the colony at the hands of the Indians and condemned the irresponsibility of Michael D. Jones and Lewis Jones of luring unsuspecting Welsh men, women and children to their certain deaths on the Patagonian frontier.[20] 'Since you will not be dissuaded from expatriating yourselves to that wild outlandish desert,' an uncle wrote in a letter to his emigrating nephew; 'I write to wish you a safe and pleasant voyage and much success in your new country. If the Indians do eat you, I can only wish them a confounded bad digestion.'[21]

While the settlers did not exactly anticipate being eaten by Indians, they were certainly nervous about the possibility of attack. So nervous, in fact, that they brought with them, amongst the wheat and wooden boards, the Bibles and shovels and ploughs, a good number of guns. Once they had established themselves in Rawson, a militia of 30 men was organised and drilled to defend the settlement against attack.[22]

Only there was no sign of Indians. The first winter passed slowly, with rain and fog and cold winds, and finally turned to spring. It was time to move out to the farms, to build houses and clear the land for sowing. But what if they went out into that vast quiet land, and the Indians were to attack? At least in the village, in Rawson, they were all together. Out on the farm, each family would have to fend for itself.

They had never met an Indian. The Argentine government had negotiated on their behalf with a number of chiefs to whom it paid an annual tribute of flour, sugar, cattle and horses as a kind of rent on the land occupied by the Welsh. In return, the chiefs undertook to leave the Welsh colony in peace. However, a letter by *cacique* Antonio, which was brought to the fledgling village of Rawson at the end of 1865 half a year after the arrival of the Welsh, claimed that things were not quite so straightforward, and might well have alarmed the settlers.

> Very distinguished Sir,
> WITHOUT having the pleasure of knowing you personally, I know as a fact that you are peopling the Chupat with people from the other side of the sea. You, doubtless, do not know that in the country south of Buenos Ayres there exist three distinct sets of Indians.

Cacique Antonio does a nice line in diplomacy here, being bonhomous, welcoming and very courteous; while at the same time establishing his superior local knowledge and the fact that the Welsh are both newcomers and ignorant of the lie of the land.

It is also interesting to read his description of the three 'distinct sets of Indians'. In the vast majority of literature and local lore about *Y Wladfa,* mention is only made of the Tehuelche as the only indigenous people in the vastness of Patagonia. In fact, as Antonio states, there were three:

> To the north of the Río Negro (Patagones) and on the borders of the high mountains, which the Christians call Cordillera, lives a nation of Indians demoninated 'Chilenos' [Mapuche]. These Indians are of small stature, and they speak the language called Chilons.
> Between the Río Negro and the Río Chupat lives another nation, who are of taller stature than the Chilenos, and who dress themselves in guanaco mantles, and speak a different language. This is the nation called 'Pampa', and speaking Pampa. I and my people belong to it.
> To the south of the Chupat lies another nation called 'Tehuelche', a people still taller than we are, and who speak a distinct language.
> Now, I say that the plains between the Chupat [today the River Chubut], the Afon Camwy of the Welsh and the Río Negro are ours, and that we never sold them. Our fathers sold the plains of Bahía Blanca and Patagones, but nothing more....
> I have a Treaty of Peace with Patagones, but that does not touch on selling lands. I know very well that you have negotiated with the Government to colonize the Chupat; but you ought also to negotiate with us, who are the owners of these lands.

You can almost hear the Welsh gulp at this point of the letter, sitting in sorry little mud huts in the middle of nowhere, hundreds of miles from the nearest town, surrounded by Indians and utterly defenceless.

> But, never mind, friend.... Our plains have plenty of guana-cos and plenty of ostriches [rheas]. We are never in want of food.
>
> Notwithstanding, if plenty of people come, we shall have to go to the plains, frightening the animals which are our property, that were given to us by our God, the God of the Indians, so that we might chase them for food.[23]

The Welsh, now thoroughly alarmed despite the overall friendly tone of this missive, sent out members of the militia as a search party further inland. The party went some twenty or thirty miles upstream where it encountered a large and impassable rock wall, through which the river had cut a narrow channel. It was an easily defendable bottleneck, and a place from which attack by a large group of Indians was unlikely.

They returned to Rawson relieved, believing themselves to live in a virtually isolated valley and thus safe. They duly went to live on their allocated land.[24]

There are two versions of the story of how the first contact finally came about. Both have been passed on orally and told as gospel, and it is impossible now to say what really happened.

The first one goes like this. On the very day of the first wedding feast to be held in *Y Wladfa*, a man on an outlying farm – who appears not to have been invited – saw a dust cloud on the horizon. Looking more closely, he observed a small group of Indians riding at a leisurely but determined pace towards the settlement. It was winter again, the June of 1866, almost a whole year after the settlers' arrival. Perhaps the valley wasn't quite as isolated as they had thought. He jumped on his horse and rode with all speed to warn the wedding party. Shortly afterwards, the Indians arrived, solemn and polite, and by means of some Spanish words and much sign language, both sides managed to inform each other that their motives were peaceful.

I like the other story better. A woman – nobody knows her name – was at home in her isolated farmstead in the valley, washing or cooking or baking or darning or hoeing the garden and looking after the children, while her husband was out in the fields. A small group of Indians on horseback appeared on the horizon and came solemnly riding towards her. Now at this time, apart from Antonio's letter, there had been no contact whatever between Welsh and Indian.

It could have been very ugly. The Indians had no firearms. The Welsh did. Had the woman panicked, had a few men with guns been there – who knows.

But it didn't happen like that.

The woman waited until the small group had arrived and got off their horses. They couldn't have communicated by words, because none of them spoke the other's language. So she did something else to show them that the Welsh had come in peace: she took the most precious thing she had, the baby that she was carrying in her arms, and put it into the arms of one of the Indian women.

Peace, said the gesture. Trust. Friends.

And the Indians understood.

The Welsh had named their first settlement Rawson in honour of Dr Guillermo Rawson, the Argentine minister of the interior who had done much to help the colony in its fledgling years. They called the second one Gaiman after the name given to the place by the Tehuelche: *gaiman'k* in their language means whetstone, because here by the banks of the river were found the best stones for sharpening knives.

In the decades before the arrival of the Welsh, groups of Indians had traded with the Argentine outpost Carmen de Patagones, exchanging feathers, skins and meat for sugar, tea and flour and most of all, cheap alcohol, the curse Europeans brought to the Americas. They relied on the trade but were under no illusion about the inhabitants of the trading post.

'Be not afraid of us, my friend,' wrote *cacique* Antonio in his first letter to the Welsh; 'I and my people are contented to see you colonize on the Chupat, for we shall have a nearer place to go in order to trade, without the necessity of going to Patagones, where they steal our horses and where the "pulperos" [tavern keepers] rob and cheat us....'[25]

To the Welsh, of course, Antonio's plains full of food was the inhospitable dusty desert. But the Indians taught them to see the land in a new way.

After the first abundant harvest of 1867, the Welsh happily traded bread with the Indians, for whom this was rapidly becoming a great and much sought-after delicacy. *Bara* – bread – was reputedly the first Welsh word spoken by a native Patagonian. In time, several Tehuelche learnt to speak fluent Welsh; and some of the Welsh learnt the *Aoniken* language.

And when a year later the harvest failed catastrophically, and the Argentine government refused to send more food, it was the Patagonians who came to the rescue. They took young Welsh men with them and taught them how to hunt guanaco and rhea and hare using the bolas, a kind of lasso with three round, heavy stones wrapped in leather at the end. Bolas were used both as weapons of war and for hunting. A hunter would whirl the lasso over his head then throw it out. The strong leather strap weighed down by stones wrapped itself round the neck or feet of his prey, immobilising it immediately.

For one entire year, 1869-1870, during which the little settlement was cut off from all contact with the outside world except for the Patagonians[26], all they had to live on was the meat they hunted, and plants and roots they grubbed up. Without the help of the Indians, the Welsh colony would have never survived.

18

I'M SITTING IN *Ar Lan yr Afon* one warm evening in early summer; in the living room with its Welsh dresser which Natalia's great-grandmother had bought from the *Compañía Mercantíl*, the Chubut Trading Co., which had it shipped across the Atlantic; its Welsh Bible verses in cross-stitch, its framed tea-towel of Llanfairpwllgwyngyllgogerychwyrndrobwllllantysiliogogogoch, its china Welsh lady on a side table, complete with stovepipe hat and daffodils. It's been a hot day, and I am sunburnt and dusty and glad to be resting inside the cool walls of the old house, before I go out later with Clara Roberts and her husband Amando for a meal in Trelew. (Amando's last name isn't Roberts; he's of Spanish extraction and called Martínez. Clara's full name is Clara Roberts de Martínez. When a woman marries in Argentina, she adds her husband's name to her own by means of a *de*. In *Y Wladfa*, I've met women called Hughes de Williams or Freeman de Jones, and even Jones de Jones.)

Sounds from outside drift through the narrow gaps of the shutters: shrill bird calls, glugs from the river, the yapping of small dogs, the revving of motors from the main road, the rustle of the wind in the poplars that line the river.

Most of those sounds should clash with the violently Welsh interior of *Ar Lan yr Afon*. But I've been here for so long now that they don't. It feels quite natural to me to speak a mix of Welsh and Spanish; to kiss people's cheeks for a greeting and ask, '*A syt 'dych chi heddiw*?' (And how are you today?). Everybody kisses absolutely everybody hello in Argentina. It's lovely.

Into my musings sounds a knock on the door. Natalia answers it; there are greetings and exclamations in Spanish and then she reappears, with a well-nourished, pink-faced, pinstriped gentleman in tow.

'Can you believe it?' she says to me, beaming. 'You will never guess who this is.'

She's right.

'He is a cousin of...'

Well?

'Che Guevara.'

'No!'

Yes. Unbelievable. There he is, pointing to the dimple in his clean-shaven chin and assuring us that *el Che* had one just like it, only you couldn't see his, obviously, because of the beard.

'But he did have one, just like this, like mine, look!'

For further proof, he tells us his family history, and *el Che*'s, of course. It sounds as though the two grew up together.

'So what was he like, as a boy?' I ask, fascinated despite myself. The man is so terribly unlike a revolutionary. But it is quite true that Ernesto 'Che' Guevara came from an upper-middle-class, conservative family.

'Ah, no,' says the visitor, not a bit abashed; 'you misunderstand me. I never *met* him. I met his father once, Ernesto Guevara *padre*. When I was a child. But we were closely related. Our grandmothers were the sisters Lynch.'

'That's an Irish name,' interrupts Natalia. 'Celtic! *El Che* had Celtic blood!'

They beam at each other.

Their grandfathers, continues the visitor (I never catch his name), the Guevaras, were also brothers. 'So you see,' he concludes triumphantly, 'two of our sets of grandparents were siblings. Really, *el Che* and me, we're practically brothers.'

'How fascinating!' exclaims Natalia. 'What a wonderful story it will make for your book. – Imogen is writing a book about Patagonia,' she explains to the visitor. 'She will want to hear all about you!'

To which there really isn't anything I can say, except to nod and express polite interest. And immediately wish I hadn't, because now *el primo del Che*, Che's cousin, launches into a story about his business activities, followed by a detailed account of the religious organisation he supports, the main function of which appears to be to combat the rising tide of secularism in Argentina. (I imagine *el Che* revolving in his grave.) The Virgin Mary comes into it somewhere, too, but his Spanish is rapid and I am tired, and find my attention drifting away. I wonder whether his skin really is that shade of pink or whether he suffers from sunburn. Virtually every Patagonian I have seen is tanned and weatherbeaten. I also wonder what on earth has brought him here. (I never find out.)

El primo del Che continues with a long story with a very boring punchline; drawn out by the fact that he pauses meaningfully after every sentence and glances round. Sentence. Pause. Sentence. Pause, meaningful glance. Finally, the punchline.

We laugh politely, which mercifully covers up the hungry growling of my stomach. Finally, a knock on the door. Amando and Clara have arrived to save me.

We drive into Trelew. The sky is black and vast and thick with stars. It's late.

'Are you sure the restaurant will be open?' I ask, and they both laugh.

'Of course it will.'

I'm used by now to going out for a meal at ten or eleven o'clock at night, but almost midnight seems to be pushing it. We have to find a space to park, and walk some way back to the restaurant; and by the time we get there it's after midnight.

And the place is packed. Whole families sit crammed around tables laden with pizzas the size of wagon wheels. There are babes in arms and toddlers and school-aged children among the adults, and everybody is talking nineteen to the dozen and merrily eating at the same time.

We talk about politics; about the economic crash that Argentina has suffered, about the big demonstrations staged by the unemployed in Buenos Aires every week, and even down here in Rawson, the provincial capital.

'I bet it's not like that in Europe,' says Amando.

Well, no, I say. But we do have demonstrations. With noise and people shouting demands and everything. And there are problems with long-term unemployment too, in the old industrial areas of northern England and south Wales and former East Germany. And even worse since the financial crisis. Empty houses, dead factories, shrinking cities, hopelessness.

Vendors come into the restaurant; they go from table to table to sell flowers and good-luck charms. Most of them are men, but just as our pizzas arrive, a small boy of no more than eight or nine appears by our table. He is selling tomorrow's edition of the local paper. I look around for an accompanying adult, but there isn't one. Amando is digging through his pockets for money, buys a copy and gives the boy a little extra. Both he and Clara are shaking their heads.

'But that,' says Amando. 'Children having to sell papers on the street to earn a few coins. You don't see that in Europe, do you?'

19

RAINY DAYS ARE RARE in Gaiman. I have seen it windy and sunny, or hot and sunny, and sometimes, not often, windy and grey and chilly. On the whole, it tends to be dry and windy. But this morning starts with a thunderstorm that shakes the roof. Which isn't all that difficult, because the roof – like most roofs in Patagonia – is made of corrugated zinc sheets.

Claps of thunder explode like dynamite. The zinc roof rattles. A flash of lightning, more thunder. The storm must be directly overhead. The lights go out with a loud *ping*. The radio falls silent. A grey, subdued light filters in through the window. Rain is pelting down, pounding on the roof with primordial force. There is nothing gentle about it. Everything beyond the window is hidden by a curtain of solid water. I could be alone in the world, just me and the storm. The air is heavy with humidity.

Then, as abruptly as it started, the thunderstorm ends. The lights come back on, the radio chatters away again, and the twenty-first century reasserts itself.

The temperature has plummeted abruptly. Heavy grey clouds move slowly across the sky. This is a face of Gaiman I haven't seen yet. I wrap up and go out into the sharp, cool air.

During my first visit, I was nervous of venturing outside the village. I found the sheer size of the land unnerving. I was afraid about not knowing the rules, worried I might step outside some boundary, trespass unwittingly. Everything was new and unknown. I had common ground with the Gaiman Welsh, but nothing to connect me to the other people of the place. I was nervous of them, and embarrassed about being nervous. I had heard stories of tourists being robbed in Buenos Aires and in Patagonia; and while my brain told me that people get robbed every day in every country, I had contrived to think of Patagonia as a sort of Wild South. I was very self-consciously aware of being a stranger. I didn't yet speak much Spanish. I would have been able to ask for the way had I got lost, but probably not have understood the answer.

Now, I feel almost at home in *Y Wladfa*. I have spent time exploring the streets of Gaiman and learning more about the history of the place. I have met people and made friends. I am no longer a stranger here. I have learnt Spanish. I've seen parts of the valley from the fastness of Lisa's car, and now I want to venture out further by myself, leave houses and roads and people behind and walk in the land under the big Patagonian sky.

When I was here before, it was autumn, the land a hundred shades of brown and gold. Now it's spring, and unbelieveably green. The wind is strong and cool and sharp, it rustles the leaves of the poplars. Gravel crunches under my feet. Teros utter their sharp warning cries. 'Tero-tero-tero!' For a while, the sound of revving motors follows me from the town. Argentinian drivers seem to believe that noise is a measure of the vigour and power of their cars, or perhaps themselves

The dirt roads run straight as a rule, seemingly all the way to the horizon. It's difficult to gauge distances. On a stretch of road ahead of me, I see a lorry that appears to be stationary; unloading something perhaps. But after a good while I see that it trails a cloud of dust: it is actually moving. Impossible to make out how far away it really is; it could be half a mile or three.

The white hills that frame the valley to the north and south, parallel to the course of the River Chubut, look as dry and dusty as ever; despite the recent downpour. The water seems to have disappeared already, evaporated or absorbed by the dry soil.

From certain points all I can see are hills and fields: no road, no houses, no telephone poles. That's what it must have looked like back in the days of the early Welsh settlers. Green pastures lie on both sides of the road, fields full of lean sheep and cattle. The air is cool and thin and smells faintly of damp earth. I feel small and far away out here, lost in the vastness of the land. And yet I am rarely further away than a few hundred yards from a human habitation. *Chacras*, small farms, lie along the road like pearls on a string.

The breeze freshens as I walk back towards Gaiman, the clouds draw together and there is a quick flurry of raindrops just before I have reached the canal with its sheltering poplars. But the rain soon stops, and a piece of blue sky shows with bright white clouds sailing through it as though in a distant vision. A ray of sunlight breaks through and paints everything golden. A rainbow hangs in the pewter grey sky over Gaiman, over the poplars that bend in gusts of wind and the brick and stone houses ducking close to the ground.

It is my first Patagonian rainbow, and I am still full of delight as I wander back into town. A young woman is standing in a doorway, looking out over the valley.

'Did you see the rainbow?' I say before I can stop myself. Instead of the strange look I expect, I get an answering smile.

'No, where?'

It is still visible, just beyond the trees on the other side of the river. She comes out into the road to look, clasps her hands in delight in a way I've only ever seen on the stage and exclaims: '*¡Es bellísimo!* It's glorious! I wouldn't have seen this without you. Thank you so much!'

We chat for a while before I wander on.

I would have forgotten about this, but a week or so later, I bump into her again in the supermarket, and she says hello. I can't place her at first, until she says, 'Don't you remember the other day? *Vos sos la chica del arco iris, ¿no?* You're the one with the rainbow, aren't you?'

After we're through the checkout, we stand in the street outside the supermarket and chat, and then we walk as far as her house and stand outside that and chat more.

An hour has passed when she looks at her watch and exclaims that she is late.

'But tomorrow,' she says, 'do you want to come round in the afternoon for a cup of coffee?'

I have never known a place like Gaiman. Not once have I struck up a friendship with a perfect stranger anywhere else in the world. Here, I seem to do it all the time.

20

THE NEXT DAY IS WARM AND BREEZY with lots of sunshine. We sit, not in Lorena's spacious living room with its windows shuttered against the sun, but on the front doorstep that looks out over a dusty gravel street. Every now and again a neighbour stops to chat. Dogs trot past, intent on their own errands, not looking left or right. Whenever a car passes, it leaves a huge plume of dust hanging in the air. Time passes slowly.

That, says Lorena, was one of the reasons she has come here to live. She's from Buenos Aires originally, but the city was getting too noisy, too dangerous, too much. Lorena wanted to leave the rat race; she wanted peace and quiet and a better life in the country. She's a yoga instructor; working from her studio in Trelew, the biggest city of the province of Chubut. It's a half-hour commute from Gaiman, less time than she spent getting from one part of Buenos Aires to another.

'And look where I live now,' she says, stretching out her arms to encompass the hills, the quiet road, the flowering trees, the dogs, the birds. One can almost guess her profession from her posture; she holds herself effortlessly upright, her movements are fluid and graceful. I might find so much perfection intimidating, were it not for the way she has of breaking out into loud shouts of laughter, or excited exclamations. Her dog, a large white mastiff, lies at her feet radiating heat and contentment.

We talk and talk, about the meaning of life, about friendship and dreams, dogs and books, Wales and Buenos Aires and Patagonia. I tell her about my writing, about the ideas for stories and books that are suddenly crowding my head, when for years and years I'd found it impossibly difficult to think up a plot. She listens with attention and real interest, and she's very good at understanding my Spanish, which is perfectly adequate for everyday use, but stumbles on teetering legs when I attempt philosophical questions. I get tangled up in subjunctive and word order, too many sub-clauses and the meaning of my life. Lorena nods, repeats my last intelligible phrase and probes for meaning. What's more, she does it without making me feel at all self-conscious.

We have more coffee, I light a cigarette and watch the blue smoke drift away on the breeze. Through Lorena, I get to see Gaiman in a different light, through the eyes of someone who is both insider and outsider: a non-Welsh perspective.

'I do love living here,' says Lorena, 'the quality of life is so much better. When I have children, they'll be able to grow up safely, play outside without me having to worry about them. The air is clean, people are friendly, Patricia has lots of space... all of that.'

Patricia is the white mastiff. Hearing her name, she thumps her tail a couple of times in the dust without lifting her head.

'But Gaiman is such a conservative place! Very closed against outsiders. It took me a long time to grasp that. And some things are just odd... there are all these empty houses in the valley. In the seventies and eighties, most of the Welsh sold their land and left their farms and moved to the city. Hardly any of the descendants of the Welsh are still farmers, you know. It's a difficult life, hard work; now it's mostly the Bolivian immigrants who do the farming, they don't mind the hard work. I've asked people why they only sold the land and not the farm houses, and they say they don't want their houses to pass out of the family and go to strangers. So they just leave them empty, to decay.' She wrinkles her forehead.

I think of Treborth, the empty house that Lisa showed me with its smell of mothballs and mouse repellent, the shrouded dining-room table, the outdated wiring. And I can understand both of them: why Lisa is so attached to the house she grew up in and all it stands for, her family history, the first settlers; her connection to Wales, even, because John Morgan James who built the house with his own hands came from Ponterwyd. If it was my house, I would hate to lose all that. But I understand Lorena's frustration, too. Why not let someone else live in the house if you no longer want to? Why cling to a past that is almost dead?

'It's as though they want to hold on to their special status,' Lorena says. 'You know, the Welsh were the pioneers, the first to settle here. They're proud of that and a lot of them still keep themselves apart from everyone else. But times are changing. There's a lot of fear of change here. People want to hold on to the old days, to how things were. They don't want people from the outside who do new things.'

I say, jokingly, 'You're from the big city, girlie, you don't understand that we do things differently here.'

Lorena gives me a startled look.

'Do you know, that's exactly what people *have* been telling me!

"You're from Buenos Aires, you don't know how we do things here."' She shakes her head. 'I sat on a sub-committee of a residents' group for a while. I wanted to go to the municipality to push them to do something on a project they were dragging their feet over. The new estate over on the other side of the hill isn't connected to the electricity grid, and nothing was happening. So I wanted to get something done. But the other people on the committee said, "No, we don't do things here that way, they won't like it if we push them." As though we were still living under the military dictatorship! The municipality doesn't own Gaiman; it's ours, we pay our taxes and we have a right to the services that we pay for.' She makes an exasperated growling sound in her throat, and Patricia the dog lifts her head, slightly alarmed. I imagine that Lorena doesn't lose her patience very often.

'They didn't like me talking like that. Sometimes, I'm getting a bit disillusioned with Gaiman, to tell you the truth. I've been living here three years now, and it's a great place to live. It's safe, too, Buenos Aires is not a safe place to live, so many robberies and everything. And I tell myself: You've made your choice, now stick with it. But, you know, sometimes....'

21

ERNESTO, LORENA'S PARTNER, owns a *chacra* in the valley, six miles or so outside Gaiman. In the summer, when everybody is on holiday and Lorena closes her yoga studio for two whole months, they live out on the farm. They often spend the weekends there as well.

It's hot in the valley, even the cool wind from the south can't change that. The air hangs heavily between the white hills. At noon, the heat of the sun beats down like a hammer. The poplars rustle dryly, their leaves fluttering silver and green. The minicab – *remis* – I'm in trawls an enormous dust cloud. I have been invited out to Ernesto and Lorena's for lunch. There is no bus going to the individual *chacras*, and it's too far to walk in the heat. So I go by *remis*.

The *chacra* has no address as such. It is simply *Chacra* No. 322. Lorena told me to tell the driver that it's on the road to Treorky, near Capel Camwy, the *chacra* with a red gate. There are no maps to the roads in the valley, and practically no sign posts. People just know where places are because they've grown up here, or learnt what is where. Or else they get lost.

We arrive. The gate is an unspectacular brown that doesn't look in any way red, but there is Lorena, outside a house with a bright red front door, red window frames and shutters. There are also Patricia and three more white mastiffs. Or more precisely, they would be white if they were clean. They are Patricia's offspring, they're just six months old and have the souls of puppies in the bodies of almost fully-grown dogs. They have been splashing about in the water of the old irrigation canal that runs alongside the farm boundary. Now they come running and throw themselves at me in delight, grinning all over their wide, ugly, lovely faces. They are dripping wet, and mucky. Within minutes, so am I. My jeans are covered in muddy paw prints. 'Don't jump!' Lorena admonishes the dogs, but to no avail. I don't mind. It's so hot, I'm tempted to join them in the cool water of the canal.

I ask Lorena about the gate – I'd thought she'd said it was red.

She laughs. 'It used to be, and everybody still remembers that. When I got here it was already brown, but this will probably be "the *chacra* with the red gate" for the next hundred years.'

We go for a tour round the *chacra* – which I thought would be a major walk, but it's just two fields long, and one wide. Ernesto fattens beef cattle. Half-grown cows arrive, stay three or four months in a corral outside the house, eat and eat and eat, then they're off to the slaughterhouse. There's money in beef, Lorena says. I haven't met Ernesto yet. He's off in the car somewhere doing farmerly things, but will be back for lunch.

I have assumed that Ernesto inherited the *chacra* from his forbears, and that he, too, has some Welsh ancestry. But he is, like Lorena, an incomer, although not one from so far away. He's from the Patagonian province of Santa Cruz to the south, and used to work in Trelew as a joiner. Then he lent someone a lot of money, and they kept not being able to pay him back.

'And in the end,' says Lorena, 'the man gave Ernesto twenty head of cattle instead, and he decided to buy the farm with the money he'd been saving to buy a house.'

She rolls her eyes, sighs, smiles.

'They gave him cows instead of cash?' I try to imagine that. 'Why didn't they sell the cows to get the money?'

Lorena shrugs. 'I don't know. I'm not even trying to understand. I guess it's a Patagonian thing. But I must say, it's worked out well. And Ernesto is happy out here. It suits him, he's not a city type.'

There are also some sheep. They were similarly meant for fattening, but arrived ill last autumn, and most of them died over the winter. The few that are left don't look too good. Then there are chickens, with chicks – little and fluffy and yellow – and three cats. The house is single-storey, built of pinkish bricks, with a corrugated zinc roof. The bricks are made just round the corner, at one of two brickworks in Treorky.

Indoors it's beautifully cool, despite the metal roof. There are muddy boots by the kitchen door – I add my own muddy trainers to the collection – a modern kitchen sink, a gas cooker, and a black cast-iron stove like the one I saw in *Treborth* with Lisa.

'We use that for heating in winter,' Lorena says with a nod in its direction.

'But you don't cook on it, do you?'

'I do in winter. When it's hot anyway, it seems a bit of a waste not to use it.'

'That must have been quite a change from how you lived in Buenos Aires.'

Lorena laughs out loud. 'I'll say! At the beginning, I didn't even know how to light this thing! Can you imagine, there's no electricity out here, there was no water... It's like another world. But I like learning. I like being able to manage with what there is out here. But I'm glad Trelew is only half an hour's drive away.'

Ernesto arrives. He's a lovely man, big and burly and smiling. He pats the dogs, greets me with a buss on the cheek, hugs Lorena, strides off for a brief survey of the cattle in their corral. Indoors, Lorena chases the cats off the sofa – Patricia promptly climbs on there instead, and is allowed to stay – and lays the table.

We eat, and Ernesto tells me how they found the well on their land that now supplies them with water.

'There are problems with the water supply in the entire valley,' he says; 'especially since the big dam was built a hundred miles upstream in the 1960s. The ground water level has sunk a lot. But we got a man to come here to douse for water, a Chilean. He is very good. He used an old silver fob watch on a chain, and in his hand held a little bottle of water from a mountain spring in the Andes, on the Chilean side – the place where he was from. And then he went all over the farm. In one place, the watch began to go round in circles, like a pendulum, and he told us that there was water in the ground there. So we sunk a shaft. At a depth of eighteen feet, we found a subterranean current of water between two layers of clay. We put a layer of gravel and sediment as a natural filter, and now the water comes out, crystal clear. Better than bottled mineral water from the shop!' Ernesto exclaims and jumps up. 'Come and see for yourself!'

He drags me off outside to the hose connected to the electric pump that draws up the water. He fills a glass straight from the hose. 'Taste that.'

The water is very cold and slightly salty, and it tastes dark, somehow, of subterranean passages and deep places in the earth.

22

IN 1867, TWO YEARS AFTER the arrival of the *Mimosa*, Michael D. Jones wrote a letter to one Thomas Benbow Phillips. Phillips, latterly of Tregaron, was living in Nova Cambria, a Welsh colony which he had established in the province of Rio Grande do Sul in southern Brazil some twenty years earlier. (What on earth had that been like: to exchange grey, small-town Tregaron for the lush subtropical jungles of Brazil?)

The Brazilian settlement had begun with plenty of funding in place, and houses built even before the first settlers arrived. By the end of 1851, there were 80 people living in Nova Cambria, but even at its peak it never seems to have been home to more than 120. And despite its grand name, it never was very Welsh. The Brazilian government made it clear very early that all the administration, internal and external, had to follow Brazilian law. The Welsh of Nova Cambria were free to speak Welsh among themselves and to their God in chapel, but other than that, they might as well have remained in Britain. When in 1854 a coal prospector arrived from Liverpool to look for coal in the mountains of southern Brazil, several of the settlers – many of whom were former coal miners – went with him. There was nothing to keep them in Nova Cambria, no heroically overcome hardship, no mad dream like the one of *Y Wladfa*. Once the first people had gone, more followed. The settlement unravelled until even Phillips and his family gave up and moved to the nearest town, Pelotas, to open a business there.[27] They were still there ten years later when Michael D. Jones' siren call lured them south to Patagonia.[28] He wanted the seasoned pioneers to share their valuable experience with the raw settlers of *Y Wladfa*. Phillips and his family seem not to have hesitated. They packed up and made their way south to the Chubut valley: a journey of some 1900 miles, which these enterprising souls made by oxcart.

In his letter, Michael D. Jones outlined the economic situation of *Y Wladfa*, then in its third year:

> About 200 Indians came down and bartered quillangoes guanaco-hide mantles, ostrich [rhea] feathers, dogs, horses and goats for bread, flour, matti [maté], tea, coffee, tobacco, etc. According to the reports we have received, this visit brought a profit to the colonists of about £1000....The visit of the Indians has evidently paid the colonists well.[29]

All those feather boas and fans, Victorian hats trimmed with ostrich feathers and feather dusters sold and used all over the British Empire meant that there existed a big demand for feathers. And so the first modest wealth of *Y Wladfa* was built, of all things, on the plumage of the rhea, the large flightless bird of the desert. (Rhea look very like ostriches, so that's what the settlers called them.)

In the late 1870s, there were no fewer than eight merchant houses in the Chubut valley, set up to trade with the Indians.[30] As late as 1881, sixteen years after the arrival of the first settlers, a full two thirds of the exports of the Chubut colony consisted of feathers. 1881 had been a bad year with a disastrous harvest. A year later, just under half of the exports was wheat – but still the larger part was made up of feathers and *quillangos*, guanaco hide mantles. Trade with the Indians was the economic mainstay for *Y Wladfa*.[31] After the first ten years, between agriculture and trade, the settlers had proved that life – European, settled, 'civilised' life – in Patagonia was possible.

Indeed, by 1875 the little settlement in the middle of nowhere was regarded as a success not only back home in Wales, but also in other attempted Welsh colonies, most of which were in the United States and Canada: so much so that further would-be settlers arrived from Wales and North America.

Emigration was a fact of life at the time, not only in Wales but all over Britain, Ireland and the European continent. The New World offered the possibility of a better life, upward mobility, an escape from poverty. In exchange, emigrants had to give up family ties, homeland, community. Welsh-speaking emigrants often lost their language within a couple of generations, went to church instead of chapel. But *Y Wladfa* had been established to prevent exactly that. Here was a little Wales beyond Wales, where morals and mores, school and religion were as Welsh-speaking and God-fearing as anyone in the old country could possibly wish. It was Utopia.

'It was a strange and unforgettable sight,' wrote William Hughes, who had arrived from Wales in 1881; 'to behold those Welshmen come to meet us on the deserted shore of a faraway, exotic land. What made it so very odd, and what caused us no little amazement, was how different it all was from what one had imagined. To hear the settlers converse in perfectly correct Welsh whilst seeing the ponchos they wore slung over their shoulders was like a dream of an enchanted land.'[32]

What did Utopia look like? I have a faded sepia photograph of Gaiman in 1906. It was taken by Henry Bowman, an English stone-mason and something of an adventurer who had drifted to the Chubut colony in the 1880s and more or less stayed. He would move away to other places in Patagonia for a few years, but eventually always come back to Gaiman. His hobby was photography. He left many records – often the only ones of their kind – of the early years of life in Patagonia.[33]

The photo shows the typical grid of streets running at right angles with a few scattered houses built of adobe – mudbrick – or rough stones quarried from the dusty, whitish hills. All in all, I can count twenty-three buildings. There can't have been more than a hundred people living in the village at the time, if that. None of the buildings has more than one storey. Most of them look like a house in a child's drawing: the front door in the centre with a window on either side and a chimney at both ends of the roof.

Other buildings in the photo must have been built by Argentines or immigrants of Spanish or Italian extraction, of whom there were a couple of dozen living in *Y Wladfa* around the turn of the century. They are rectangular, with a high, red-brick front and a flat roof of corrugated zinc which slopes towards the back. There are buildings like that all over Patagonia; as typical for the region as the semi is for the U.K.

And then there is, oddly, what looks exactly like a terrace of workers' houses on the edge of what will later become the central *plaza*. They might have been taken off any street in the South Wales valleys and moved to Gaiman. Were they built by homesick miners from Merthyr or Tredegar? They look incongruous in the middle of the flat, dusty landscape of Patagonia.

The streets of this Gaiman of the past are as wide as motorways, but there isn't a single vehicle to be seen on them. The most substantial thing in the picture is a line of bushy poplars on the horizon.

23

IN 1885, A GROUP OF FARMERS, craftsmen and – perhaps oddly – a couple of religious ministers decided to set up a co-operative trading company, which became known as *Compañía Mercantil del Chubut*. (The Chubut Trading Co.) Now the settlers could join together and sell their rhea feathers, *quillangos* and wheat directly in Buenos Aires, instead of having to rely on middlemen. They sent their own representative to negotiate with the merchants in the capital and to hire boats which would take the grain to Buenos Aires and, on the return trip, to bring all manner of goods to Patagonia. Suddenly, there was a shop in Rawson which sold furniture and agricultural implements, tools and fabric and crockery: things which most people would take completely for granted, but which the Chubut colonists had now done without for two decades.

The *Compañía Mercantil* was a roaring success. Wheat from the Chubut valley turned out to be top quality. It famously won gold medals, a fact which everybody in the valley today will proudly recount: one in the Paris Exhibition of 1889, and two at Chicago Exhibitions, in 1893 and 1918 respectively; and the company could demand high prices for it in Buenos Aires.

Construction of the railway began a year later, in 1886. The first trains ran from Rawson to the newly founded town of Trelew (named after Lewis Jones: *Tre* meaning town in Welsh and *Lew* being short for Lewis), and on from there to the harbour at Porth Madryn, as the New Bay had now become.

The population of *Y Wladfa* had grown to almost 3000 by this time. There were three villages in the Chubut valley: Rawson, Gaiman and Trelew with its brand new railway station. After over two decades of struggle, things were looking good.

Then the river flooded.

There had always been floods in the valley. Every few years, *Afon Camwy* – the river Chubut – burst its banks. It was something of which the Tehuelche had warned the Welsh from the start. But now, the colonists had lived in the valley for many years. They knew it. They had constructed a network of irrigation canals with which they could control the flood water. Or so they thought.

The canals worked in most years. But in 1899, the last year of the old century, thirty-four years after their arrival, it began to rain and rain and rain and didn't stop.

'The rain fell day and night in terrifying silence,' recounted Eluned Morgan, writer and educator and the daughter of Lewis Jones. 'Even the animals appeared to sense that something un-natural was happening; they would stand in small groups on the higher ground, away from the constant, unfamiliar dampness.'[34]

The river rose higher than ever before. Finally, in the middle of winter at the end of July (by bitter irony the very time when usually there were celebrations to commemorate the landing of the *Mimosa*) it burst its banks and flooded the entire valley.

> A dark winter night; the rain fell steadily; and youths on horse-back galloped from house to house to raise the alarm: 'Run to the hills, the waters are coming!'... It is hard to describe this strange exodus. At times, there was only a quarter of an hour's notice in which to collect enough food and clothes to stave off cold and hunger. Often the waters had already begun to arrive by the time the cart made its getaway; and there was nothing for it but to whip the horses and race away, while behind the waves were rising up like mountains.[35]

Animals were drowned, seed and hay were spoilt. And almost everything that people had not managed to load on a cart and take with them was lost: furniture and clothes, food supplies and tools and books. And two years later in 1901, exactly the same thing happened again.

If those floods had happened twenty years earlier, they would probably have been the last nails in the coffin of the mad dream that was *Y Wladfa*. But now, more than thirty years on, things were different: there were three thousand people living in the valley, not just 153. There was infrastructure: roads and the railway and a regular, comparatively quick connection to the outside world. Even after two devastating floods in three years, nobody seems to have suggested that they give up and go elsewhere. *Y Wladfa* was firmly rooted in Patagonian soil, and nothing was going to shift it.

24

I'M HALFWAY BETWEEN heaven and earth, sometimes seemingly flying, at others swaying, through a cloudless blue sky past golden hills. For the past three hours, the view has been uniform: flat, greyish-white soil showing through the sparse grey-green shrubs like skin through thinning hair.

I am not on a plane, but on the upper deck of the long-distance coach to Comodoro Rivadavia, a city some 400 kilometres – 250 miles – south of Trelew and Gaiman. For miles and miles and miles, hour after hour, nothing changes. I doze, read, doze, look out at the unchanging steppe.

The coach sways and rolls in the buffeting wind like a ship on the high seas. The road runs ahead as straight as a ruler to the horizon. Puddles of heat shimmer like mirages on the tarmac. It is December – early summer – and the temperature is set to climb to 33 degrees in the shade. There is no shade at all on the bare, baking tableland.

Finally the land moves aside like a woman lifting her skirt for a moment, and I catch a glimpse of a bay: blue glittering sea water, white-capped waves, framed by rocky fjords. Even just the sight of the sea from afar feels refreshing after so many miles of dusty land.

As the road descends from the tableland towards the coast, it appears to experience a moment of madness: it coils in sudden hairpin bends and curves, hills and dips, left and right and up and down as though we were skirting the Pembrokeshire coast. It makes a lovely change after hours of straightness. The only thing is – I'm not sure that the driver has noticed. His driving is no different at all from when we were the only vehicle on a straight road with a visibility of several kilometres. The coach merrily overtakes cars and lorries just before sharp bends, oblivious of dips and blind summits. I clutch the arm rests of my seat and don't dare take my eyes off the road, as though that might somehow help. (It's a good job that I don't know, at this point, that several coaches have in fact careered off just this stretch of road and crashed down into ravines due to reckless driving and high winds.) After some kilometres of this roller-coaster ride the road regains its composure and reverts to its previous flat, straight self. I sit back and breathe again.

Outside the coach windows, hammer-shaped black metal cross-beams move busily up and down, pumping crude oil out of the ground. It all looks a bit unreal to me, like something out of a Hollywood film set in 1950s Texas. Comodoro Rivadavia is best known in Argentina for producing the bulk of the country's oil. It even has an oil museum. The first pumps started work here in 1910.

The city looks as uncompromisingly modern as the oil pumps looked old-fashioned: it is all tower blocks and new, blindingly white, angular buildings. At first glance I can see only three colours: a dazzling cornflower blue for sea and sky, the blinding white of the buildings, and the calm grey-brown of the Patagonian steppe in the background.

Comodoro's street pattern is, as everywhere in Patagonia, laid out on a regular grid. Away from the city centre, the tarmac roads downgrade to gravel and finally peter out altogether like the threads of a piece of coarse-woven cloth with no hem. Comodoro's noisy, busy roads under the beating sunshine have a whiff of frontier town, of the oil rush about them. This place feels raw and new.

I have dinner that evening in a restaurant on the seafront. The building consists, so it seems, entirely of windows. The formal and pricey and the food is unspectacular. Unlike the view. The sun sets while I eat bland ravioli in cheese sauce, and I am transfixed by the changing colours in the immense sky: blue fading to green and turquoise and purple while the sea reflects clouds of burning gold and red and crimson.

I want to break into applause when finally the dark curtain of night descends.

25

IT'S NOT AN EASY TASK next morning to find the *Museo Histórico Regional*. Everyone I ask wants to direct me to the *Museo del Petroleo*. Finally I locate the *Museo Regional* on an island in the current between two busy, noisy roads. It is a square whitewashed building with beautiful dark wooden shutters covering its windows like closed eyelids. The sunlight bounces off the walls with glaring brilliance. The interior is dusty and gloomy and beautifully cool after the hot, hot sunshine. Traffic is audible as a constant rushing noise in the background.

The exhibits don't appear to have changed since the *Museo* was set up in the late 1940s: dusty artefacts and fossils in glass cases, accompanied by faded inscriptions on little cards. There are the obligatory whale and dinosaur bones. (Patagonia is famous for dinosaurs past, and whales both past and present.) There are stuffed cormorants and penguins that have seen better days, and swarms of prehistoric flint arrowheads mounted on wall boards. The Visitor Book records visits of school classes and the odd university student bent on research. It looks like a museum showing what museums were like fifty years ago.

The second of the two exhibition rooms houses the section about indigenous peoples. By accident or design, this room has whitewashed walls and unshuttered windows that allow daylight to stream in and brighten everything up. I feel back in the twenty-first century here. The glass cases contain photos and books about the culture and language of the Tehuelche and Mapuche; silver jewellery, pottery, textiles and musical instruments.

'I put all of that there,' says Oscar Payaguala. 'Every single thing comes from my own collection.'

Oscar Payaguala is the director of the *Museo Histórico Regional*. He is also a protest singer and a Tehuelche. Being Tehuelche is not only his ethnic origin, it's something of a full-time job.

Which is why I have come to see him. The descendants of the Welsh settlers of Gaiman are always ready to acknowledge how much their forefathers were indebted to the Indians for their support during the rough early years, and how proud they all are of the friendship that developed between the two peoples. But the Tehuelche are only ever talked about in the past tense. *The*

Tehuelche were. The Tehuelche did.

In the present, the Tehuelche are not. They have disappeared. Some time after my second trip to Argentina, as I was reading about Patagonia and planning my third visit, this fact suddenly struck me. History books about Argentina only mention the immigrants: Italian and Spanish, Russian and German, Syrian and Polish and Welsh. It is as though they went to an empty land. I decided to find out what had happened to the Tehuelche.

'Actually, my people is called *Aoniken*,' Payaguala tells me. 'The Mapuche called us Tehuelche, and that's how we went down in history. In the Mapuche language, *tehuel* means wild, recalcitrant and *che* means people. So we were the Fierce Folk. But we call ourselves *Aoniken*, People of the South.'

Payaguala takes me up to his office. We climb a wide, white marble staircase. One storey. Two. Three? And emerge on the roof in a sudden burst of air and sky, heat and noise and light. Oscar Payaguala's office is located in a sort of little cottage on the flat roof of the building, like a bird's nest atop a cliff.

Outside are hot sunshine and much sky, dust and the noise of the city. Inside, the walls are covered with photos of Oscar Payaguala. Oscar Payaguala with his guitar. On stage, singing. On stage, taking a bow. Oscar Payaguala in Venice, in Barcelona, in Hanover, in Stockholm. Oscar Payaguala in Patagonia. Oddly, some of them appear to be autographed.

Along the length of one wall run shelves with cassettes, CDs and books. Another wall is covered by a variety of musical instruments: a guitar, a kind of tambourine, a horn of some description, something that resembles a couple of gourds, a sort of long-handled trumpet, a drum a bit like an Irish bódhran.

On the desk, under a sheet of glass, more photos of Oscar Payaguala.

'That's me in Germany,' says Oscar Payaguala, pointing out a group of photos in case I might have overlooked them. 'They think very highly of us abroad,' he tells me, half bragging, half wistful. He refers to his band and to his people. 'But here in Argentina...' He waves his hand, dismissively.

'I have actually read,' I say, feeling unkind as I point it out, 'that there are no Tehuelche any more.'

He gives a short bark of a laugh.

'Lots of us,' he says, 'are living in the province of Chubut and the neighbouring province of Santa Cruz to the south. There are some 7000, maybe 10,000 Tehuelche. Oh yes. What is true though, sadly, is that not many of us still live in the ways of our ancestors. Most of my people have migrated to the cities, looking for a better life, for work. Why? Because most of our land has been taken away from us. Many of our people have died. But our culture did not die.' He bangs his hand down on the desk, on the glass sheet and the photo showing himself out in the country, in the midst of a group of people I would, at this point, describe as *Indios*. I learn later that they themselves don't care for that word. They refer to themselves as *Indígenas*, the Indigenous, or *Pueblos Originarios*, the First People: much in the same way the Native Americans and the First Nations do on the North American continent. Stressing their seniority, their older claim.

'The future,' says Payaguala, 'the future will be ours. All we need for the Argentinian state is to allow us to be who we are. We're not asking for help. All we want is our land back, our own land that has been taken away from us; and for an end to discrimination. It's not much to ask, is it? The freedom to live life our own way, to express our faith, to use our traditional medicine, to live in the old way, using our own wisdom. We can end droughts, we can make rain, did you know that?'

Thankfully, he doesn't seem to require an answer.

'We understand the earth, we know how to treat it. The land, the earth, it doesn't belong to us: we belong to it. It's where we came from, where we will return to. It's a continuous fight to reclaim our lands. To struggle for equality and diversity in a country that opened its arms to immigrants from all over the world, but that stole from its own peoples.'

He's been delivering the last few words looking out of the open door, now he turns and fixes a gimlet eye on me.

'I've been to Europe, and I don't believe that the European countries close the doors to their own populations and instead give preferential treatment to those coming in from outside, eh? But that's what's happening to us here. We're the underdogs. We have no lands, no work, not much education, not much access to health-care – the very basics.'

It is an uncomfortable but instructive hour I spend in the company of Oscar Payaguala. He shows me a side to Patagonia that had been invisible to me. Or rather: unnoticed. Of course, I have passed through the outskirts of Trelew: the almost-shanty town, *la villa*, as they say in Argentina, short for *villa miseria*: misery settlement, literally. In Argentina, the town and city centres are bright, attractive areas where people work and live and shop; whereas the undesirable areas are found outside the centres, ringing the city like a besieging army, trying to get in.

And in passing through the *villa* outside Trelew I saw, without thinking about it, that most of its inhabitants were on the whole darker-skinned than the people in the city centre, and the people of Gaiman. In contrast, on all the advertising and public information posters I have ever seen in Argentina, the people depicted were white. In his office, and in his museum, Payaguala is attempting to restore some kind of cosmic balance that has gone badly out of kilter for himself and his people.

Of course, not all the poor in Argentina are *Indígenas* and not all *Indígenas* are poor. But the correlation is strong. The Peróns referred to the masses of the dispossessed as *Cabecitas Negras*, the black-haired ones; because by and large, they are. Evita, the angel of the poor, caused dark-skinned dolls to be manufactured for their children, for the first and so far only time in Argentinian history.

A few weeks later, in a café in Trelew, I fall to chatting to the man who occupies the table next to mine. He is a perfectly nice, charming man, an educated man. We talk about travel and books, about Germany and Argentina. He tells me, in all seriousness, that all Argentinians are of European extraction and appearance.

'If you see a dark-skinned or a black person on the street, they will be from elsewhere – Bolivia or Peru,' the nice man says pleasantly. 'Argentinians are all white.'

26

A SOUND LIKE AN ELEPHANT fills the tiny office on the rooftop. Oscar Payaguala has taken one of the musical instruments off his wall and is giving me a spirited demonstration.

The instrument in question looks like a young alpenhorn: a slender neck perhaps three or four feet long, at the end of which sits what appears to be a cow's horn.

No, corrects Payaguala. Not a cow's horn. A calf's. The *trutruka* is a ceremonial instrument. It is not played for pleasure, but for religious purposes only. And, when played more gently, it sounds like a trumpet.

Unlike the *trompe*, says Payaguala, and jumps up once more like a Jack-in-the-box. Twanging sounds fill the office. The *trompe* turns out to be a mouth-harp. I always thought these were European originally; I have a vague idea that they were played by travelling folk back in the Middle Ages. Apparently, the Mapuche had a very similar instrument, a kind of bow made of wood and a gut string, instead of which they adopted the mouth-harp and gave it the old name.

'It's an instrument used for meditating, to relax, to de-stress. Everybody is stressed these days,' says Payaguala, talking in the slightly unnerving way peculiar to people who are very aware of history. When he says 'these days', I get the feeling that he talks as one who has been around for several centuries.

There is certainly a soothing quality to the *trompe* as he plays it. Its twanging sounds bounce round the walls of the office like small rubber balls. It sounds like an instrument that doesn't quite take anything seriously. Nothing's all that bad, now is it? is what the *trompe* appears to say.

'It's the most important instrument of all,' Payaguala tells me. 'When two *caciques* meet, chiefs; or two *longkos*, elders, they play *trompe* to clear their minds, so as not to rush into anything.'

Perhaps if George Bush and Tony Blair had sat down and played the mouth-harp for a while instead of all that posturing...

'And this is the *kultrung*.' It is the drum I saw earlier. Its front is painted with abstract symbols in blue and yellow. 'It represents literally thousands of years of our culture,' Payaguala tells me. 'Christopher Columbus came to America believing that the earth was round, didn't he? But we, the *pueblos originarios*, the original inhabitants of America, have known for twelve thousand years that the earth is as round as the *kultrung*. We paint the four points of the compass on every single one of our percussion instruments. They symbolise the Mother Earth, who can get by just fine without us. And you see, there is no man and no woman in this representation. Nature and the animals can live very well without us. But we cannot live without them, without Mother Nature. That's the difference.'

I have no problem identifying the last instrument that comes off the wall. It's a guitar. Oscar Payaguala is going to sing for me. I brace myself. I'm not sure what to expect after the visual overkill of all those photos. But I needn't have worried.

Payaguala's music is one-man-and-his-guitar-type folklore, singer-songwriter stuff. It's beautiful. As is his mellow, surprisingly powerful baritone. But there's nothing Tehuelche about the song, nothing new and unfamiliar; which to me is somehow at once a relief and a disappointment. That's until I start to listen to the words and I realise that I don't understand a single one of them. This isn't Spanish.

I ask about the Tehuelche language. Does he speak it? I have heard that it, too, is extinct.

'Oh yes,' says Payaguala. 'I speak both languages, Tehuelche and Mapuche.' And then he bursts into a short speech in Tehuelche. It sounds staccato and guttural and utterly foreign.

'I said there, Welcome Imogen Herrad to Patagonia, may your stay be fruitful and successful. May you be well and healthy and happy here so far away from your loved ones back home.'

It hadn't sounded that long when he said it in Tehuelche.

'The Tehuelche language is very concise, every word can have a lot of different meanings. We don't have a mass of verbs, there aren't that many words in our language, but it is the more direct for it. The Mapuche language can be more wordy, more flowery even.'

And I get another burst of language. I can't make out a word of this, either, but I can tell that it sounds different from the first. Smoother somehow, liquid almost, less guttural; it flows. As far as I can tell, Payaguala doesn't speak either of those languages with a Spanish accent. They sounded, both of them, like nothing I've ever heard before.

Before I leave, Payaguala guides me through the two rooms of his museum.

There are photos which show a group of people and horses out in the countryside. Flags are fluttering in the usual Patagonian breeze. The people carry instruments which I can now identify: a *kultrung*, various pipes and flutes, and the long alpenhorn-like *trutruka*.

'These,' says Payaguala, 'are our rituals, you can see how they are carried out, following the old rules. Nothing has changed.'

Another glass case contains a flag, the same as the one in the photos: it has three horizontal stripes, blue, white and yellow, and in the centre a stylised blue arrowhead, similar in shape to the Stone Age arrowheads in the next room.

'This is the flag of the Tehuelche and Mapuche of Chubut,' explains Payaguala. 'The blue represents the sky, the yellow the sun and the white the harmony of the universe. The arrow is a symbol of our on-going struggle for our rights.'

There are assorted textiles woven with elaborate geometric patterns – some, if I understand him right, signifying joy, others sadness. Mourning, perhaps? Payaguala casually sends a whole stream of information my way, in which I flounder. There are all the unknown words in the Aoniken-Tehuelche and Mapuche languages, place names, dates fired off in too-rapid Spanish.

A map. 'There' – he points – 'you can see the distribution of our various communities, the places where Tehuelche communities live although it is said that the Tehuelche are extinct.' Again that short bark of a laugh. 'And the Mapuche communities. You can see that they are much more numerous than we are. But we're still here. We're still here.'

We arrive back at the case with the photographs. They are arranged chronologically, sepia to black-and-white to colour.

'That's my family, back in the 1800s,' says Oscar Payaguala, pointing. Another, somewhat blurred, picture seems to show a group of men running after something. 'And there we are, playing football. The English will tell you that they invented the game of football, but there we are, years and years ago, playing football. We also played hockey, way back; we played all sorts of things. They didn't invent anything!'

Payaguala is not fond of the English. Earlier in his office, when he pointed out all the places in Europe where he has played his music, Germany and France, Spain and Scandinavia, I asked him why he didn't go to London. I was sure he'd find an interested audience there, too. At that, his face closed.

'I will never go to England,' he said, biting off the words. 'My brother died in the war.'

It took me a moment to get that.

The Falklands War. *La Guerra de Malvinas*. I was fifteen at the time it happened, a German teenager. It wasn't my war. It meant nothing to me.

But of course, in Argentina (and in Britain) it means a great deal. People died. Were killed. Not faceless soldiers, statistics, numbers.

People like Payaguala's brother.

27

AT THE END OF THE NINETEENTH century, only a few small communities of European immigrants existed in Patagonian frontier country on the eastern side of the Andes. With the exception of *Y Wladfa*, none survived. They were attacked by Pampas Indians and Mapuche who stole cattle and abducted women and children. It was thought that over a thousand white people were held in captivity by Patagonian tribes. Some tribes believed that a cachet was attached to having a *Cristiana*, a white woman, in their tents.

Then again, from the seventeenth century onwards there had been regular incursions by the Spanish military on both sides of the Andes, with the express aim to capture Indians to be used as slaves. 'I had great luck,' reported one Sergeant Major Juan Fernández in 1627, 'in capturing 130 pieces [*sic*] and with them 30 horses; and hanged the surplus Indians from the trees, all this with the loss of one single soldier.'[36]

The Mapuche were behaving no worse than the *Cristianos* themselves. Not that it was seen like that at the time. In the 1880s, hysterical stories appeared in European papers, warning people not to settle in Argentina.[37] The stream of immigrants arriving in Buenos Aires dried up.

The Argentine government was not amused. Argentina laid claim to all territories south of the Río Negro and east of the Andes mountain range: all of Patagonia. (Or, to be precise, eastern Patagonia.) This included not only the inhospitable south, but also large swathes of fertile pampas.

The problem was, so did Chile. In 1830, the improbably-named Chilean republican and liberator Bernardo O'Higgins wrote: 'I consider the Pehuenche, Puelche [Mapuche] tribes and Patagonians [i.e. Tehuelche] as our compatriots... who will like nothing so much as to represent the civilisation of all the sons of Chile on both sides of the Cordillera, united in one big family.'[38]

When the Welsh decided that they wanted to settle in the infertile wastes of the deep south, the Argentine government probably thought they were mad. But then there was the success of *Y Wladfa*, only a few years later, in growing wheat in what had until then been regarded as desert. At around the same time, the Argentine explorer Francisco 'Perito' Moreno spent several weeks in the tents of one of the most famous Patagonian *caciques*: Sayhueke, who reigned over a large area of land in the foothills of the Andes, several hundred miles to the west and north of *Y Wladfa*. An immense and immensely fruitful territory, undreamed-of beyond the inhospitable desert: bursting with rich grasslands and fruit trees and crystal mountain streams.

'A new Switzerland,' an enchanted Moreno reported back upon his return to Buenos Aires. It would be, he thought, 'the richest province of Argentina.'[39] Suddenly, there was land worth having in Patagonia.

Successive Argentine governments had negotiated over land and made treaties with the leaders of several indigenous tribes – among them Sayhueke. In exchange for ceding land in the valley of the River Chubut for the Welsh settlers, he received a bi-annual payment from the government that consisted of '1000 head of cattle, 20 kilos of sugar, 16 kilos of *yerba maté* (tea), 12 kilos of tobacco, 2 reams of paper, 10 kilos flour, 8 demijohns of gin.'[40]

But these contracts were only feasible with individual tribes – and only with those that were willing. Not all Indians were inclined to make treaties with the government and allow strangers to settle their lands. And even if they had been, paying them rent indefinitely would have been an expensive business for the government.

So when the European papers were full of bloodcurdling tales about the Indian menace and immigrants began to stay away, the Argentine government decided to clear the suddenly desirable south of its indigenous inhabitants to make way for what it was pleased to call 'progress'.

It sent a rag-tag army south, composed to a large extent not of regular, trained soldiers, but of adventurers and mercenaries who joined in the hope for spoils.

The express aim of the so-called *Conquista* or *Campaña del Desierto* – the Desert Conquest, or Desert Campaign – was to open up frontier country for settlement by removing the people who so inconveniently already lived on the land. Over a period of nearly eighty years, altogether thirty 'desert campaigns' were carried out, the most notorious ones in the last two decades of the nineteenth century under General Roca, later twice president of Argentina.

'The wave of barbarians,' wrote Roca in 1883 in a breath-taking reversal of the facts, 'who for centuries swamped the wide and fertile plains of the pampas and forcibly kept us cooped up in limited spaces, who made us pay them shameful tributes, has finally been destroyed or at least pushed back into their primitive camps beyond the mountains.'[41]

Nobody knows for sure how many people lived in Patagonia before the arrival of the white settlers. In 1881, while the 'Desert Campaign' was still well underway, an Argentine government report estimated that an area of the northern Patagonian province of Neuquen must have been inhabited by at 'least some 15,000 souls, because over the course of the Campaign, more than 14,000 have been killed or taken prisoner.'[42] Estimates vary wildly, but it was certainly a very sparsely populated territory, with probably no more than 100,000 people living there before 1900. (That's rather less than the population of Newport, Gwent, spread out over some 300,000 square miles. The entire U.K. is 95,000 square miles.)

In the years between 1850 and 1930, *three million* European immigrants streamed into Argentina. Around half of them left again after a few years because they couldn't make it in the New World. One and a half million stayed, settled and started families.

In order to make space for them, Tehuelche, Pampas and Mapuche men were killed, pressed into the navy or taken to work as forced labour on farms to the subtropical far north of Argentina, two thousand miles away (about the distance between London and Moscow). Women and girls were distributed as prizes amongst the soldiers or given as servants to upper-class families in Buenos Aires.[43] A few hundred were herded together in reservations, as in North America, on pockets of the poorest land in places which the whites didn't want. Many were baptised en masse upon capture, by Catholic clerics who travelled with the military.[44] The *Indígenas* weren't even allowed to keep their own souls.

And this was happening to people who prized their individual freedom to the point that one of them had rejoiced on his deathbed that he had taken orders from no one.

28

THE WELSH COLONISTS knew about the 'Desert Campaign'. They heard it directly from the Indians themselves, some of whom were their friends. In 1881, Sayhueke sent a heartrending letter to Lewis Jones.

> And now my friend, I have to tell you about the terrible attack made on me on 19 March, when 3 armies set upon my bands, killing without warning a large number of my people. They came armed and stealing into our tents, as if I were an enemy and a murderer. I have serious agreement with the government for many years, and therefore cannot fight nor contend with the armies, for which reason I retreated with my band and tents, thereby attempting to avoid sacrifice and wretchedness... I now find myself ruined and sacrificed – my lands, which my father and God left me, stolen from me, as well as all my animals to the extent of 50,000 heads which include cattle, stallions and sheep and herds of useful horses... I am not a criminal – but a noble *Criollo* i.e. a Creole, [a term whites born in Argentina used for themselves] and by obligation the owner of these things – not a stranger from another land, but born and raised on the land and an Argentinian faithful to the government. For this reason I cannot comprehend the tragedy that has descended upon us. ... I never undertook any attacks, my friend, nor killed any one, nor took any prisoners – and I therefore beg you to intercede on my behalf with the authorities, to protect the peace and tranquility for my people, to return to us our animals and all our silver possessions, but mainly my lands.[45]

At the time, the colony, dependent though it was on the goodwill of the Argentine government, was shocked by what happened. The settlers sent a petition to Buenos Aires. Of which the government took no notice whatsoever.

> Without interfering in any way in the measures which you saw wise to adopt, we hope that, as ones who were long acquainted with the native people, we can express our hope that you can show them every compassion and assistance that are consistent with your obligations. We have received much kindness by the hands of these natives; in reality, the Indians have been a source of protection and assistance to us. We hope

that you will see possible, while understanding your military obligations in accordance with your wisdom, to leave our old native neighbours in their homes while they remain as peaceful and harmless as has been their custom. (Signed by all the colonists 20 July 1883.)[46]

As a German, when I read Sayhueke's letter, I cannot help but be reminded of the reaction (the lack of it) of German middle-class Jews to the oppression and persecution they faced in 1930s and '40s Germany. They were middle-class Germans. Just as Sayhueke referred to himself as 'a noble *Criollo*, an Argentinian faithful to the government'. Neither could believe that their own government, their own *country*, would set out to destroy them, mercilessly.

There are only a handful of Patagonian Indians about whose life we know a little. One of them is Sayhueke. His full name was Valentín Sayhueke, although I'm not sure whether Valentín was his first and Sayhueke his last name in the European fashion, or whether the one was his Spanish and the other his Tehuelche name. Or indeed his Mapuche name. Nobody seems quite sure exactly which tribe he belonged to. Some accounts state that his mother was Tehuelche and his father Mapuche.[47] (He certainly spoke both languages.) Others claim that he was part Pampas, part Araucano – Mapuche.[48] He personifies perfectly the multicultural, multi-ethnic indigenous society of Patagonia in the second half of the nineteenth century.

Mapuche, Pampas and Tehuelche cultures were oral. His name was written down by Spanish speakers, and there are about a dozen different versions of it: Sayhueque, Sayhweke, Saihueque, Shai-Hweké, Saibúeque, Sayeweke, Saygüeque and even Cheoeque.

The 'standard' version which is commonly used these days is Sayhueque. I've chosen to spell him Sayhueke after the manner of some modern Tehuelche-Mapuche activists who use instead of 'qu' the letter 'k' which is unknown to Spanish spelling; in order to lessen, symbolically at least, the impact Spanish culture has had on their culture, their ancestors, and their own lives.

According to a much-repeated story first told by the explorer Francisco 'Perito' Moreno, Sayhueke's Mapuche father had exhorted him early on to make his peace with the white people.

'His father Chocorí,' the scientist reported, 'upon his death counselled Sayhueke that he should never fight against the Christians, because the very first clothes he wore upon his birth were Christian; and he added that, but for the Christians, they would still go about naked as in previous times.'[49]

Perhaps chief Chocorí saw the signs of the times and hoped that his people would have a better chance of survival through an alliance with the whites than by fighting them. In Chocorí's own lifetime, in the 1840s and 1850s, there had been one 'Desert Campaign', led by the Argentine dictator Juan Manuel de Rosas. (Indeed, according to some records Chocorí himself had been killed during that campaign when Sayhueke was in his infancy. Nobody seems to know for sure.)

Chocorí's – later Sayhueke's – tribe were ideally placed in the foothills of the Andes, in an area called *País de las Manzanas* – Apple Country – after the fruit trees that grew there in profusion. It was abundantly fertile land, well protected by the mountains and inaccessible from anywhere that was settled by Cristianos. At the same time, it was near enough to both Chile and Carmen de Patagones to allow for trade in both directions. The *Manzaneros*, as his immediate tribe were known – the Apple Tree People – must have thought of themselves as pretty much unassailable. The white people lived far, far away. So they believed themselves safe.

During the 1860s and 1870s, Valentín Sayhueke rose to unequalled heights of power as Lord of the Apple Country. He became the most influential and powerful chief in all of Patagonia, a kind of overlord or high king to whom most lesser chiefs answered.

Sayhueke firmly thought of himself as Argentinian. In 1872, the Chilean government sent an envoy who presented him with a Chilean flag, but the chief politely refused the gift, pointing out that he was an Argentine citizen.[50] Hadn't the Argentine government sent him communications like this one?

'The Government wishes to show chief Saibúeque that he is highly esteemed and considered as a true and loyal friend, wherefore it is undertaking to pay him a monthly salary of 600 pesos from the first day of this month May 1859.'[51]

Why on Earth wouldn't he think of himself as a noble *Criollo*?

29

AFTER THE ATTACK on his tribe in 1881 – the one about which he told Lewis Jones in his letter – Sayhueke decided to fight back. His men, armed mostly with lances and faced by regiments with Remington rifles, were formidable warriors. Even with those odds they won several battles. But the end was inevitable. In 1884, all the (surviving) Patagonian chiefs held a final big gathering: Inakayal, Foyel, Chagallo, Salvutia, Chikichan, Rayel, Nahuel, Pichi Curuhuinca, Cumilao, Huichaimilla, Huenchunecul, Huicaleo and Sayhueke.[52] They were Tehuelche, Mapuche and Pampas, united in the face of the biggest threat their people had ever faced. They swore to resist to the last. Within the year, all of them had been killed or captured. Altogether, General Roca – later twice president of Argentina – claimed that 1313 indigenous fighters had been killed and 1271 captured in the campaign, along with a further 11,500 Indian captives: men, women and children.[53]

Sayhueke was among the last to surrender, on 1 January 1885. He was taken to Buenos Aires, where he was regarded as something of a curiosity, a sort of 'native' king. He was well treated and became a celebrity, much reported in the newspapers and gaped at in public. There are photos of him at this time: his hair cut off at about ear height; he wears European clothes, a military uniform, boots, a hat. His face is shut down, unreadable. He went to visit his friend, the explorer and scientist 'Perito' Moreno, in the latter's elegant flat overlooking *calle Florida*, today the main pedestrianised shopping street of Buenos Aires.

Moreno helped him to arrange a visit to the *Casa Rosada* – the presidential residence – and an interview with General Roca, who was not only the instigator and sometime leader of the ethnic cleansing campaign, but also now the president of Argentina. And there Sayhueke went, to talk to the man who had set out to destroy the indigenous nations of Patagonia.

He had lost everything, his land, his standing, his freedom. It must have taken a lot to sit down with Roca, the man who had destroyed the life of not only Sayhueke, but of all the Indians of Patagonia.

I wouldn't blame Sayhueke if he'd pulled a gun on Roca or if he'd gone for him with his bare hands. But he didn't. He was still responsible for the lives of his tribe: the 700 men and 2500 women who had surrendered alongside him on New Year's Day, 1885.[54] At least they hadn't been dragged off to prison camps, the way the tribes of Inakayal and Chikichan and Foyel had. But Sayhueke was the only one who could prevent a similar fate for them. He could not afford a grand gesture of revenge. So he talked to Roca. He asked for land where he and his people might live in peace, outside the city, back home in the south, in Patagonia.

It took ten long years for his wish to be granted. For *ten years* he and his tribe lived in limbo, waiting to hear where they would be allowed to live permanently. Finally, the Argentine government set aside 150 square miles of land for Sayhueke and his people near what is today the village of Tecka, in the province of Chubut, in the dusty emptiness of the desert.[55] There he lived out his remaining years on dry and stony ground; four hundred miles south of the Apple Country. Sayhueke died in 1903.

He, at least, died in freedom.

Inakayal was a Tehuelche chief whose tribe had once inhabited the area in the foothills of the Andes where at the turn of the century the Welsh would establish an offshoot colony of *Y Wladfa*. He had attended that last great gathering of the chiefs, and had surrendered with his warriors in 1884, a few months before Sayhueke. He, too, had been visited and written about by Francisco Moreno. And when Inakayal was in captivity, Moreno intervened and talked the authorities into releasing him and his immediate family. (Only him, not the rest of the tribe, the commoners.) They were released, but not into freedom. Inakayal, his wives and their children became inmates, living exhibits of sorts, at the great Natural History Museum which Moreno had established in the city of La Plata near Buenos Aires. The museum had already collected, and was exhibiting, plenty of bones of the Patagonian 'natives'. Inakayal and his family were made to undergo anthropometric measurements and photographic sessions.[56] There are frontal and profile photos of the chief's expressionless face. They look like prison shots. Which is what they are. Inakayal's crime was to be a Native American in a country of immigrants. He never regained his freedom.

'One day in 1888,' wrote Moreno's secretary, Clemente Onelli (later to head the Buenos Aires zoo) in his memoir, 'as the rays of the setting sun painted the front of the building purple, Inacayal appeared at the top of the monumental staircase, supported by two

Indians. He took off his clothes: the clothes of those who had invaded his country, and bared his golden torso. He made an obeisance to the sun; another, much longer one, towards the south. That same night, Inacayal died...'[57] After his death, Inakayal's skeleton, brain, scalp and death mask were kept by the museum as exhibit number 5438.[58] They were put on display alongside other specimens of 'indigenous anatomy'.[59] His remains were not buried until over a century after his death, in 1994.

To this day, the collections of the La Plata museum include the skull of Mapuche *cacique* Calfucurá, along with those of a number of other Indians whose names are unknown.

It is hard to believe that this campaign of ethnic cleansing, this – surely – state genocide against the indigenous population of the Patagonian steppe, is still largely spoken of in Argentina today simply as the 'Desert Campaign'. Very few people get angry over it, except for the Mapuche and the allegedly extinct Tehuelche. There are no Pampas Indians left at all who can get angry.

It is equally hard to believe that to this day statues of General Roca, the architect of the 'Campaign,' stand on the *plazas* of virtually all towns and villages in Patagonia. (Scrawled over, often, with graffiti by Mapuche or Tehuelche activists.) He is still seen largely as a hero who brought civilisation to the wild wastes of Patagonia.

30

I MEET RODRIGO GÓMEZ in the *Amgueddfa Gaiman*, Gaiman's small local museum, on a Tuesday afternoon. He is there most Tuesday afternoons, because that is the day he visits the smallholdings of people who live in the countryside around Gaiman, in the *chacras*. After he has finished his business with them, he often has an hour to kill before the next bus leaves for the city of Trelew, where he lives. So he is in the habit to going to the museum for a round of *maté* and a chat with Miguel – the affable young man who spends his life mysteriously doing nothing but to learn. And, it appears, to mind the *Amgueddfa*. I have called into the museum with much the same end in mind as Rodrigo; barring the *maté*, of which, despite trying, I am not fond. Miguel, who knows that my interests in Patagonia now include indigenous as well as Welsh culture, introduces us. He thinks Rodrigo's job might interest me.

Rodrigo is the joint manager and founder of a not-for-profit organisation called *Banco de Lanas*, The Wool Bank. 'We supply spinners and weavers of Mapuche-Tehuelche origin in the region around Gaiman with micro-credits,' he explains. 'People for whom this kind of work is part of their culture. We pay them for doing something they do well, and that helps preserve the cultural heritage. Most of our producers live in small, isolated communities here in the region or on the tablelands near the Andes. The money that the Wool Bank provides means that they can stay on their land, within their culture, if you like, and won't have to up and leave for the city, where they'll be cut off from everything they know.'

Miguel, who had wandered across to the window to observe the street outside, returns.

'The Trelew bus is coming round the corner.'

'Why don't you come with me to Trelew?' asks Rodrigo. 'I could show you our premises, and you could meet Lía, my partner.'

No! I think. It's six in the evening and I'm tired, I went for a run at 7.30 this morning and I've been on the go pretty much ever since before dropping in to the museum for a breather. What I want to do now is to go home and put my feet up, read a book, see nobody, do nothing. Instead, I say, 'Yes – why not?'

The bus wheezes up the hill, past the large hoardings advertising Gaiman's tea shops, past the small chapel that overlooks the roundabout and the rusting Coca-Cola hoarding that has quite probably stood there since the 1950s. Gaiman ends abruptly: one moment we're in the town, the next we are out on the open road with nothing but grey scrubland left and right. The white hill of Bryngwyn rises up to the right, bordered by a green line: poplars and willows growing by the edge of the river.

Trelew with its population of 120,000 is the largest city in the province of Chubut. It's laid out in the grid pattern typical of cities in the Americas: wide, perfectly straight roads intersecting at regular intervals. Every *cuadra*, or block, is one hundred metres long. It's all very beautiful and logical; a system that makes it almost impossible for anyone (even for me) to get lost. There are no crescents in Patagonia.

The lake behind the bus and coach station is named in honour of a chief of Pampas Indians with whom the Welsh were on friendly terms: *Laguna Chiquichano*. The large green square in front of the station contains a giant statue of Lewis Jones, in whose honour the city itself is named. There are hotels and souvenir shops, cinemas and cafés and restaurants.

Rodrigo and I get off the bus at a street corner and walk a few *cuadras* to the shop and office of *Banco de Lanas*. The window boasts a couple of mannequins wearing cardigans, shawls and ponchos. The word poncho, he tells me, is in fact derived from a Mapuche word; *pontró* in the Mapuche language Mapudungun describes a wrap or mantle.

Inside the shop it's warm and a little stuffy. The air smells of dust and wool. At the back, in a tiny office, hopelessly crowded with furniture and office equipment, sits Lía, Rodrigo's partner in the Wool Bank and in life, typing at a computer. Rodrigo takes a small, dented kettle from a wall cupboard and proceeds to boil water for *maté* (for him and Lía) and tea (for me).

'These days, I use my full name, Ñancufil Musa,' Lía explains while the kettle begins to sing. 'My father was Arab and my mother Mapuche. I use both their surnames. When I grew up, nobody said, "I am Mapuche" or "I have Mapuche ancestors". It wasn't something you'd want anybody to know about. Our grandparents learned to keep quiet. There has been so much pain, so much loss. They learned to turn inwards, not to hold their heads high, to disappear within themselves. And that hurts. One can feel it still today, in our people. I myself can feel it.' She looks at me for a moment, her face serious, her eyes remembering. 'A lot has changed. Take me, for example: I was lucky, because I had the grandmothers of our people who guarded the traditions. They taught me a lot. I began to read about us. I used to be ashamed to say: "I am Mapuche". Then I started to learn about the past, to find out who I actually am. And I found such a rich heritage in our culture. So much that is worth preserving and passing on. So much that we must defend and protect, so that it won't get lost.'

Doors open in me while Lía is talking. I can feel echoes in myself of her sadness over the lost years, the needless shame of the little girl she once was.

'It makes our work quite hard sometimes,' says Rodrigo, who is bearing *maté* and a cup of tea. 'Most of our members find it difficult to stand up for themselves. They have become so used to having a boss, to following orders, as it has been for so long. We try to give them the freedom to act for themselves, but it's not easy.'

'It is getting easier now,' Lía says. 'The young Mapuche are beginning to look at themselves...' She stops for a moment, reconsiders. '*We* are beginning to look at *our*selves in a different way, to re-evaluate what is ours, our culture. We're beginning to throw off the shame. We're learning the language again. And we're beginning to realise that our culture really was a great and valuable culture. That we had our own gods, our own way to connect with nature. There was a connection with nature that gave us protection. And through the imposition of another culture, all of that was lost. Our identity. But now, we're beginning to stand up again. To try and understand what we are about. To work on healing the wounds of the past that way and also, on the other hand, to learn how to coexist with the other culture, the white culture.'

It is as though the walls of the stuffy little room at the back of the shop have fallen away. The landscape of the past is all around us, reclaimed by the Mapuche of today who are learning to hold their heads high, to be proud of their people, their culture, their past. And the landscape of a present in which the young are beginning to leave bitterness behind, and open themselves up to approaching and claiming for themselves their own culture, with pride and without shame.

'As a small girl, I kept trying to understand who I was, I even picked up a few words of our language from the grandmothers. And today, when I need to be able to speak Mapudungun, I find that the words are still in me.' Lía gives me a brilliant smile. 'When I was little, I couldn't understand why I had a Mapuche surname. Sometimes it made me furious, I didn't understand why the other children at school made fun of me for it. Until a teacher told me what my name meant. Ñancufil is composed of the words *ñancu*, which means hawk, and *fil*, snake in Mapudungun. "You are named," that teacher told me; "for the wisdom of the snake and the wisdom of the hawk. And when you need help, you can call on them and they will come and help you and guide you." That changed my whole life. I often dream of hawks. When I am low and I need help, I call them and they come to me.'

Lía turns in her swivel chair and taps out some commands on her keyboard that open a number of images on the computer.

'We took those the last time we were in Epuyen, in the Andes,' she explains.

Photos appear of a glorious mountain landscape, white peaks and green wooded valleys. And in the foreground stands Lía, her head tilted back, looking up at the sky from which descends a large bird. A hawk. Over the course of several pictures, it comes closer and closer, until it finally alights on her head.

She laughs at my astounded face, a laugh of utter joy.

I have never seen a large bird of prey sit on anybody's head. Not ever, not even on T.V.. (Maybe Oscar Payaguala was right about being able to make rain, too?) Rodrigo hovers in the background, smiling.

Working with Rodrigo in the Wool Bank is not Lia's only job. She is also a teacher. She teaches traditional crafts in the schools in the poorer neighbourhoods on the outskirts of Trelew.

'There are lots of children there of Mapuche origin. Spinning and weaving is part of their heritage. The thread that we spin is a connection to the grandmothers and grandfathers. I learnt spinning from my grandmother, and now I am passing it on to the children of today. That's how it always was. Today, the grandmothers and grandfathers are not held in high regard, because they're old. With the work I do, I hope that the children will learn again to respect their grandmothers, and their culture. They have a right to know who they are.'

31

A FEW DAYS LATER I visit the Gaiman museum again where Miguel is on duty once more. I sit at the table in the back room with a stack of newspapers. When there are visitors, he disappears to the museum's front room to welcome and guide them round. When there are none, he sits in a tiny little room, hardly more than a cupboard, off the back room, reads and listens to the radio.

Today, nobody comes into the museum all afternoon.

Halfway through my stack of early twentieth century Welsh newspapers, I remember that I want to buy a book. The museum has a little shop – that is to say, a book rack in Miguel's cupboard which must be larger than it looks, because it somehow manages to contain most books published in Spanish about *Y Wladfa*. I want the Spanish translation of Eluned Morgan's account of her trip west across the desert at the turn of the last century, *Dringo'r Andes*. I'm struggling with the Welsh original.

I announce my intention to buy the book.

'Ah,' says Miguel and emerges, two books in hand. 'You want to buy this one as well.' *This* is a history of some of the women of the colony. '*Vos escribís sobre estas cosas del feminismo, ¿no?* You write about this feminism stuff, don't you?' He says it with a sidelong glance.

'I've already got that one,' I tell him. 'And yes – I am a feminist.'

We drift into a conversation. He asks me how I got on with Rodrigo, and I tell him about Lía and the hawk, and thank him for introducing me to Rodrigo. We talk about Patagonian Indian cultures, and Miguel says – I get this only slowly – that he really shouldn't talk about this topic. He speaks faster than usual, and because of this I find it harder than usual to follow his Spanish. At first, I naturally assume that he – like Rodrigo, like Lía, like me – feels that more justice for the Mapuche and other indigenous peoples is necessary. But it turns out that he doesn't.

Quite the contrary, in fact.

'What kind of culture did they have anyway before the Europeans came?' demands Miguel – rhetorically, because before I can answer, he sweeps on. 'They have exactly the same civil rights as all other Argentinians, but they don't want to be Argentinians, they say they're Mapuche not Argentinian....'

What the hell is this about? What has ruffled his feathers? I've never seen Miguel other than chilled.

I say that I can understand that some *Indígenas* don't necessarily identify with a state which ordered their destruction, even if it was over a hundred years ago.

'The Desert Conquest, don't talk to me about that,' Miguel says when I call it a genocide.

It wasn't a genocide, he argues, because a genocide is the illegal killing of a group of people, whereas the 'Desert Conquest' was decided by the Argentinian Congress, which passed a law about it. So it was legal. And anyway, it was decided upon because the Indians had attacked European settlers and settlements. So it was justified as well.

'Yes, but excuse me,' I say, finally getting a word in, 'those settlements were on the land that belonged to the Indians!'

'But they didn't even *work* the land,' says Miguel, as though there was any logic in that. 'They just moved about on it, they weren't settled or anything.'

'And?'

'And now they demand all that land back from the state; and they still don't do anything with it. There are some who have a *chacra* in the Andes, and what do they do? Nothing. What is a farm for, working the land and making money, isn't it? Not for just sitting on the land staring at the sky and doing nothing.'

I remember that a couple of days ago Miguel himself said that Rodrigo was always trying to get him to work and it was no good, he and work are incompatible. And now he accuses others of laziness!

'They want their land back,' Miguel continues, 'but how, of whom? They don't have any written deeds, nothing to show it is theirs. It now belongs to other people, and do they want to disown those people to get their land back?'

'Of course not,' I say, 'that wouldn't work, they did that in East Germany, returning the lands of people who had been disowned or who had fled in the 1940s and 1950s, after the War; and the East German state gave that land to other people. After reunification, it was taken off those people and returned to the heirs of the original owners.' I want to say, "That would be committing a new wrong to right an old one", but I haven't got the words for that in Spanish and, anyway, Miguel is in no state to listen.

'I know what you think, you think it's a simple thing and it isn't.'

'I don't think that, actually...' But it's no good.

'I am a descendent of the Welsh, of Lewis Jones, Llwyd ap Iwan; the Welsh were given land by the state back then, my family owns a farm and lands in the Andes – they would want those back off us too, I suppose.'

Is that at the root of his outburst? Does he fear being seen as someone who benefited from the 'Desert Campaign'? Or does he fear that someone will take his land away and restore it to Indian ownership?

'Today, the Mapuche language is written down,' says Miguel. 'But that's only since the Europeans came and taught them how to read and write. They didn't even have that before.'

I've got an answer for that one.

'Neither did the Celts – your forbears, they had an oral culture for centuries, they had legends and tales and laws and everything, the *Mabinogion*, all that was transmitted orally.'

Miguel waves Celts and *Mabinogion* aside. 'People say the Mapuche have a great culture, great music – but show me the instruments, show me the culture,' he says '– they had nothing, *nothing*!' And he slams out of the room to put on the kettle for his *maté*, which has gone cold.

A part of me is almost scared by Miguel's uncharacteristic outburst. It's as though a friendly, lazy dog had suddenly jumped up, growling and baring its teeth. I don't like violence, even as low-key as this. I know about violence. I know about people you thought you could trust suddenly turning round and behaving in ways you'd never think possible. Trust is not something that comes naturally to me. My old survival instincts tell me to be on my guard now against Miguel. What might he do next?

At the same time, I think: This is interesting. His reaction has nothing to do with me. This is about him. But I still don't understand it. Without realising, I must have pushed one of Miguel's buttons. A big red one.

I decide to go back to my newspapers, bury myself in the past. I will tune Miguel out for a bit.

He comes back with the kettle filled and retreats into his cupboard like a hermit crab into its shell. (It must be about as tight.) He even closes the door.

Nothing happens for a while, and I think that all this is *muy raro*, very strange.

A while later, he opens the door again and we talk a bit, cautiously, pretending that his strange outburst never happened. We talk about reading, I buy the Eluned Morgan book, he compliments me on my Spanish. I go back to my articles once more and he retires to his cupboard again, but leaves the door open. Indicates the radio: '*Estoy sufriendo.*' I'm suffering.

He's listening to a football match and his side appear to be losing.

'All I want is a draw, but...'

Things don't look good, apparently. He keeps the volume down, he says, so that he can't hear the commentary properly. This is in case something terrible happens, so that he won't have to hear it.

I immediately perceive the flaw in this.

'Something good might happen, and you won't hear that then either.'

'*No importa.*' Doesn't matter.

'But it does,' I argue. 'The good is as important as the bad, *¿no?*'

He gives me a long look. I brace myself for another argument.

He turns the volume of his radio up a bit.

The game ends one all.

32

UNTIL NOW, I HAVE SEEN Patagonia in summer, when the air is hot and dry and dusty; in autumn, when the wind is cool despite the heat of the sun; and in spring, when the fresh green of the valley is a feast for the eyes after the harsh dry greyness of the desert and the dusty white hills. So for my next trip, I go in July, in the middle of winter: to see what the place was like when the Welsh first arrived.

I have decided to travel south by coach again. I once travelled from Berlin to London on a coach. The trip that took twenty-four hours and seared itself into my memory as the most uncomfortable thing ever. But for some reason, I think of the trip from Buenos Aires to Patagonia as a diverting adventure. I am positively looking forward to sitting on my rear for twenty-one hours on a swaying coach full of strangers.

In the central coach station in the Retiro area of downtown Buenos Aires people are strolling, walking, running. Couples sit, gloomily and silently, with just too much space between them, staring in opposite directions, or down at the floor, not communicating. (The end of a visit, an affair, a marriage?) Harried mothers try to manhandle howling children and mountains of luggage at the same time. Weeping families see off a loved one. Buses disgorge people from the provinces who have come to the city to make their fortunes. Not only their bodies, even their faces look stiff from travelling. They glance around at the huge new city with wary, tired eyes, uneasily aware that they are newcomers here. They don't know the rules. There are bigger, sharper, more experienced fish in this pond who will regard them as prey.

Outside the coach terminal stands a street market. Bars and cafés offer last-minute fast food. Stalls sell bags of every description, handbags and huge rucksacks and trendy wheeled suitcases in bright colours. You can buy clothes and toys and food, CDs and newspapers.

Vendors with small mobile ovens bake and sell bread rolls. There is an almost visible aura of warmth around oven and vendor. You can see the live charcoal glowing, smell the almost painfully delicious scent of the baking bread. I discover that on a cool winter's day like this, nothing is better than some fresh *chipa*.

Chipa is a Paraguayan speciality, the vendor tells me, made with cassava and maize meal and cheese. Paraguay, a small, landlocked country to the north, is to Argentina what Poland is to the U.K.. Lots of Paraguayans come to Buenos Aires looking for work, most of them on the coaches. That's why the *chipa* sellers congregate around the terminal. This one eyes me curiously. Not many foreigners travel by coach, he says.

'Didn't you tell me that you're from Paraguay?' I ask. 'So you're a foreigner too, in Argentina, *¿no?*'

He grins, shakes his head. 'Not from as far away as you.'

He doesn't mean 'foreigners' exactly. He means *Gringos*: Europeans and North Americans.

Behind the market, side streets lead off the big, multi-lane main road on which traffic roars past the old railway station and the coach terminal. They are narrow, dirty, pot-holed lanes criss-crossed by disused railway tracks from the old days, before coaches replaced trains for travel to all corners of the country. These streets lead to another world. Behind the coach terminal stands the most (in)famous of all Argentina's shanty towns: Villa 31, squeezed between the railway tracks and the urban motorway. Infamous: because Retiro is a prosperous neighbourhood with glittering shops and office towers. It's like having the back streets of Hackney or Deptford within spitting distance of Kensington; except that Villa 31 is a hell of a lot poorer and more drug and crime ridden than the worst sink estate in Britain.

I always imagined a shanty town to be an anarchic huddle of ramshackle huts; beaten-earth floors and open sewers and gangs of abandoned children and dogs. Villa 31 at least isn't like that. It is a small town in its own right, bang there in the centre of Buenos Aires. There are houses that look no different from those in any small town in Argentina: simple whitewashed cubes. There are shops: most have the nature of their business painted on the outside wall, *Carnicería*, butcher; *Panadería*, baker, and even *Locutorio*, an internet café. But the normality stops when you look up at the second or third floors, which have clearly been put there without the benefit of planning permission: Most are built of bare bricks and breeze-blocks, with window-frames crammed in anyhow. Most houses sport satellite dishes.

That is as much as I can see from the main road. I don't actually go down any of the side streets. It's not a clever idea to visit a shanty town by yourself. I don't really feel like a foreigner any more in Argentina, but I am one; and thus, by definition, rich. I can afford to travel here, to travel for fun. Venturing into the Villa by myself would be more than foolhardy. Although back in Europe I may feel as though I don't own very much, in comparison with the inhabitants of Villa 31 I am wealthy. I'd resent having my wallet stolen by one of them, but I can see why they would think it OK.

I never used to see this side of Argentina. I loved Retiro from the first time I caught a coach here. For me, it was – it still is – a place where journeys and adventures start, somewhere exciting and romantic. But once when I was burbling about this to Lorena, she gave me a funny look and said, 'Have you never seen the street children begging outside? The druggies? The kid prostitutes?'

I hadn't. I hadn't seen the houses of Villa 31 either, although now I wonder how on earth I managed to look through them.

Sometimes, Argentina is a tricky place. I love it, that hasn't changed. I am learning more about it all the time, and while I feel at home here now, more familiar with place and people and language, there are still times when I am out of my depth.

33

THE COACH BUMPS OVER the last ramp on the road out of Retiro coach terminal, lumbers over the abandoned railway tracks and gathers speed to roll through dull, wintry Buenos Aires onto *Ruta 3*, which runs for almost two thousand miles south, south, south, all the way to Tierra del Fuego.

This time, the journey seems to pass much faster. The endless pampas don't appear much changed from the way they look in summer: they are still green and unnerving in their vastness.

Darkness falls early, so I read, and doze, and wonder what Patagonia will be like in the depths of winter.

I wake up in the middle of the night. The lights are dimmed. Blanket-covered forms huddle in their seats like Antarctic explorers buried in snow drifts. Outside the windows, all is darkness. The coach hums and sways; tinny tango music drifts up the stairs from the drivers' radio. I rearrange my crumpled blanket and try to go back to sleep.

But then the coach slows down, and now I can see the odd streetlight outside. Houses. I locate my left arm and check the time. It isn't the middle of the night, it's six o'clock in the morning.

We're not due to arrive until past eight. The coach comes to a stop, and the driver calls out something I don't catch in my still sleep-befuddled state. Perhaps we've broken down? Flat tyre? Snow-bound road? People are unwrapping themselves from their blankets, stretching, pulling on shoes and coats and getting up. I scramble downstairs to enquire what's happening.

Not a breakdown. A fifteen-minute break.

'*Para tomar un cafecito,*' says the driver with a broad smile. A coffee break. His teeth glint in the lights reflected from the dashboard.

Yawning figures clamber off the coach into the Patagonian darkness. I climb the stairs back to the top deck to get my cigarettes, my comb and my toothbrush.

It's cool outside, the pre-dawn dark is dense. A fine rain whispers. The air smells of damp sand and open spaces.

I wander in the soft drizzle, past dark houses whose occupants still lie asleep. Pine needles and sand and small stones crunch underfoot. I feel a sudden mad happiness at being back here. Back home, I almost think, then catch myself. Don't get carried away, I warn my romantic self. Patagonia isn't home, it's the very opposite of home; it's a vast desert with a handful of towns dotted about it like oases, of which I know just a few.

And yet, there's something here that makes it mine, although I've never properly lived here. When I return to Buenos Aires I don't feel like this. I love Buenos Aires, but it's all one-way. Buenos Aires is a beautiful woman who might flirt with me in passing, but she won't remember my name, or even my face.

I stand for a moment alone in the darkness, in the cold south wind and the rain, and exchange greetings with Patagonia. Then I go blinking into the brightly lit service-station and brush my hair and my teeth, have a coffee and a cigarette and wake up.

When the light of dawn finally floods the eastern sky, I'm long back on the coach, and it's not far now to Puerto Madryn. The brown scrublands on either side lie half hidden in mist. Low stunted bushes grow on the grey, sandy soil, black in the dull light and wet from the rain. Clouds of drizzle swirl and eddy in the wind. A thin line appears on the horizon and steadily grows more substantial, expands and separates itself into squares and rectangles. Houses. Buildings. Puerto Madryn. Behind them, a thick, hazy grey line. The sea.

Puerto Madryn, where the *Mimosa* made landfall, still bears its Welsh name and even boasts a tea shop or two. It got its name from Lewis Jones and one of the major financiers of *Y Wladfa*, Love Jones-Parry Esq., whose family estate near Nefyn on the Llŷn peninsula was called Madryn. (Jones-Parry's Christian name really was 'Love,' birth certificate and all. It must have been very trying for his wife when she was cross with him. "Oh do shut up, Love" just doesn't properly convey ire.)

These days, its name is about as Welsh as Puerto Madryn gets. Lewis Jones and Love Jones-Parry had already named the place back in 1863, but the city wasn't built for another twenty years, in the late 1880s, around the natural deep water harbour in the sheltering arms of the New Bay, the best harbour in all of Argentina. In its heyday, the railway ran 150 miles south-west from Madryn, stopping at Gaiman in the station that is now the museum, on through the famous tunnel and across the desert as far as the small settlement of Las Plumas. But the heyday of the Patagonian railway is long past. The trains stopped running in 1961.

The harbour, on the other hand, is still very active; and the main business of the city is still connected with the sea, although in different ways. These days, Puerto Madryn is famous for its wildlife. Colonies of elephant seals, sea lions and penguins live on the nearby Península Valdés, and summer visitors flock to catch a glimpse of them. Cruise liners on their way down to Antarctica call in for a day, and their passengers are given a Welsh tea, and time to wander around the souvenir shops. In the winter, Southern Right Whales visit the bay's deep, cold waters to mate, and to stock up on the plentiful fish; as they have done for millennia. Just a few decades ago, they were hunted nearly to extinction. Now, people travel to Madryn from all over the world simply to look at them.

34

IT'S ONLY HALF PAST EIGHT as I walk out of Madryn's coach terminal, and I'm feeling cold and tired and excited.

Madryn's streets are wide and straight, laid out in grid pattern. They're lined with two- and three-storey houses with red brick or stuccoed fronts in pastel colours. Most buildings are low, so that even in the middle of the city I can see the sky without having to look up.

Souvenir shops, cafés and restaurants line the streets downtown, together with a surprising number of ice-cream parlours. All of which are open, despite this being the middle of winter. Lots of businesses offer excursions to Península Valdés to see the wildlife. As I walk, I can see the seafront at every intersection. It puts me in a holiday mood.

The hostel at which I'm staying is basic but beautifully cheap, and the staff are friendly. There is also, I discover, an added bonus. Julián has blond hair and melting brown eyes and a sweet disposition. Intelligence is not his strong suit, but he has a way of jumping up and licking people's faces that would charm a stone. Julián is a golden labrador.

'Our watchdog,' says the woman in the hostel, with an eyeroll and a laugh, and drags an over-enthusiastic Julián back by his collar.

I dig out an extra fleece and stuff my bag under my bunk bed by way of unpacking. I meant to go for a coffee to warm up, but instead I find my feet carrying me to the beach. There's a chance that I might spot a whale – a slim chance, the woman in the hostel has warned me: they tend not to come into the bay much when it's overcast. There are excursions, of course, boatloads of people go out every day to whale-watch. But although all the trip organisers stress that they give the whales a wide enough berth so as not to bother them, I'm not sure that they do. I prefer to take my chance from the beach, where I won't get in their way.

Ballenas, whales, are big in Puerto Madryn: the gift shops along the seafront sell whale T-shirts and whale mugs, whale-shaped knitted hats, whale soft toys and whale calendars. A photo shop sports a neon whale over the door to advertise its one-hour developing service. One sweet shop even sells whale fluke-shaped chocolates filled with that most wonderful of Argentine inventions, *dulce de leche*. I think that chocolate filled with caramel must surely be a horrendously sweet affair, and buy a *cola de ballena* ('whale tail') to find out.

Happily I am wrong. The 'whale tails' are delicious, and – together with ice cream and coffee – will form the basis of my diet over the next couple of days.

The beachfront is lined with multi-storey buildings for as far as I can see. It's not exactly Miami, most of them are just five or six storeys. The majority seem to contain holiday apartments. Big colourful hoardings advertise special mid-winter deals: *Whale-watching from your bedroom!*

The beach itself is huge, a flat expanse which stretches in a wide arc in both directions. A cold, blustery wind is blowing and grey clouds hang low in the sky. The headlands north and south of the beach are visible, the ones beyond almost hidden in the murk.

The water is grey and empty. No whales.

But it doesn't matter. I'm just happy to be back in Patagonia, and by the sea: the smack and hiss of the waves, the smell of salt on the air; walking on the damp, firm sand by the water's edge. The wind is exhilarating. It seems to blow right through me, whipping away the close, confined night on the coach. I lean into it and stride on.

There is something oddly pleasant about walking in freezing wind and rain *in July*; perversely pleasant, perhaps, since I'm losing out on summer back in Europe. But I love walking in the rain. I love to feel the strength of the elements. For a while, and with modern amenities in easy reach for when the elements become too strong. Madryn is the perfect setting. There are a dozen cafés within five minutes' walk to which I can retreat. And so, in the secure knowledge that shortly, I'll be having a big cup of tea (with a dash of rum, possibly) and then a hot shower, I throw myself into the teeth of the wind with abandon and delight.

I check the water every now and then for any sign of whales, but nothing. Promising black specks invariably fly away after a while, revealing themselves as birds.

The beach curves, slowly. It's even longer than it looks. When I turn back to check my progress I can see that I am quite a distance from my starting point. But the buildings at the far end of the beach don't appear to have come any closer at all.

Out in the bay, there's something black again, and a spray of white. I peer out over the grey waters, but I see nothing more. Just a wave, probably. But I still keep looking in that direction. And there: a cylindrical black shape with a blunt nose rises half out of the water and throws itself back in, producing an enormous splash. A whale!

White spray flies everywhere as the huge creature sinks back beneath the waves.

A whale. I've seen a whale!

I stand there on the cold, windswept beach of Puerto Madryn, jumping and whooping and watching a real live whale out there in the sea, just a few hundred yards away.

For a mad moment I am very, very tempted to throw myself into the sea and swim out there to join it.

There are more. Quite far out: six, seven, eight hundred yards away maybe, but even so they're clearly visible. A yacht lies at anchor near where they're sporting, and the whales are about the same size as the boat. Their sheer size is impressive. (I look them up later: an adult female Southern Right Whale can grow to a length of 18 metres, around 60 feet. That's *big*.) Perhaps that is why I find myself so unexpectedly touched by their presence: They're so huge, and so peaceful. We could learn a thing or two from whales.

As I walk towards the end of the beach, I see several more whales: whales rising up and throwing themselves back in the water. I see large, black, curved backs rising briefly above the waves and exhaling a large plume of spray that drifts off on the wind. And I see, finally, that iconic image: the whale fluke rising out of the water and – that's what it looks like – waving. It moves vigorously back and forth a few times, and then crashes into the water with an almighty splash, as though a giant had slammed his open palm down on the water. (Apparently nobody knows why the whales wave their tails about in this manner. I like that. There are a few mysteries left in the world.)

I pinch myself at one point: I'm seeing *whales*. In reality; eye to eye, so to speak, not in a photo, not on T.V. *Real* whales, here, now. The world is a place full of wonders and beauty and surprising and unexpected things, and I'm out here in it, standing on a beach by a bay with a whale in it.

35

IT'S RAINING. Everybody is commenting on it, which is unusual. As a rule, Argentinians don't talk very much about the weather, because there doesn't tend to be all that much of it. The eastern part of Patagonia is usually either bright and windy, or cloudy and windy, and nearly always dry. Annual rainfall is around seven inches, twenty-odd millimetres. People from Gaiman who've been to Wales have commented to me on how the British tirelessly talk about the weather. The Patagonians regard this as an eccentricity.

I'm in Gaiman, because today is the 27th July and tomorrow will be the anniversary of the landing of the first Welsh settlers in the *Mimosa* in 1865: a public holiday in the entire province of Chubut which today celebrates its foundation. There's a local transport company named after it, all of whose buses have the venerable date emblazoned on their fronts and sides; and there's even a village called *28 de Julio*. The first time somebody told me they lived there, I thought I had misunderstood. ('Where do you live?' – '28 July.') 28 July is A Big Thing in Chubut, a sort of equivalent to Thanksgiving in the US, I suppose. And I have come to Gaiman to witness the festivities.

Except, as soon as I arrive there after a ninety minute bus journey, Clara Roberts the choir mistress, with whom I'm staying this time, tells me that the most interesting celebration will take place in Puerto Madryn, whence I have just come. There will be a pageant of sorts with a Mapuche-Tehuelche religious ceremony tomorrow morning; and later in the day a staging of the actual arrival of the Welsh, with people dressed up in nineteenth century garb rowing ashore, to be greeted by smiling Mapuche-Tehuelche.

It will be a pleasing distortion of history, and of course no mention of the 'Desert Campaign' will be made.

'To be fair,' says Clara, who knows my views well; 'at the time, the Welsh and the Indians actually did co-exist very peacefully. They would have been all right if the government had left well alone. The Welsh tried to intervene, you know.'

'The pageant is going to be a lot more fun than that bromide we'll be going to tomorrow,' Clara's husband says gloomily. Amando used to be mayor of Gaiman, and a bank manager too; he and Clara won't be able to wriggle out of any public functions.

'I'd go to Madryn if I were you,' he tells me. 'Of course, they might cancel the event because of the rain, but if not, it should be great fun.'

'They wouldn't cancel it just because of a bit of rain?'

'Half the teas in the valley have already been cancelled because of the weather,' Clara says. 'Most of the chapels are *en las chacras*, in the country, where only dirt roads go. They are impassable when it gets really wet. Mud slides, the lot of them.'

Still – the roads to and in Puerto Madryn are tarmacked; and surely a shower or two won't stop the festivities for the Founding Day of the province. I don't take her warning too seriously.

28 July dawns cloudy, but breezy and dry. I get up early to catch the bus back to Puerto Madryn.

Dawn creeps up slowly as we leave Gaiman, and between Trelew and Madryn, as we traverse the endless, flat, bare steppe, the sun peeps through the clouds.

Sitting on the bus, my nose pressed against the window, I try to conjure up the past. I would so love to witness their arrival, to stand hidden at the edge of the beach and see them come ashore in the *Mimosa*'s small boat; splashing through the last few yards of water. Standing there, surveying their new homeland.

We bump into the bus terminal of Madryn only a day after I left it, and I clamber off the bus and back into the present.

It's started to drizzle and the sea is heavy and the colour of lead. A whale sports far out, and I want to wave to it. I don't know why it cheers me up so much that a whale is out there in the water, without the least idea that I exist; and even if it did what would it care? But I'm heartened, and pleased, and only mildly miffed when I hear that the pageant on the beach has, indeed, been cancelled.

Actually, I find it quite funny. This is Patagonia, the Deep South, one of the last wildernesses of the world... and they cancel a parade because people might get wet?

An hour later, I understand a little better. There has been a sudden, brief downpour of no more than perhaps ten minutes. But the roads in Madryn's city centre are flooded. The gutters can't cope at all. This place isn't built for rain.

So I catch yet another bus back to Gaiman. There is to be a big celebratory community tea in the old Capel Bethel in the afternoon, with a concert to follow in the evening, just like the communal teas and concerts of old. Capel Bethel stands in the middle of Gaiman, and so this tea will not be cancelled. I am very keen to experience at least one of the famous festive teas of *Y Wladfa*.

36

I MAKE MY WAY to the chapel alone. Clara and Amando are being politely bored at some official function in the village of 28 de Julio. I rang Dudú from a phone shop in Puerto Madryn to ask whether she would go to the tea in Capel Bethel, but she said No – it wasn't her kind of thing. Lisa, who would be in her element at a Welsh commemorative tea ceremony, has decided not to travel all the way to Patagonia this year for the festivities, but instead to remain in Buenos Aires. I haven't bothered to ask Lorena. I don't think a celebration of the Welsh pioneers is quite her scene.

There is a queue outside Capel Bethel. As all the other chapels in the valley are closed, everybody is coming here. Only as many people are allowed into the chapel as there are others leaving it, because there aren't enough seats to go round.

Already half a dozen bedraggled figures are sheltering in the porch. It is drizzling again, and the bare branches of the poplars bend in the wind.

Finally, my turn arrives.

Boards have been laid over the backs of pews to make tables. People sit facing each other and eat cake. Young girls run about busily replenishing tea cups and bearing trays of cake and bread-and-butter. The bread is home-made, of course, as are all the cakes. There is the wonderful cream cake which looks so misleadingly like cheese cake but consists entirely of cream and sugar and egg yolks. And tastes *divine*. There is apple pie and scones and Swiss roll (made, an Argentinian touch, with *dulce de leche* instead of jam), lemon tart and the famous *torta negra*.

The floor of the old chapel is made of thick, uneven planks of wood, worn smooth by the feet of many generations. On the walls hang oil paintings that make up in fervour what they may lack in talent: the recently arrived Welsh on the beach in Puerto Madryn, Bible in one hand, pointing with the other towards the desert. There stands the Reverend Abraham Matthews looking like a Biblical patriarch compete with bushy beard and stern gaze. A portrait of Michael D. Jones, the spiritual father of the whole mad scheme, who himself prudently stayed at home in Wales – although, to be fair, he did donate large amounts of his own money to the cause. Or, perhaps, The Cause.

What I hadn't quite grasped is the extent to which this is strictly a social occasion for the Welsh. Entire extended families sit and chat and demolish cake. Absolutely nobody except for me has turned up by themselves.

The thing is, until now, I haven't felt like an outsider in Gaiman. I've been coming here for years; coming and going, admittedly. I'm not actually Welsh, but I speak the language and I have learnt Spanish, too; I have studied the history of *Y Wladfa*, have explored the country, spoken to its people. I feel at home.

But I'm not. Not here, not today.

For the first time, I feel like a stranger in Gaiman.

I don't belong here. I'm nobody's daughter, niece, wife, mother.

The people with whom I share a pew ask where I'm from, about my family. I hate that question. How to respond? "I haven't been in touch with my family for fifteen years because they're respectable middle-class abusers who beat the hell out of me throughout my childhood and never ever apologised" is truthful but a bit of a conversation stopper. I know. It's how I used to answer when I was younger and my feelings were much more raw. For a while after that, I would say they were dead; it seemed less extreme somehow and people would be sympathetic instead of disconcerted.

By now much time has passed. I have made my own life. I'm working on making some of my most cherished dreams come true. I have friends who are, I suppose, a sort of elective family. I'm my own person, and usually I care much less about being different, about what people might think. Usually, I just say firmly that I'm not in touch with my family and that my life is the better for it; and let people make of that what they will.

But here in Capel Bethel, I find it difficult to hold on to that. In the face of the gathered clans, I feel again like a piece of unclaimed baggage; the way I used to feel as a child, when nobody cared enough to protect me.

I feel rather alone in Capel Bethel.

I think of Dudú and suddenly understand her wry tone when she told me this morning that the commemorative tea wasn't her kind of thing. How many of the people here knew of her prison of a marriage? Of her husband gambling away their money, her struggle to get herself and her children out into a decent life? How many looked away, then blamed her for the break-up of the marriage?

Who among those assembled here knows of a woman or a child being beaten behind closed doors, but won't interfere because the family is more important than the well-being of an individual?

I finish my tea and cake as quickly as I can, and leave. I will give the concert a miss. Instead, I walk by the canal in the fresh cold air, with only the wind and the bare trees for company.

And a while later, when I feel fit for human company again, I call in on Lorena and Ernesto and their brand-new baby daughter, and Patricia the mastiff. I spend the rest of *28 de Julio* with the four of them, drinking velvety red Argentinian wine and talking about dogs, and babies, and the meaning of life.

Desert

37

WHEN THE WELSH FIRST ARRIVED in Patagonia, they were alarmed and intimidated by the vastness of the land, and nervous of its indigenous peoples. After some timid exploring they found that the valley where they had chosen to live appeared to be virtually sealed off from the desert. Relieved, they returned to Rawson: they were living in an easily defendable cul-de-sac. The desert – and the Indians – couldn't get at them.[60]

It's easy now to smile at both their alarm and their naïveté. Yet I remember the first time I was in Gaiman. I didn't dare leave the village for almost the entire length of my stay. Everything outside was big and strange and potentially dangerous. All kinds of threats might lurk there: rabid dogs (possible), pumas (unlikely), robbers and desperate characters (very unlikely), the alarming emptiness of the desert (undeniable). Beyond the safe circle of Gaiman lay outer space. I might be sucked into emptiness and never return.

On the last day of my first trip, daringly, I went for a walk outside the immediate centre of Gaiman, in a kind of grey area between the village and the desert. It was before dawn when I set out; which, in autumn, made it just before seven. I felt as though I were venturing into the jungle, the Sahara, the Antarctic. After a short while the tarmac turned into to a gravel road that struck me as a whole lot less trustworthy. You know where you are with a tarmac road. This gravel business was unfamiliar, and somehow seemed less substantial, as though I might encounter a patch of quicksand along the way, or an elephant trap.

I laughed about it later, as soon as I was safely back in the garden of *Ar Lan yr Afon*, with a cup of coffee and a cigarette. But at the time, I was genuinely (unnecessarily) afraid. The valley was grey as cobwebs when I got there: grey ruler-straight roads. Grey poplars, rustling in the pre-dawn breeze. Grey scrubby thorn bushes. Although I couldn't see any houses or farmsteads, I could hear cocks crowing and dogs barking and the occasional lowing of a cow.

I encountered a few people, bemused figures walking or cycling to work, or to catch a bus in Gaiman. I nodded good morning, but only a few returned my greeting. I didn't know then that Argentinians absolutely don't walk unless they have to. The concept of 'going for a walk' for recreation or enjoyment isn't understood except in big cities which have parks for the purpose. In the country, only those who can't afford a car – or a horse – or at least a bike, have to walk. 'Going for a walk' in the valley at dawn would have struck the people who encountered me as a very odd thing to do.

I didn't stay out there long, just long enough to watch the sunrise. Light suffused the sky. Colours changed from black to inky blue to green to pink. For a time, the whole of the eastern sky was the most improbable, amazing hot pink. Birds flew up, cawing. When I looked up, the sky directly above me shimmered like a crystal.

It sounds as though I was on LSD, but I hadn't even had a cup of coffee.

It's easy to look at the vast, dusty steppe with the eyes of a recently arrived European and see empty desert, unclaimed land waiting to be irrigated, worked and made fruitful. But for the people who inhabited it, whose forbears had done so for millennia, it already was fruitful. 'Our plains have plenty of guanacos and plenty of rheas. We are never in want of food,' the *cacique* Antonio had written to Lewis Jones.

Once friendly relations had been established, things improved greatly. Here were people who knew the land, who lived in it and off it and understood it. They taught the Welsh where paths ran; taught them to hunt and search for water and survive in the desert.

During the lean years, the young men would ride out hunting with groups of Pampas or Tehuelche Indians, several days' worth deep into the desert. They learnt which animals to hunt, how to shoot, how to use the bolas to bring down a rhea or a hare or a guanaco. Finally, they felt safe enough to go forth by themselves. Understanding came gradually. Early attempts failed when they ran out of water or encountered impassable territory. But they persevered, and travelled a little further each time.

Apart from sheer curiosity, there were two main motivations for exploring the desert: land and gold.

In the early 1880s – almost twenty years after establishing the colony – there was still arable land to be claimed in the lower Chubut valley. But new settlers continued to arrive. Indeed, they arrived in larger numbers than ever before, now that the valley had proved fruitful. By 1883, the population of *Y Wladfa* had risen almost tenfold to 1300, and still more were coming. Land would have to be found for them all. The Indians had told tantalising tales of a fruitful, green landscape many days' travel to the west, in the foothills of the mountains.

Among the new arrivals were some who had been prospecting for gold in Australia. Gold fever was in the air: these were the years of the California Gold Rush. Why shouldn't the Argentinian West turn out to be just as rich in gold?

It's astounding what an effect a soft yellow metal will have, even on otherwise quite sensible, unworldly people. The majority of the Welsh settlers in Patagonia were unworldly in the best sense of the word; they were deeply religious, without much interest in material goods and riches. But the possibility of gold in the Andes led to a rush to explore.

Perhaps not all. But there were certainly numerous small groups that set off along the courses of the rivers Chubut, Senguerr and Chico, panning as they went. They didn't find much, certainly not masses of gold, and no fertile land for several years. But that didn't stop them trying.

38

THERE IS A PLACE a hundred miles west of Gaiman, out in the dusty steppe, known today by two names. Officially and on maps, it is *Las Plumas* in Spanish and *Y Plu* in Welsh: The Feathers; probably named after the rhea feathers in which *Indígenas* and Welsh traded.

Unofficially, especially among the Patagonian Welsh, it's known as *Valle de los Mártires*: The Valley of the Martyrs. Whereby, as you might expect, there hangs a tale.

In 1883, a band of four young men left the Welsh settlement to go west and look for gold. One had grown up in *Y Wladfa*, the other three were recent arrivals one of whom had experience of panning for gold in Australia. They left in July, during the height of winter when the weather was cold but damp and there was a chance to capture rain water to drink. Each had several pack horses with provisions, and spare horses to ride. For months they travelled all over the desert. They found small but promising amounts of gold in several rivers; so promising indeed that they named one place after it: *Hafn Aur*, Gorge of Gold.[61]

This was the same time that the 'Desert Campaign' of ethnic cleansing of the Indians of Patagonia was in full swing. Just before they departed that July, the four explorers would have signed the petition against the persecution and killing of Tehuelche which the Welsh sent to the government in Buenos Aires.

It's difficult to know how much the inhabitants of *Y Wladfa* knew about the extent of the 'Desert Campaign'. For General Roca in Buenos Aires – and for us with hindsight – it was an orchestrated campaign to sweep the south clean of the 'savages' who possessed the effrontery to have lived there first. The Welsh knew, in some detail, about what was happening in the Chubut valley: they had heard about the attacks from the Indians themselves. It is unclear whether they were aware of the similar attacks on other indigenous peoples all over Patagonia.

The fact is that, at the very time General Roca's army was waging war against the Indians of Patagonia, the four young Welshmen were on an extended trip through the desert, looking for gold and new lands to settle. By the end of the year, when they had been travelling for about six months, they met a group of soldiers engaged in the 'Desert Campaign', who told them that the plains had now been cleared of Indians.

In this the soldiers were wrong, because a few days later the Welshmen came across a couple of Indians. From this point, the accounts vary. Some identify them as Mapuche fleeing from the persecution of the Chilean military – which was engaged in its own war against the *Indígenas, La Guerra de Arauco*, the Arauco War – and bent on revenge. Of course, they might have been Mapuche fleeing from the persecution of the Argentine military. Other reports state that they were Tehuelche, but from a group who did not know the Welsh.[62] The *Günün A Künna*, the Pampas Indians, appear to have vanished from history already at this point. There is no way of knowing, now. We possess no account from an Indian point of view.

The four Welshmen had travelled up to 300 miles away from the Chubut valley, near the foothills of the Andes: a long, *long* way from home. They decided to return home with all speed. There were angry Indians about, and although the majority of the Welsh deplored the genocide and had taken no part in it, they were still white, like the soldiers; and the colony would still, in all likelihood, profit from the newly depopulated land. So they didn't hang about.

Some accounts say that the four had recently bought new clothes from a travelling merchant: and that at least some were parts of military uniforms. So perhaps the Indians who ambushed them thought the young men were soldiers. Perhaps they knew them for Welshmen and wanted to take revenge against those first white settlers, now that a whole army was mercilessly driving all Indians off their own land. Perhaps they didn't care one way or the other. Eluned Morgan wrote in 1901; twenty years after the event, and still enraged:

> The illustrious senators who rule Argentina determined that the only way to bring development and progress to Patagonia was by completely eliminating the old Native peoples, and it was this end which the great campaign served, the campaign that happened just at the time of those four young men. The hunt had been merciless and the treatment given by the soldiers to their captives such that hundreds of Indians preferred to throw themselves off mountains into lakes and rivers, rather than fall into the hands of such terrible enemies. The few hundred who had managed to escape the soldiers were hiding in the mountains, maddened by fear, all their faculties possessed by

the demon, their hearts filled with but one desire: to avenge the blood of their loved ones. And what Welshman could blame them?'[63]

The four gold seekers were within a hundred miles of home when they happened into – what? An ambush? A group of Mapuche? Tehuelche? No-one knows, except that it was a group of Indians armed with spears – no guns – and that they were out for blood. The Welshmen tried to get away, but their horses were already tired. Only one of them escaped, because his mare managed to jump a wide trench which slowed his pursuers for long enough to allow him to get away. The other three were killed and their bodies mutilated beyond recognition.

Bruce Chatwin reports that their genitals had been stuffed into their mouths.[64] I have no idea where he got that interesting detail. It may be true. It may not be. After the end of the genocide, big *hacienderos*, land owners, would offer 'piece payments' per killed Indian, and there were a handful of professional hunters.[65] Proof of a killing were ears, testicles or breasts, as scalps were in the North American West.[66] It would make sense for Indians killing whites to mirror those mutilations on the corpses. But those 'piece payments' happened years later, after the end of the 'Desert Campaign'.

There is no doubt that the Indians vented their fury on the three victims. 'The peaceful pagans of old had been converted, by the good works of civilisation, into ferocious, blood-thirsty outlaws,' Eluned Morgan commented bitterly.[67]

Communication and contact between Welsh and Indians was at this point effectively over. The eastern stretches of the province of Chubut were soon declared void of indigenous life. Survivors were driven hundreds of miles south, into what is today the province of Santa Cruz, where one single Tehuelche reservation was established; and west, into the foothills of the Andes. In the west, there were still skirmishes, and the Argentine army still sent out hit squads against groups of Indians many years after 1885, the official end of the 'Desert Campaign'.[68]

The story of the Welsh 'martyrs' is told to this day, but the many, many more indigenous martyrs are hardly ever mentioned.

39

THE FIRST WELSHMEN (to the best of my knowledge, they always *were* men) who rode off into the unknown depths of the desert, did so more or less haphazardly. One of the first – perhaps the very first – to put exploring on a more scientific footing was John Murray Thomas, an accountant latterly from Merthyr Tydfil. Not the most likely candidate, you would have thought, for saddling up and turning his horse's head towards the sunset. But that was exactly what he did. (Not alone. Lone Ranger figures were always more fiction than fact. Incidentally, do you remember the name of the Lone Ranger's Indian companion? When I learnt Spanish, I was astonished to find that *tonto* in Spanish means *stupid*. Nice.)

John Murray Thomas would travel with a small group of men. They took with them several horses each, and large amounts of provisions. Being a systematic kind of bird – all that accountancy paperwork, no doubt – John Murray Thomas was the only one of them who kept a diary.

Thursday, 2 August 1877
Rose at 9 am and washed. Just in time. Since Friday 27 July, we had only been washing our hands on the Sunday. This morning at breakfast we used up the last of our bread.
I caught a couple of the horses and went down the canyon together with Pugh, T.O.T. and Severo towards the River Chubut, a distance of some eight miles from our encampment. Near the river, we spotted the tracks of some horses which had passed there recently, some 18 to 20 days previously.

Look at the Welsh. This is a mere twelve years after they have arrived in Patagonia, disoriented and frightened of the vastness of the unknown land. And here they are in the desert, reading tracks like Buffalo Bill.

We cut our names into the bark of some trees.
On the way back from the river, T.O.T. and I separated from Severo and Pugh in order to hunt a hare with "Guess", which we managed to catch. Severo and Pugh attempted a rhea but failed to bring it down without their dogs. When we reached the camp once more, T. Roberts had the soup and meat ready.
We found some pieces of petrified wood and some clay.

Very cold last night with frost; today quite mild, we slept comfortably.[69]

When I read this for the first time, I wondered why clay was worthy of mention in a diary. But when you live in a place where you have to make all your own crockery – and, indeed, all your own bricks – I suppose clay is a pretty exciting find.

John Murray Thomas and his merry men didn't have a map. None existed, yet, of the places they exploded. They had compasses, and they knew that they weren't going to fall off the edge of the South American continent because they had spoken to the Indians who'd travelled all over the steppe and knew it as they knew the backs of their own hands. But being told by someone who knows a place, and going there yourself without a map, are two very different things. How did they even know how to find the way back? How *did* they manage to find their way back?

Then again, sometimes they did get lost, too.

Friday, 24 August 1877
Got up before dawn. Piercing cold with intense frost.
Towards mid-day, much milder. Left camp late and went towards the coast, avoiding as much as possible the chasms. I made a detour towards NNE to see whether I could find any evidence that our companions had passed this way, but found that I had kept too far E, without allowing for the distance my companions would have covered.
Night fell without my having caught up with them. I thought I saw smoke towards the East and went in that direction, until night fell and I was forced to make camp for the night, with only my dog for company. Nothing to eat or drink and not much fire wood, what there was being thorny and green. Very cold.[70]

John Murray Thomas undertook three exploratory journeys, accompanied by assorted different companions who never play a huge role in his diary. The bulk of the entries describes the kind of territory they passed through, features of the landscape like rocks or streams, and the distance covered: between twenty and thirty miles each day.

For the convenience of future explorers he drew up a list of what each traveller took for provisions:

50 pounds flour
2 cheeses of 15 pounds each
10 pounds rice
$^1/_2$ pound bicarbonate of soda
3 pounds salt
6 pounds butter
15 pounds *maté*
15 pounds sugar
15 pounds semolina
$^1/_4$ mustard [a quarter? a quart?]
2 dozen matches
3 pounds ground coffee
6 pounds tobacco
1 flint and steel
2 pipes
3 pounds bacon
1 comb
1 towel
1 whetstone
2 spoons: one large, one small
1 strong enamel mug
1 kettle
1 large cooking pot
2 compasses
2 knives
1 revolver
1 sail, in case of rain
Fishhooks for fishing in summer; none in winter.
Ropes, hobbles, bridles.
Needles and thread.
Small axe and strong saw.
Sunglasses in summer
Quantities of spurs, whips, leather straps.
Cinches for pack horses, bags, saddlebags etc.
In winter, dogs; none in summer.[71]

40

For the first twenty years of its existence, *Y Wladfa* existed in a happy sort of power vacuum. The settlers were nominally subject to Argentine authority, but the government in Buenos Aires was too distant to interfere. The Welsh provided their own administration, set up their own systems of education and justice, and largely ran their own lives. They had known from the outset that there could not be actual independence: the agreement had been for a settlement within Argentina, not an autonomous colony. But they must have *felt* pretty autonomous. Then *Y Wladfa* became, in some ways, a victim of its own success: the small community proved that there was a living to be made in Patagonia from trade and agriculture. The Argentine government was mindful of the fact that the Patagonian territories were similarly coveted and claimed by the neighbouring state of Chile; and that Tehuelche, Pampas Indians and Mapuche by and large didn't feel much allegiance to either state, having lived on the land long before either Argentina or Chile existed. The success of the Welsh settlement prompted the Argentine government to take a hand. In 1884 – when the 'Desert Campaign' was almost over and the plains had been declared clear of Indians – Argentina put Patagonia firmly on its own map, by creating the five provinces that make up the territory to this day. From north to south, they are: Neuquén, Río Negro, Chubut, Santa Cruz and Tierra del Fuego. Provincial governors and judges were appointed by the government in Buenos Aires.

The Welsh of *Y Wladfa* weren't overjoyed by this development. They'd become quite used to being their own masters. Indeed, one Argentine official referred to them, unfondly, as 'those people who are accustomed to doing as they please'.[72] A compromise of sorts was reached when Luis Jorge Fontana, an Argentinian, became governor of the newly created province of Chubut, and in return, Lewis Jones was given the title of Commissioner of the colony.

The so grandly named new Province of Chubut at this time had a total population not exceeding 1600, all of whom were living in and around the two villages of Rawson and Gaiman on the eastern edge of the region. That is to say, a *white* population of 1600. There were still not inconsiderable numbers of Mapuche (several hundred, at least) and isolated groups of Pampas Indians and Tehuelche in the western half of the territory, but they would be removed if the authorities could do it; and so did not count, and were not counted.

Patagonia had yet to be properly mapped, although clearly the military must have had maps of some sort in order to find its way around. The federal government in Buenos Aires was desirous that the new governors should explore and settle their new territories, especially the Andean region, where the soil was richest (Moreno's 'new Switzerland') and there beckoned the possibility of finding gold. It promised an area of fifty leagues (around 175 square miles) of free land to be set aside for settlers in the Andes.

This was well received by the Welsh, who had used up all the arable land in the Chubut valley. There must also have been those who found the idea of living somewhere remote and far away from the government attractive; and others who had caught the pioneering bug and were attracted by the thought of settling 'virgin' lands.

(Almost all travellers in nineteenth-century Patagonia, even the best of them, exclaim at some point in their writings how *thrilled* they are to be standing in some spot where no person has stood before them. What they invariably mean is, of course, no *white* person. Thus indigenous people are rendered simultaneously invisible and not-quite-human.)

Fontana, the new governor, would have liked to explore his new province but couldn't because, frankly, he didn't have the means. Apparently the government in Buenos Aires had contented itself with creating the provinces and their administration without providing sufficient funding.

John Murray Thomas was probably keener to go west than any other inhabitant of *Y Wladfa*. After all, he'd already been out there. Fontana didn't have the money to go? No problem. Thomas sent a hat round Rawson and Gaiman, and within the space of months had raised the very considerable sum of 6000 pesos from individual contributions.

In October 1885, the expedition set off. It was made up of some thirty men (most of them Welsh, also a handful of Argentines, a couple of Germans and one U.S. citizen), and duly headed by Luis Jorge Fontana, with John Murray Thomas as his right-hand man. The horsemen were not only equipped with vittles but also carried a sabre and a rifle with a hundred shots each.[73] Were these for hunting? Or did the Welsh expect trouble? But they weren't just *the Welsh* any more, they were officially part of Argentina now, riding under the leadership of an Argentine governor, at a time when the state-run war on the Indians was still going on. Two years had passed since an Argentine general had marched a group of captured Tehuelche through the Chubut valley[74], since the deaths of the three young Welshmen, the 'martyrs'. Much more than previously, this part of Patagonia had become frontier territory. So they carried sabres and rifles. Today, the expedition is known under the martial name *Rifleros de Fontana*, Fontana's Riflemen.

41

TO BE PERFECTLY HONEST, I'm not all that interested in the *Rifleros*. Not even in John Murray Thomas, although many of his diary entries make intriguing and diverting reading in between the rather dry geological and scientific observations. Somebody in Gaiman suggests that I go and visit John Murray Thomas' elderly granddaughter who edited and published the diary, but I am not keen.

I used to be in love with the image of a hermetically sealed, little piece of Wales in big, foreign Patagonia. But now I want to look beyond the frontiers of *Y Wladfa* into the rest of Patagonia. Do I really want to talk to Señora Olivia de Mulhall, who will doubt-less tell me yet more tales about the heroic doings of the early Welsh settlers? But in the end the seductive whisper of 'Why not?' wins.

Olivia de Mulhall lives, not in Gaiman, but in the big city, in Trelew. It is the biggest city in Chubut today, with a population of around 120,000.

Her house stands in an old residential area on the edge of the city. The streets are pleasantly tree-lined, the pavements cool with the speckled shade of rustling leaves. Tree roots have pushed up and cracked paving stones in many places. It's quiet, and the air, even here in the city, carries the faint taste of the dust of the desert. There are small shops, greengrocers, bakeries, butchers. The occasional garage promotes its services by means of the word *Gomería* (tyre repair shop) stencilled in white on a large black tyre propped up by the side of the road. Advertising slogans are painted directly on garden or house walls. One of them catches my eye: all rendered in blue and white (the colours of the Argentine flag) on a windowless house wall are a large bottle of mineral water and the words, *Soda Malvinas – Bien Argentina!* Malvinas soda water – very Argentinian! *Malvinas*, of course, is the Spanish name for the Falklands.

I have rung Olivia de Mulhall's house beforehand, but not actually spoken to her. Instead I talked to her daughter-in-law, who looks in on the old lady every day, and who, after some hesitation, agreed that I could come and talk to her.

'She's quite elderly,' said the daughter-in-law. 'She does love meeting people and talking about history, but she gets very excited, and it tires her. Please don't stay too long.'

She has also asked me not to use the front door of the house, but to go to the grocer's shop next door instead. I assume Señora de Mulhall is none too mobile and has trouble walking to the front door, and that the lady in the shop will have a key and let me in instead.

I walk into the shop and explain, feeling a little silly amid stacks of biscuits and chewing gum, household cleaning products and a bunch of mops that brush against my elbow, that I have come to meet Señora Olivia de Mulhall who lives next door. The shop lady jumps up from behind her counter, locks the shop door from the inside and disappears into the interior reaches of her shop, no doubt to get her bag. I wait politely.

'Señora! Aren't you coming?'

Is she talking to me?

I take a few hesitant steps around the counter, look beyond it.

She is half-way down a corridor, about to turn into a doorway on the left.

'This way!' she calls encouragingly when she sees me.

Feeling a little bit like Alice in Wonderland, I plunge into the corridor after her. Where *are* we going?

Through the doorway, along another corridor, up a few steps, through a door into a large, cool, shuttered drawing room full of heavy Victorian furniture. From the next room, a T.V. blares. The shop lady marches purposefully towards the din of the telly.

'Llegó la escritora para usted!' she announces loudly. The writing lady has come to see you.

A small lightbulb appears almost visibly over my head. There must be an internal connection between the shop and Olivia de Mulhall's house, in whose drawing room I am now standing.

'¡Pase, pase!' calls an old voice. Come in, come in! The T.V. is turned down a few decibels.

I walk into an equally dark, cool, shuttered and over-furnished room. Its walls are hung thickly with paintings. I experience a sinking feeling, not at all sure that it was a good idea to come here.

'Well, there you are,' says the lady from the shop, beams all round and departs.

Olivia de Mulhall sits at a heavy dinner table which is flanked by a small stand with the T.V. on it, on which flickers some daytime show. On the table in front of her are an empty plate and a cup, stacks of magazines and a couple of books.

'Come, sit down,' she says, gesturing at another chair.

I had mentally prepared myself to explain what I'm doing, why I have come to see her, what I want to know from her. But she launches straight into a narrative about the life and works of her grandfather. Her voice is cracked with age, but vigorous still. Every sentence ends with an exclamation mark.

'My Papa told me all about John Murray Thomas, and I have all the documents here to prove that he told me the truth. It's incredible what that man achieved! He rode out into the desert, spending six months at a time without his family, without any news whatsoever from them. No water, nothing! What he must have suffered. In 1886 *he* discovered the Andes, but will they believe a word of that here? They say it was Fontana, but I ask you, who paid their expenses? Eh, who? My grandfather, he did everything! *¡Era el único, él!* He, alone. But nobody here will believe it, nobody. They have no idea. No culture. *¡Brutos!*'

It's easy to see why her daughter-in-law warned that Olivia de Mulhall gets excited when people come to see her. On and on goes her tale, looping endlessly around her two central concerns: the numerous achievements of John Murray Thomas, and the ingratitude of a world that refuses to acknowledge even a single one of them.

Her complaint is this: In the history books, it is governor Luis Jorge Fontana who is credited with having led the expedition of the *Rifleros*, in the course of which the western reaches of the province of Chubut were 'discovered' and an offshoot colony of *Y Wladfa* was founded in the fruitful lands which the *Günün A Künna* and Tehuelche had described to the Welsh. But Olivia de Mulhall wants the credit to go to her grandfather, and is incensed by the refusal of the authorities to comply. 'They would not even name a road after him!' She repeats this, much affronted, several times.

I would like to hear about her own life, but she keeps jumping back a generation or two, to talk about her grandfather or her father. And yet I find myself warming to Olivia de Mulhall. She has a real enthusiasm for history. She is continually jumping up to bring more books to the table, soon I sit behind a small hill of them. There are photocopies of old maps, photos, newspaper articles carefully clipped and folded.

Then she suddenly abandons the books and presses an *alfajor* on me: a small sweet cake. They are immensely popular in Argentina, most shops sell them like they do chocolate bars. There are lots of different sorts of *alfajores*: large and small; covered in milk chocolate, dark chocolate, meringue, made of cornflour, wheat flour...

'Here, take a tea towel.' She points to where a small pile of tea towels lies, incongruously I had thought, on the table; then takes it herself and spreads it over my lap. 'It will crumble, it's coated in meringue, you know.'

The *alfajor* is sweet and sticky and filled with *dulce de leche*. A small snowstorm of tiny meringue crumbs drifts downwards and settles on my black fleece while I eat.

'Good, isn't it?' she asks with satisfaction. 'Here, have another. One for the road.'

It *is* good. I lick sugary white dust off my lips and wonder whether I should politely refuse the second *alfajor*. But she seemed genuinely pleased that I enjoyed the first one, and pleased to have another to give.

'Yes, please,' I say. 'And thank you very much, it was delicious. *Era riquísimo.*'

She produces a high-pitched giggle, like a teenage girl, or a witch. With this giggle she has won me over.

I hope that I will be giggling like that when I am old.

'Papá vivió en el campo...' Olivia de Mulhall says. 'Papa lived out in the country, near Dolavon.'

Dolavon is the third settlement in the Chubut valley, a few miles west of Gaiman; begun in the early nineteen-hundreds when the land around Gaiman had all been claimed and settled.

But already she's off again, talking about John Murray Thomas.

'He was the first paymaster of the province of Chubut, the first photographer, the first everything! How could one man do so much?' She thumps the stack of books next to her, causes a small avalanche of loose photocopies on another part of the table. 'The first merchant. Postmaster in Rawson. Why don't those Welsh talk about that? Why don't they want to know?'

Almost towards the end of our conversation, she mentions in passing that a street *has* now been named after John Murray Thomas, in the town of Esquel in the Andes. One of her nephews unveiled the street-sign and a plaque only last year. But it is as though that had been much too little, much too late for Olivia de Mulhall. She has lived in a state of righteous indignation for decades, and indignant she will continue, regardless.

And then, suddenly, she switches back to the subject of Papa. It's as though she has to get the outbursts about John Murray Thomas out of her system periodically.

'Papa did everything. Everything! *¡Papá era terrible inteligente!* He was terribly intelligent. We lived there with him for a while, on a little farm by the river outside Dolavon. He worked near Dolavon for seven years, seven years out there, in the middle of nowhere! *¡Lejos!* So far away, in Laguna de Vaca, Cow Lagoon. And all alone, he was. He lived by himself most of the time, because it was so remote. Sometimes Mama went to stay with him for a while, with my sisters, so that he wouldn't be lonely. They would help him teach, Mama and my sisters.'

Ah. So he was a schoolmaster, out there in the *chacras*?

'There was an *estancia* nearby, a ranch, and the people from there came to be taught by him. Such poverty! Papa not only taught them, sometimes he gave them a little to eat, from what he had. There was a girl he taught, and she's now working in Rawson, and when I meet her, she always says: How well your Papa taught us, Señora de Mulhall! That's what she says.'

She stops talking and just sits there for a few moments, looking vaguely around the table; like a wind-up mechanism that has run down. I wonder whether the tiredness her daughter-in-law has mentioned is now setting in; whether I should take my leave.

But then she looks up again, as vigorous as before, and enquires whether I would like a cup of tea.

I answer truthfully that I would rather hear more about her life. I'm afraid that a trip to the kitchen to boil the kettle and brew a cup of tea now will interrupt her train of thought.

What was it like, I ask again, growing up *en el valle*, in the Chubut valley, all those years ago?

'Ha!' she exclaims. 'It was hard work! Clothes were washed by hand until recently, everything was done by hand! If you wanted to do the washing, you had to take a horse and cart out into the country to collect firewood to heat the water. We went once a week, every Saturday. Then there were the cows to be milked, every day: ten, twelve cows, before school!'

Until now, I had pictured her childhood in something like this house, in Victorian splendour. But I have no trouble imagining her in the country, running out before dawn with her hair in untidy braids to see to a dozen cows. It's easy to imagine her as a girl. She is so alive still.

'Young people these days, they have it too easy,' she grumbles, the universal refrain of the older generation; but with perhaps more justification than most. 'They don't know where their water comes from, their electricity. We had to go to chapel three times a day. And milk the cows beforehand! Then in the cart as far as the river, get a boat across and walk to chapel. Three times a day! These days, they hardly go the once. And things are worse, for all that their lives have become easier. We used to go to Capel Moriah, the very first chapel. The very first!' she repeats, fixing a sudden gimlet eye on me. 'A historical place. Have you been there?'

I admit, shamed, that I have not.

'The Welsh,' she says, off again on another track, 'in Gaiman. They're very closed there. They cling to their language, even the Indians had to learn Welsh because the Welsh refused to learn to speak Spanish. They're fanatics, even now. Last Sunday when I went to church, there was one lady who told me to speak Welsh. "Look," I told her, "even in Wales, Welsh isn't spoken everywhere. English is the universal language of commerce, not Welsh, you know!" That's what I said to her.'

I have to laugh, and she shoots me a quick look and giggles.

'Ooh, the women!' she says, shaking her head, and I brace myself for another tirade. But no. 'They worked hard, the women. Everybody had to work. I helped in the fields, milking the cows, making butter, with the washing – I did all that, and school on top! Papa had not even been able to go to school. He worked in the fields all day, and then he went across the river into Trelew to night school. And look how well he turned out.

'He had the first automobile in Chubut, Papa, a Ford.' She smiles proudly at the memory. 'I went with him to the shops. I was the eldest. They had these big wooden counters where they sold things, and Papa would stand me on top of the counter and I would sing – I was little, three, four years old. And there I would stand and sing.'

And she sings a nursery rhyme with her old voice.

Una niña bonita
que del cielo bajó
con sus alas doradas
y en su pecho una flor.

Para qué tantas flores
si no son para mí
yo me muero de amores,
y me muero por ti.

A pretty little girl
who came from heaven down
with a pair of golden wings
and a flower her crown.

Look at all the flowers,
all for me, can it be true?
I'm dying for love,
I'm dying for you.

I sing this to Lorena, later, back in Gaiman, to make sure I have remembered all the words correctly. She bursts out laughing when she hears the second stanza.

'You must have got mixed up,' she tells me. 'Dying for love, in a children's song?'

But I remember especially those lines, because they had struck me as odd too.

'It definitely doesn't go like that,' Lorena assures me.

I don't care. I bet Olivia de Mulhall got plenty of flowers from admirers in her time. Listening to her singing, I wish that that I'd thought to bring her some.

42

'GUESS HOW OLD I AM,' she says, coquettishly.

I consider. Olivia de Mulhall is clearly old, and somewhat frail – probably more so than she appears at the moment, buoyed by excitement at having a new audience.

'Eighty?' I hazard. 'Eighty-something?'

'*Noventa*,' she says with satisfaction. 'I turned ninety this year. Oh, you should have seen the party they threw for me! I'll show you.' And up she jumps again to fetch a photograph album. The television blares on in the background, ignored. 'Here – Osian, my brother arranged it all... he's a poet, he writes me a poem every year.' She leaves through the album, showing me photos of children, grandchildren, cousins, nieces, nephews; pasted newspaper clippings, Osian's poem written out in an immaculate flowing hand.

'One hundred and ninety guests! Can you believe that so many people came? How they all love me.' This might sound pretentious, as though she's showing off, bragging about her fortune; or else seeking confirmation that they do indeed love her. Instead, she radiates a sense of happy contentment. Life is a bit dull these days, she is old and can't get about much, but for her ninetieth birthday, one hundred and ninety people came and showed their love.

'I didn't even know that they were planning a party! It was a complete surprise when suddenly everybody showed up.' She gives her girlish, witchy giggle again, lost in memories. 'I danced all night. All night!'

She gets up to show me out. 'There, down that corridor is my front door,' she says, pointing straight ahead. Then disappears through a doorway on the right. I hesitate, thinking that perhaps she has gone to fetch another book, a last photo to show me.

'Come along,' she calls from somewhere inside the labyrinth of the house.

More Alice in Wonderland. I follow her, wondering what is to come. And find myself in a small, dark kitchen.

'My sewing machine,' Olivia de Mulhall says, patting a shrouded shape. 'I have two, one mechanical, the other electric.'

From beneath the cover peeks a cast-iron pedal. Olivia de Mulhall whisks round another corner, out of sight again. This feels like the oddest game of hide and seek.

'Here,' her voice calls. 'Come and see my papers!'

'Here' is a study. There are boxes full of papers, stacked on a bookcase behind a curtain.

'*El escritorio de papá*,' she says, removing another dustsheet. 'Papa's desk.'

The desk is covered with piles of papers. In a glass-fronted bookcase rest yet more books, old, cloth-bound volumes; and about two dozen copies of John Murray Thomas's diary which she edited and published. On top of the bookcase, yet more boxes of papers.

A young man appears suddenly from the recesses of the house. He is dressed, oddly, in a white smock. Olivia de Mulhall is talking non-stop, about the books, the papers, *Papá*, John Murray Thomas...

The young man – her nurse perhaps? – and I say hello and exchange smiles over her stream of words. Then she turns abruptly and does her vanishing act again.

'Come on through!' she calls, and when I do – followed by the unexplained young man – I find myself standing in what I take, at first, to be her front room.

'The first chair Papa won in the Eisteddfod,' she says and proudly points at a large wooden throne. *Y gwir yn erbyn y byd – Eisteddfod y Chubut 1942* is carved into the wooden back. A faded red ribbon tied between the armrests indicates that, despite the (also faded) red cushion on the seat, this chair is not for sitting. (*Y gwir yn erbyn y byd*, Truth Against the World, is the motto of the Bardic Circle of Wales. There is still an Eisteddfod held in Patagonia every year, and the author of the best poem in Welsh still wins a carved chair and is ceremonially enthroned.)

'He won this one for me, the eldest. And then another one for my sister. But then after the War there was no Eisteddfod for fourteen years.'

The walls of the room are covered in large, framed sepia photographs.

'John Murray Thomas,' says Olivia and points. 'Look at the face of that man! And that one there, that's Papa.' Papa is fair-haired with the face of an aesthete.

There is yet another shrouded piece of furniture.

'The piano. The very first piano in the province of Chubut!'

On the wall opposite, the photo of a Victorian lady with a sweet face, her dark hair gathered up in a bun.

'Mama. She played the organ in chapel. She was a very fine organist.'

Underneath the photograph, bizarrely, I see a white porcelain basin and a leather chair with a high backrest. It looks like a chair you might find in a barbershop or a hairdressing salon. There is a framed newspaper article on the wall, the headline goes: *Peluquería El Museo*. The Museum Salon.

This place is a *hairdresser's*. In Olivia de Mulhall's house? I remember now that I did pass a hairdresser's on my way here, next door to the house. There must be another internal door. After all, I came in through a shop.

'This is Manuel, the owner of the salon. He's from Chile,' says Olivia de Mulhall, introducing the young man much as she did each of the photographs. 'He speaks Welsh.'

'My wife is of Welsh extraction,' explains the hairdresser. He has a lovely smile. His white smock makes sense now. 'At home, we mostly speak...'

But Olivia de Mulhall has already swept on, taking framed photos off the walls, off the piano, introducing their subjects. For her, there doesn't seem to be any difference between Manuel and the photos of people long since dead. I'm not at all sure that they are dead, to her. Even those whom she never met, or only as a small child when they themselves were already old, like John Murray Thomas, seem rather more real to her than Manuel or I. Most of the time, we are merely her audience, her listeners.

I nod, smile, try to follow. My head is swirling with ancestors.

43

THE WELSH NAME FOR THE fertile lands in the West of the province of Chubut, in the foothills of the Andes, is *Cwm Hyfryd*. The story goes that this was what one of the *Rifleros* under the leadership of Luis Jorge Fontana (or John Murray Thomas) exclaimed upon rounding a bend: '*Dyna cwm hyfryd!*' What a beautiful valley!

There are several words in Welsh for several types of valleys. *Dyffryn* is a wide, fertile river valley like the lower Chubut valley: *Dyffryn Camwy*. A steep, narrow valley is called *cwm*: like the south Wales Valleys, and the rocky valley spotted by the *Rifleros* on their exploratory trip out west: *Cwm Hyfryd*.

In Spanish, it is called *Colonia 16 de Octubre*: 16 October Colony. Argentines like naming things after dates.

16 October was the date on which the valley was 'discovered'. Once this had happened, and it had been duly named and a surveyor had visited, there was land to be had: fertile land in a green valley surrounded by mountains. Large tracts of Patagonian land had been given to the – regular and irregular – soldiers who had fought in the extermination campaign against the *Indígenas*, but an area of fifty leagues (around 175 square miles) was specifically set aside for Welsh settlers. There would be no lean years of trial-and-error experimental farming here. This was first-rate soil, ideal for growing crops or grazing animals.

The valley lay four hundred miles away from the coast, and no road whatsoever connected one to the other. The distance was easily – more or less easily – covered on horseback, but anybody intending to live there would need to move themselves and their possessions – tools, clothes, furniture, farm implements, animals – across the trackless desert and a number of rivers.

Wagon trains of up to eight vehicles would make the crossing from the Atlantic coast to the Andes together; the trip took them six weeks. In some places, the ruts left by the iron-tyred wooden wheels in the arid soil of the desert are still visible today.

It must have been an odd time in *Y Wladfa*. On the one hand, progress and modernity were arriving in Gaiman and Trelew and Madryn: the railways and the *Compañía Mercantil* made consumer goods available and affordable: Welsh dressers and mantelpieces were shipped across the ocean from Wales, furniture and china and clothes from the metropolis of Buenos Aires. Around the stations in Trelew and Madryn, hotels and cafés sprang up. And on the other hand, there were the pioneers rumbling off in wagon trains to start new lives from scratch in the remoteness of the 'Beautiful Valley', in their log cabins with no running water, no roads, no shops, no trains.

The Reverend William Hughes, who had come to Patagonia for his health in the 1880s (and had started his sojourn there by digging irrigation ditches in the middle of winter), decided in the early years of the twentieth century to make the crossing to the other side of the steppe. At that time, the wagon trains had been going for almost twenty years and the journey was more or less a matter of routine.

Or at least, it was if you were a seasoned pioneer. It seems the Rev. Hughes, for all his twenty years in Patagonia, was not. In his memoirs, he quotes the diary he kept during the crossing of the desert.

> Thursday, 22 December 1904
>
> Journeyed from Gaiman as far as the beginning of the north-ern irrigation canal, 18 miles; and a most unpleasant journey it was. The horses refused to do their work: March in the centre doing his utmost to fluster the Black Colt and Pinky, who were harnessed on either side of him. They caught his mood and began to fidget, whereupon the wagon overturned and fell into the ditch we were attempting to cross. Everybody off and into the mud, attempting to pull the wagon free. Impossible. Managed it at last, with help.
>
> When we arrived at the meeting place, there were John Murray Thomas and E.F. Hunt, awaiting us in their carriages; Wm. Henry Thomas with his family, and E.F. Hunt, both with loaded wagons; also Alfred Hunt and Henry Thomas on horse-back[75]

The Rev. Hughes, who frequently shows himself as a rather stiff Victorian figure in his writing, all probity and side whiskers, comes to glorious life in those paragraphs. I can see him sitting on the wagon glowering at that headstrong nag March; climbing off into the mud in disgust, tugging ineffectually – and doubtless in an increasingly filthy temper – at the overturned wagon. Throughout his travel diary, there are accounts of his nemesis March escaping at night and running away, drawn by the green, green grass back home in Gaiman. March refusing to let himself be caught and harnessed in the morning. March in harness but in a foul mood, infecting the other horses with his insubordination. To the very end of the trip, the Rev. Hughes – in a quite endearing display of ineptitude – fails to get the better of this four-legged saboteur.

For all my dreams of venturing out into the desert, in which I picture myself in perfect harmony with nature, I cannot help feeling, when I read his account, that this is how it would actually be: recalcitrant horses, lost items of luggage, mosquitoes, nights disrupted by stony camp sites and howling foxes.

The wagons travelled six days a week, from Monday to Saturday. Sunday was strictly a day of rest and prayer only.

That's if you were a man.

'It wasn't exactly a rest that awaited us women,' observed Eluned Morgan wryly, 'as Sunday was also the day for baking bread.'

Eluned Morgan, founder of the oldest secondary school in Patagonia (Coleg Camwy in Gaiman) and daughter of Lewis Jones, made the trip across the desert on horseback a few years before the Rev. Hughes, in 1898. She had been born on board ship en route to Patagonia and grown up in Rawson and Gaiman. Although she was educated at a ladies' college in Dolgellau, she spent her formative years and indeed most of her life in Patagonia.

> How does one bake bread in Patagonia?, it will be asked. ... One digs a shallow pit, filling it with large amounts of wood and lighting the latter. Once the wood has been reduced to ashes, these are removed from the pit and the mould with the bread dough placed inside it, well covered with a lid, which latter in its turn is covered again with the hot ashes. After one hour, one has a splendid loaf of bread.[76]

On my list of things to do before I die, this is among the top ten: to bake a loaf of bread in the ashes of a fire in the Patagonian steppe.

44

THERE IS A DAILY BUS from Trelew to Colonia 16 de Octubre. Or rather, it is a *nightly* bus, and its destination is the town of Esquel, the biggest town in the western part of the province of Chubut. Every evening, the bus leaves Trelew, travels nine hours across the steppe and reaches Esquel early the next morning. There is also one bus a week which goes during the day: leaving Trelew at noon and reaching Esquel at nine in the evening. It is not very popular, because it means that you lose a whole day travelling. Except with visitors, who want to *see* the desert. I take the daytime bus.

The first time I make this trip, during my first stay in Patagonia, I am the only passenger on board the bus for the first hundred miles or so. Other than me, there are two drivers and a blaring T.V. which plays Hollywood movies with Spanish subtitles. Also the radio, at a similar volume, which the driver has tuned to a local station which seems to specialise in asinine advertising jingles. I wish they'd play something more suited to the landscape, Patagonian folk music involving guitars perhaps.

I sit on the right-hand side of the bus, in the boiling hot sunshine. Later, when a handful of other passengers comes on board, all of them sit on the other side, in the shade. For good measure, they also close the curtains on the windows, and promptly fall asleep. Those curtains annoy me, you can't tie them back properly and they interfere with the view.

I suppose they're meant to. The plains that for me are beautiful and exciting, exotic and wild, are probably just an everlasting expanse of too much empty space for the people who live here, who see them every day.

I sit, my open book – Eluned Morgan's account of her trip west across the desert – forgotten on my lap, eyes glued to the window. The sky is unbelievably blue. The land stretches away on all sides, endless, vast, empty. At first, while the road follows the course of the River Chubut, there is still much green: grass, trees, bushes. Later the soil gets drier. The land is drenched in sunshine. I hadn't known there were so many shades of brown: ochre, tan, copper, gold, yellow, sepia.

After a while, I become aware of something vaguely bothering me, but I can't work out what it is. Something is not quite right. And then it slowly seeps into my consciousness: we're travelling in the wrong direction. We should be going west: from the coast towards the Andes mountain range. But here I am and the sun is on my right. It's just after noon, the sun must be almost exactly in the south. But if we're going west, the south should be on my left. And it's not.

Have I got on the wrong coach? Doubt nags at me until I get up and walk to the front and ask the driver who is not currently driving when we will be arriving in Esquel. (I don't want to ask outright *if* we're going to Esquel, that would make me feel even more foolish.)

'*A las nueve, más o menos,*' the driver says, with a friendly smile. Round about nine.

I'm on the right bus. But how can that be? Finally, the penny drops. I'm in the southern hemisphere. Which means I'm south of the equator. Which means that at noon, the sun is in the *north*.

At times the bus stops in what appears to be the middle of nowhere: no settlement, not even a house, no crossroads, *nothing*. Somebody clambers down, throws a word of thanks and farewell to the drivers, and walks off into the immensity of the desert. The first time this happens, I watch the tiny figure until it disappears from view. As the coach moves off, I can just make out a roof in the middle distance, a small huddle of buildings: the farmstead towards which the lone figure is heading. An irrational wave of fear washes over me, and just for a moment I can't breathe. How do people manage to live out here, a hundred miles away from the nearest town, the nearest doctor; all alone in the emptiness of the desert? What *do* they do when they have a toothache? Apendicitis? An accident?

I use the term 'cabin fever' sometimes, jokingly, when I feel a bit isolated after having spent all day at my desk, working alone at home. *This* is a place where you would get real cabin fever: so far, far away from the world.

I couldn't do it. I'd go stark raving mad within months.

Suddenly I understand the blaring television, the inane radio jingles. They're proof that the rest of the world out there still exists, the infuriating, annoying, beautiful world of noise and colours and contact and people.

Hours pass. I have just started to doze off when the bus slows down.

We have reached a stop for a coffee break in a small village along the road, Paso de Indios: dusty gravel roads, children walking home from school. Inexplicably, a larger-than-lifesize statue of a sheep at the junction of two roads. We enter a nondescript, whitewashed, one-storey building with the word *Café* painted on the wall. Inside it's as dark as a cave. Behind the bar an old Pepsi-Cola sign blinks on and off. A few tables and chairs stand on rough wooden floorboards. Two men play pool without enthusiasm. The air is heavy with dust and cigarette smoke and days passing slowly.

Back onto the coach. More hours of travelling.

Strange rock formations appear on the horizon: *Los Altares, Yr Allorau* – The Altars. They are two, three columns of rock, striped grey and brown as though somebody had taken the trouble to paint them.

I wish the bus didn't move so fast. I wish I had time to get out, to walk for a few hours in the clear blue air, in the cool whistling wind and the hot sunshine, the unbroken silence. I wish I could make this journey by car so that I could set my own pace. Better still: on horseback like John Murray Thomas and Eluned Morgan; on foot like the ancestors of Sayhueke and Inakayal and Antonio. I want to see the land as they did: to be filled with its silence, with the blue and gold and browns of the days, the absolute, star-encrusted blackness of the nights.

The coach moves on through the long hot afternoon.

It is almost dusk, the shadows are long and the light has turned from gold to purple, when we stop in the middle of nowhere. Three people stand by the roadside, and a horse.

A horse?

I rub my eyes and look again. Definitely a horse. And three gauchos standing by it. Two of them board the coach, bringing with them a smell of woodsmoke and horses and leather. The third mounts the horse and rides off into the sunset.

One of the two gauchos on the coach wears a hat: a hard, flat, black hat of the kind that I've only ever seen on photos with the caption 'Typical Argentinian gaucho'. I duck behind the seat in front and try to get a better look without seeming to stare. I've never seen a real gaucho before.

The gaucho turns round, scans the other passengers on board. He sees me. He sees my eyebrows (green) and my hair (blue strand). He stares.

He can't believe it. Maybe he's never seen anyone with blue hair and green eyebrows before. He stares.

West

45

CIVILISATION BURSTS IN on us from all sides. It's only Esquel coach terminal, but it comes as a shock after a day filled with nothing but far horizons. I clamber off the bus, blinking and bewildered.

It's 9pm and night has fallen outside, but in here reigns the harsh glare of bright lights. The air is filled with the noise and exhaust fumes of other coaches. There are people *everywhere*.

Someone is calling my name. It's Dana Williams.

Dana was my first Patagonian. We met at the stall of the Welsh-Argentine Society on the National Eisteddfod field in Wales. There is a timeless vitality about her, a no-nonsense straightforwardness. I liked her at once. We talked in Welsh and I promised: 'I'll come and see you some time in Esquel.'

Dana laughed. 'They all say that!'

Somebody in Gaiman has told her of my presence in *Y Wladfa*. She runs a B&B near Esquel, and I will be staying with her.

We go outside to her car. I can just make out the mountains beyond the glittering lights of Esquel: huge dark shapes against the starry night sky. They look like massive cloud banks. There's a nip in the air. It feels much colder here than in Gaiman.

I'm in a strange place again, just when I had got the hang of Gaiman. This is my first trip, and Patagonia to me is still huge and unknown; thrilling and frightening. I'm shivering with cold and with excitement.

We eat in Dana's living room by the side of a gigantic fireplace, so high I can stand up inside it. The flames hiss and crackle, fill the room with a wonderful aroma of woodsmoke. After dinner, we sit up over glasses of heavy Argentinian red wine and talk until long past midnight. I feel at ease talking to Dana in a way that makes me forget that this is only the second time we've met.

Dana is fluent in Welsh. It was her first language when she grew up on a farm in the *chacras* outside Gaiman. But at the time, she didn't like it at all.

'We had to speak Welsh at home when *Nain* and *Taid* were there – my grandparents. They spent every Sunday with us, and all day long not a word of Spanish was allowed in the house! I hated it. I spoke Spanish with most of my friends. And of course in school and in the town, everything was in Spanish; and you only heard

Welsh round the chapel on Sundays, for the service and the Sunday school. *Oedd Nain a Taid yn grac pan oeddwn ni'n siarad Sbaeneg!* Nain and Taid got furious when we spoke a word of Spanish. They pretended they didn't understand, although they did really. They couldn't speak Spanish, but they understood it all right!' She laughs, shakes her head. 'And now look at me, I've taken up studying Welsh again, finally! I like it now, it's a part of who I am. I've been to Wales quite a few times, near Bala where my great-grandparents came from. And do you know, I still speak with that local accent.'

'How strange is that,' I say, and she laughs again.

'I'll tell you what's strange: you're German and you speak Welsh. Here we are, an Argentinian and a German, and we're communicating in Welsh!'

Communicating in Welsh isn't nearly as easy in the Andes as it has been in Gaiman. Hardly anybody here speaks *yr Hen Iaith*.

Next morning I catch the local bus to the nearby town of Trevelin: the older and smaller of the two main towns of *Cwm Hyfryd*. Trevelin means Mill Town. For decades the flour mill was the focal point of the new settlement.

The air smells of pine trees and wet soil, and, deliciously, of autumn, of falling leaves and wet earth. The landscape is grandiose after the dry flatness of Gaiman. The mountains rear up beyond grey-green hills, brown stone crags topped with snow.

I wander the streets of the town, call in on a couple of Welsh tea shops where nobody speaks Welsh. I feel forlorn and quite alone. I have hardly any Spanish, and nobody here speaks English or Welsh.

It starts to rain. The mountains are hidden by low-hanging clouds, mist drifts across hills. Dripping sheep and a couple of bored horses stand in a field. In a weed-infested yard a rusting pale blue truck is seeing out its days. Someone has spray-painted the words *Punk Rock* across its side panels, but it doesn't spice things up much.

I want to find the old Welsh chapel and the manse which serves, these days, as the abode and schoolroom of *yr athrawes Gymraeg*, the Welsh teacher. Every year, the British Council bankrolls two teachers to come out from Wales to Patagonia for a year, to help strengthen the weakening grip of the Welsh language in Argentina.

Twice I ask for the way, and am told it by helpful passers-by. But they tell me in Spanish, and somewhere among the right and left turns I get lost. (In Spanish, *derecha* is right and, unhelpfully, *derecho* is straight on.) I trudge on through the cold, unwelcoming rain; dreaming of the *panad o de*, the cuppa I will get if I ever find the chapel.

Finally, when I've almost given up hope, there is the chapel like a vision of Wales: a squat brick building like a young barn standing in a field by itself, against a backdrop of wet, mist-wreathed hills. A little apart under a stand of dripping trees, light shines from the windows a low house that seems to duck against the elements: the old manse, now home to the Welsh teacher.

'I do wish you'd had a chance to meet my father,' says Jane Lamb regretfully. 'He knew everything about the history of Patagonia. About the Welsh. Everything.'

We're sitting in the kitchen. A clothes-line is strung diagonally across the room. On it hang jolly red-checked tea towels and mushrooms drying on a piece of string. The windows are steamed up, and on the hob a dented tin kettle is just beginning to sing.

Jane Lamb, despite her name, is not the current Welsh teacher. She is a Patagonian of Welsh and English extraction who grew up bilingually with English and Welsh and, later, Spanish. We're talking in Welsh. My once-rusty spoken Welsh has become so beautifully fluent again that I can have quite intelligent conversations. Jane's Welsh is a joy, pure and rich and a little old-fashioned, and with no trace of a Spanish accent.

She grew up on a farm, and I want to hear all about her childhood. Except she doesn't want to talk about herself, but continues to tell me about her father, lamenting that I cannot meet and talk to him instead. In this respect, she rather resembles Olivia de Mulhall, but Jane possesses none of the older woman's oomph, none of her enthusiasm. I don't exactly know what she's done with her own personality, but it's not very much in evidence. Perhaps she keeps it at home in a drawer, well ironed.

I want to know what life was like in this remote corner of the world thirty, forty years ago. Dana has told me a little, but she grew up near Gaiman, where they had electricity and paved roads and other such luxuries. Out here progress arrived much later, and much more slowly.

'If only you'd come last year,' says Jane. 'He could have told you so much.'

'I'm sure so can you,' I say encouragingly.

But she shakes her head, doubt all over her face. Behind her, the shadow of Timothy Lamb rears up, dominating the room even in his absence.

Shoo, I want to say to him.

In the room next door, Sarah the Welsh teacher is practising verbs with a small group of adult learners. One of them is Jane's younger daughter. I'm surprised that Jane doesn't speak Welsh with her children.

'Well,' she says, 'it's complicated. Back in the old days, the Welsh would marry each other and pass the language on, but these days that's all changed. I'm married to a Spaniard, so at home we speak Spanish. I did speak Welsh with my eldest when she was a baby, and these days she finds it easy to learn the language. But the younger only ever heard Spanish, so it's harder for her...

'My Mam grew up here in the valley, and my Dad on a farm between Trelew and Gaiman. Both of them spoke Welsh as their first language, and we never spoke anything else at home. I didn't know any Spanish until I went to school when I was five, six years old.'

'What was that like?' I want to know, and expect a speech like the one I heard in Gaiman: pride in the survival of the language, the achievements of the ancestors, *yr Hen Iaith*, that kind of thing.

Jane hesitates. 'Well. Having two languages is good, yes, but there is also a price to pay. We had to speak Welsh even though it seemed rather pointless. What on earth should we speak Welsh *for*? Nobody ever came here. We didn't feel much of a connection with Wales. The only contact was by letter. My Auntie would write to my mother; and I sent her letters sometimes too, even though I didn't know her at all, I'd never met her. I just wrote to her because she was my Auntie.'

I try to imagine what life was like for the child Jane in a valley in the Andes, speaking the language of a faraway place that wasn't even a country; of a place that nobody she knew had ever even seen, that only existed in old stories and a few faded photographs. Perhaps it's not so surprising that she decided not to burden her daughters with the gift of *Cymraeg*.

46

'AND THEN, OF COURSE, there were the other children, in the town, and in school. They only spoke Spanish. Children can be cruel sometimes, make fun of those that are different, that do things differently, you know?'

She shakes herself, as though shaking off her memories.

'These days, our young people see young people from Wales coming over here, and they themselves can go to Wales. So suddenly it's interesting and exciting. But years ago, people didn't travel. It was too far, too expensive. *Globalisation* hadn't arrived yet.' She pronounces the English word doubtfully, as one might a Latin term for an ailment or a newly discovered insect. 'It was only in 1965 that things changed. It was the centenary of the *Mimosa*, see. A big crowd of people came over here from Wales, sixty or seventy, for the first time. So then a door had been opened. But before, there was hardly any visiting. You had to take a ship. It took weeks and weeks, and it was so expensive. The first time I went to Wales was by boat. In 1966. The world was different back then.'

I blink. 'You went to Wales on a *boat*? How old were you?'

Jane laughs. 'Thirteen. I went by myself. My Dad was determined that all of us children should go to Wales for our education. He was a grandson of Richard Berwyn, you know, the first teacher of *Y Wladfa* who had come across on the *Mimosa*.'

There is the shadow of Timothy Lamb again. I scowl at it. The man had a nerve, sending a thirteen-year-old girl across the Atlantic by herself.

'So what was it like for you then, seeing Wales for the first time, the land of the ancestors?'

She laughs again. 'To be honest, Wales didn't make much of an impression. I mean, look at it – I'd come from a farm and a small town – Trevelin – where people spoke Welsh and went to chapel on Sundays.... and I went to Tregaron. A small town surrounded by farms, where everybody spoke Welsh and went to chapel on Sundays.' She makes a face. 'It wasn't frankly that much of a change. But the journey... oh, you can't imagine. It was the first time I'd ever left home, the first time I'd left the valley. I travelled all the way to Buenos Aires to catch the boat. Buenos Aires! I'd never seen a big city before. And then Europe, London... the whole wide world. I watched television for the first time. The Beatles!

You can't imagine,' she says again; her eyes shining with the memory. 'After that trip, all the doors were open.'

'Weren't you tempted to stay there? In London, or in Buenos Aires?'

The light in her eyes goes out as though somebody had thrown a switch. 'Oh no. I couldn't have. It wouldn't have been home. My Dad always said, *Cas y gwr na gar ei wlad*. A bad man he who loves not his homeland.'

It's still raining, and darkness is beginning to fall. The short, gloomy autumn day will soon be over. I've gone out to look round the chapel; to try to get a sense of the place and its past. Raindrops whisper in the grass, ping off an old rainwater barrel. A smell of woodsmoke hangs in the cold air. The lights of Trevelin are hidden in the gloom. It should be easy to imagine myself back in the early days of *Cwm Hyfryd,* a century ago. But it's not. I can't get a handle on it at all. It's all I can do to hold on to the here and now.

I've been on the road for too long, by myself, in a place where it's autumn in April and the sun stands in the north at noon. I'm lonely and cold and fed up. I want nothing so much on earth as to go home.

I've been wanting to like Patagonia, to enjoy this dream-come-true; I willed myself to love every minute of this trip, my first time in Patagonia, utterly and passionately. And I *have* loved most of my time here more than I would have thought possible. But now I've come up against a place where I just don't feel comfortable.

I can't make *Cwm Hyfryd* work.

And I won't try any more.

I stand in the field surrounded by hills. Stand with my head tipped back staring upwards into the trees as they go from dark green to grey to almost-black as dusk falls. Look at the pattern made by droplets of rain on the surface of the water barrel. I won't think. Won't plan. Won't try to cope.

47

AFTER THAT FIRST VISIT, I didn't return to Esquel, Trevelin and the Andes for a couple of years. I spend time in Gaiman, but the vastness and foreignness and the sheer otherness of the *Cordillera* spooked me more than I want to admit. And yet the Andes stay with me. The landscape has imprinted itself on me in a way I cannot explain. I miss the shapes of the mountains on the horizon, even while I shy away from going back.

And then it reappears on my radar. When I talk to Rodrigo Gómez and Lía Ñancufíl Musa from *Banco de Lanas* in Trelew about their work with Mapuche and Tehuelche weavers, they mention communities in the west of the province of Chubut. Oscar Payaguala in Comodoro Rivadavia gives me a name and phone number in Esquel and urges me to look up a man whom he describes as *un cacique importante*, an important chief. It begins to look as though I should take another trip out west.

I go on the same coach again, the one that travels during the day to arrive in Esquel in the evening.

Only it's not the same one. Clara Roberts looks at the ticket which I have just booked in the small Gaiman office of the transport company – in a shop just off the main street that sells agricultural implements and bags of fertiliser – and exclaims: 'You're never going on that coach! *¡Ese va por todas las rutas de tierra!*' (*Rutas de tierra* are unpaved, gravelled dirt roads.) It turns out that this coach goes by the most circuitous route possible, starting in Trelew and arriving – eventually – in Esquel, but taking in many dirt roads along the way that serve small settlements far from the main, direct route. The trip will take me eleven hours.

'I'll be seeing parts of the country I haven't before,' I say excitedly to Clara. 'It'll be fun!'

She shakes her head at such madness.

At first, everything is the same as before: the endless straight road out of Gaiman, the flat landscape, first green, then brown. But not so brown this time, because it's December and early summer; whereas before I was travelling in autumn. Even away from the River Chubut large swathes of the desert are green now. Clumps of bushes are dotted with intensely yellow flowers. Snow-white plumes of pampas grass nod in the breeze. The whole place has exploded into life and colour. The stony soil is parchment pale, almost white in places; in others an improbable rich red. The sky is immense, a huge blue embrace.

I remember how last time, I looked through the window wishing I could go outside, into the desert. Now, when the bus turns off the main road onto the *ruta de tierra*, I feel that I have come a little closer to that dream. I'm still on the coach, I'm still being carried far too fast to look at things properly. But there is no layer of tarmac now between me and the ground, and somehow that seems significant. And at least we're travelling more slowly; because on the gravel road there's only so fast you can go before the shock absorbers give up.

The landscape slowly changes. Hills appear, the first outposts of the foothills of the Andes. They are the most amazing colours: wine-red rocks, hills striped red and green and grey, each layer sharply defined. Some of the rocks look like ruined palaces, like the tumbled-down remains of an ancient, lost civilisation. One of them almost exactly resembles the Sphinx, except that it's crimson. There are rocks shaped like columns, like the carved palaces of Petra or the temples of Angkor Wat or a Roman amphitheatre. With a sudden startled movement, a group of guanacos bursts out from behind the amphitheatre and runs away into the steppe, white tails bobbing.

We stop for coffee in a village whose name I don't catch. When I light a cigarette, I discover dust in the crumpled pack of cigarettes, dust in my lighter, gritty dust in my mouth, even.

On we go. The road begins to climb. Not much, not steeply, but instead of the flat expanse of the desert, the land is undulating now: we're surrounded by a frozen sea of wave after wave of hills. The air changes, becomes sharper, cooler, contains a hint of moisture.

A chain of translucent mountains appears far away on the horizon. Clouds hang over the land. A lake by the roadside. Something pink flashes and flies away. Flamingos!

Sheep graze on the grey-green vegetation, horses, cattle. Every now and then, an isolated farmstead is visible: a house and outbuildings, a windmill for power, water tanks, corrals.

We're on the *altiplano* now, the tableland that precedes the *Cordillera*. The hills are rocky and brown; the mountains previously on the horizon much nearer, much larger, shining eerily, spectrally white with snow.

It's a good while since we passed the last settlement, when the coach stops in the middle of nowhere along a stretch of road. I half expect a gaucho to climb on board; but instead, it's a swarm of teenage girls. At least, they look like teenagers, but some of them carry small children. They all have long black hair and dark eyes; and they wear beautiful dangling silver earrings. They sit together, chatting and laughing. I prick up my ears, but they speak Spanish, not Mapuche.

There are no more hills now, just the huge snow-capped mountains in front of us, rearing up and filling most of the sky. The road winds down from the *altiplano*, becomes wider, less bone-shaking, almost respectable; it smoothes itself down and joins the main, paved road. We're in Esquel.

48

IT'S THE WEIRDEST FEELING, being back.

The air is pure and cool and clean and scented with pinesap and snow and so rich that breathing it feels almost like drinking cold, fresh water. The water is amazing, too. I have a terribly sweet tooth and will normally not drink just plain water. I want something with a taste. But while I'm in the *Cordillera*, I'm off the sweet stuff because the water is so wonderful. It's deep and rich with layers and layers of flavours; as though you could taste all the different types of rock and soil through which it has flowed.

I spend a day walking around Esquel. The town centre is full of touristy shops selling woven textiles, chunky wooden objects, silver jewellery, chocolates. There is a strong Swiss-German element in western Patagonia.

Last time, I didn't venture beyond the town centre. I was alarmed by the wildness of the scenery, intimidated by my lack of language; but also by what I thought was the rough aspect of some of the houses further out. I was afraid I might wander into a shanty town and be robbed. I had no way of gauging the meaning of buildings or roads. Everything was foreign.

For reasons I cannot explain, I am delighted to be back. I have missed the mountains, the air, the very atmosphere of *Cwm Hyfryd*. I walk through the centre and towards the end of town where the streets straggle into the mountains beyond. The road goes from tarmac to gravel. This is what I used to think was the poorer part of town. But there are houses of all sorts here: One is built of bare breeze blocks on an unkempt lot where drunkenly leaning, rusty sheets of corrugated iron serve as fence and garden gate, and another sheet as the roof. But right next door stands a smart little building with gabled windows, the outside freshly painted, and flowers in the garden. A cornershop operates out of a window of the next house. *Minikiosco*, a handmade sign says. There are some vacant lots covered with weeds. In one of them a lonely horse is tethered. On the next corner stands a large house inside a big garden with shrubs and a few small trees on the well-tended lawn.

There are many dogs: a vigilant rottweiler guards the garden of the big house, a couple of small terriers yap in the concreted-over front yard of a smaller house a few doors down. But most dogs are free to roam; they wander along the road on some business of their own. Some trot quickly as though on their way to a rendezvous. Others amble, stop every now and then for a sniff or to visit a friend in a neighbouring house. Lots of dogs sleep or doze on the rough grass or the dusty sidewalk, some curled up with their tails over their noses, others stretched out on their sides, fast asleep, their only movement a twitching ear to dislodge a mosquito.

Small children are running and playing in a schoolyard, all wearing white, thigh-length tunics over their clothes: *guardapolvos* (dustguards), the Argentinian school uniforms. Teachers wear them too.

Some houses are a peculiar triangular shape with roofs reaching all the way to the ground. They look like the letter A or a wedge of cheese standing upright. I've seen tourist cabins shaped like that around Esquel and thought they were a gimmick. But perhaps this is a shape somehow typical for the region. The ones I have seen previously were made of wood and very decorative, while these cabins are built of corrugated zinc sheets – the poor home owner's version, perhaps. Then again, cars are parked outside them – and indeed, there are cars parked outside the breezeblock cubes, too, indicating that these won't be poor people's houses. (Owning a car is a sign of a certain amount of financial comfort in Argentina. I remember how struck I was, after my return to the U.K., to hear a politician on the radio talking about poor people and their cars.) Once I look, I see lots of houses in Patagonia that have corrugated zinc roofs. So perhaps this isn't a rough part of town. I still can't read it right; and I'm still a bit nervous out here. I walk briskly as though I know where I'm going, and I clutch my bag tightly.

Eventually the dirt road peters out altogether and becomes a track. I have arrived at the foot of the mountains. Broom covers their lower slopes, its blossom bright gold. And everywhere, there are exuberant lupins growing wild in the fields: pale yellow, pink, violet, red, blue, purple. The sun is hot but a cold, cold breeze is blowing straight off the snow-capped mountains. The wind sighs and whistles in the trees like a living thing, a spirit that lives on the mountain.

49

I'M STAYING WITH Dana Williams again, in her lovely modern house in the pine forest a couple of miles outside Esquel. Dana had the house built less than twenty years ago, but the kitchen is dominated by an old, cast-iron, wood-burning stove that might well go back to the very early days of *Cwm Hyfryd*. Apart from a couple of months in high summer, it is always on. The muted crackle and hiss of the flames and the warmth they spread make it seem almost alive: an old Welsh dragon perhaps that's come to live out its days in Dana's kitchen. An ancient chair with a disreputable off-white fur cushion stands next to the stove. Next morning at breakfast, the cushion unfurls itself, stretches, yawns pinkly, curls up and goes back to sleep.

I haven't seen Dana in two years, but it feels as though I was here only last week. We sip our hot drinks – *maté* for her, coffee for me – and talk. Dana grew up in Gaiman, but moved out to Esquel as a young woman.

'It's the mountains,' she says. 'Gaiman is all very well, but it's too flat. And don't you think it looks like Wales here?'

I can talk about Wales with Dana, and about *Y Wladfa*, and discuss the vagaries of Welsh grammar. But her interests go beyond *Y Wladfa*. Dana has no patience with parochialism. In that, she is unlike a lot of Patagonian Welsh, who look at me askance when I explain that my interest in Patagonia has shifted to include the Mapuche and Tehuelche.

'I remember,' says Dana, 'when I first moved here, there was this old doctor who lived on a farm *yn y cwm*, in the valley. His sister kept house for him. They kept themselves to themselves. I think they were Welsh, but I forget the name now, it's a long time ago. People were saying that back in the old days, at the beginning of the century, he would pay people for every cut-off ear of a dead Indian that they would bring him. Their *chacra*, their farm, was on land that had belonged to the Tehuelche.'

This is the first time I have heard of a Welshman paying others to kill Indians. It might be rumour, a distortion, a misremembered tale. It might be true; a story that everybody knows and nobody talks about, because it doesn't reflect well on the community.

Later, I hear about this doctor and his sister from other people, and it turns out he wasn't Welsh at all, but of Syrian extraction.

There is a sizeable Syrian-Lebanese community in Argentina.

'Later,' Dana continues, 'the doctor and his sister adopted a small Indian boy, an orphan. He worked for them round the house for years, and they didn't treat him very well. He wasn't beaten or anything, but they would call him names, 'dirty little blacky', that sort of thing. And when eventually the sister died – the doctor was already dead, he went before her – it was found that she had left all her money to the church. There was nothing at all for the boy.'

I imagine the boy – an adolescent, a young man – creeping back into the house in the night after the funeral: kicking down doors, breaking windows, wrecking furniture; systematically destroying every possession of those two who stole his land and his life and left him with nothing.

Dana doesn't know what became of him.

'Most of the Welsh weren't like that,' she says. 'To have others killed over a piece of land.'

Dana and I talk about most things under the sun; politics and people and books, music, travel, the meaning of life. And cookery. We swap recipes for cakes and jams and chutney. Dana is an inspired cook and baker, without appearing at all domestic.

I have one of the best meals of my life in her house one evening: spaghetti doused liberally in olive oil, accompanied by a huge amount of fresh basil. That's it. And it's divine. Basil and olive oil explode on my tongue, followed by a quiet murmur of pasta, a red velvet swish of wine. Every mouthful is a revelation.

I have a coffee and a (so to speak) post-coital cigarette after this delight, outside under the soughing pine trees in the last lingering warmth of the day, and think back to Aberystwyth, fifteen years ago. *There'll be somebody in the college giving a talk about Patagonia tonight.* And how I'd thought, between disbelief and curiosity and delight: Welsh people in Patagonia? I want to see that!

I've still not come to the end of the journey that began in Aberystwyth a decade and a half ago. I couldn't even say where it is I'm going. But it won't be long now. I can feel it.

50

ALL I KNOW ABOUT Ambrosio Ainqueó is his name, his phone number and that Oscar Payaguala has told me that he's an important Mapuche chief in Esquel, and that I should talk to him.

Except that he is not a chief. I have gone to meet Ambrosio Ainqueó at his house in a quiet part of Esquel. We sit at a heavy wooden table in a shady alcove off his living room. The shutters are closed against the sunlight. The outside world seems far away.

'No, no,' he says, shaking his head slowly. He does everything slowly, unhurriedly, with deliberation. 'I couldn't be a *cacique*, because I have no community. I was taken away from my community when I was six years old, back in 1937.'

He thinks that I have come to hear his life story. He is famous for it. Ambrosio Ainqueó is one of the last survivors of a particularly unpleasant act of government oppression against the Mapuche. I had no idea, and his story is like a blow.

'I was little. I didn't have a word of Spanish. I only knew *Mapudungun*, the Mapuche language. I'd never seen a car or a lorry in my life. But suddenly there was this noise – now I know that it was a motor – and a man jumped down, and then three more, and they began to tear down our house. They tore off the *chapa*, the corrugated metal sheets, and threw them on the ground. You mustn't believe that we lived in tents! No, we had a good solid house made of adobe, with a *chapa* roof and everything. We weren't savages, whatever people believed. But there they came and started to tear our house down.'

I don't know how to even begin to comment on what he's saying. Who gets to decide that somebody else is *a savage*? On what grounds? And that it's permissible to throw a savage out of their tent, but not a civilised person out of their house?

'Why?' I ask him. 'Why did they throw you out of your house?'

'At the time, I didn't understand what was happening because I was so small, but Mama said to me, in *Mapudungun* of course, she said, "They're going to throw us out, son, because apparently this land doesn't belong to us".'

'Our community had been living on that land since 1908! And this was '37. That was the Mapuche community of Nahuel Pan. Three hundred people they took away from that place. They threw the wood and the *chapa* from our house on the back of their lorry, and when only the *adobe* walls of our house were left standing, they threw water over it all. I thought it was water, but it was petrol. They set fire to it and burnt it all down. I can still see it burning, now. I dream about it sometimes. We were crying, my sister and I. And then they put us on the back of the lorry too and drove us away. The whole community was scattered.'

I assume that Ainqueó's community had been living on the land unofficially; that they had, perhaps, been driven out of their original settlement by a late action in the 'Desert Campaign' and gone to live on unclaimed land in 1908 which was then, almost thirty years later, claimed and cleared by its owner.

But it wasn't like that at all. The Nahuel Pan community was living on land (some 19,000 hectares, to be precise) which the Argentine government had granted to them by decree as a reservation in 1908.[77] They were entitled to be exactly where they were. But in 1937, a big absentee landowner who already owned large tracts of Patagonia wanted even more: in particular, the land of the Mapuche community of Nahuel Pan. So he pulled strings in Buenos Aires to have the Mapuche removed from it. The national government, at the time under the rule of military dictator General Agustín P. Justo, was happy to comply, declaring that the reservation was not being put to its intended use because of 'the lack of a work ethic by its residents, who live their lives precariously and in a state of great abandon, without order or morals.'[58] This absentee landowner was, in fact, none other but the son of the doctor who had paid a prize for the ears of dead Indians. The family is still around, and still rich.

In the same year the enlightened Argentine government declared the Southern Right Whale a protected species, and the millenarian forest on the slopes of the mountains around Esquel a nature reserve. No protection was granted the indigenous peoples of the region.

Ambrosio Ainqueó's insistence that his people weren't living like savages makes sense now. I feel, not for the last time, ignorant and naïve confronted with the realities faced by the Tehuelche and Mapuche in Patagonia.

'They put us on the back of the lorry and drove us away, and then in a field outside Esquel, they put us down and threw the wood and the corrugated *chapa* sheets on the ground. And then they drove off and left us there, Mama and my sister and me. It was in

May, the middle of winter. There was snow, a hard frost. Mama put the wood up as best she could, and the metal sheets, and built us a shelter like that. And there we spent that night. The next days, we went to cut branches off the willows that grew there, and Mama wove them like this, and put clay on them, and constructed a house for us. Well, a house – it was a hut, it only had the one room for living and sleeping and cooking. And there we were: Mama and my elder sister, who was nine, and me. Two months later, my sister died. Nine years old, and she died from hunger and sadness.'

Ambrosio Ainqueó looks up, looks at me.

'I don't usually talk about this much,' he says, matter-of-factly. 'It's too painful. I'm telling you because you've come from so far away.'

The room is full of pain, it hums like a current.

'I think back then, people didn't look at us, the *Indígenas*, as human. They thought we were animals. I can't think of any other reason why they would have treated us like that. To let a child die of hunger. I would have good reason to hate white people. I don't. And I'm not bitter, despite the terrible things that happened.'

I can still feel the pain in the room, like a living presence, like a ghost that won't go away. Perhaps it *is* a ghost; the ghost of a little girl who died in the snow more than seventy years ago. Ainqueó is full of pain when he recalls the past. But at all other times, there is a great sense of calm about him. He is a man at peace with himself. Not with the world, but he uses his pain and his anger to tackle the world, to work on its wrongs.

'The worst of it is that my father was *un blanco*, a white man. My mother was Mapuche, but my father was an Arab merchant here in the town. A wealthy man. And yet my sister died of hunger.'

The front door suddenly bursts open, and we both jump.

A girl whirls into the room, a teenager in jeans and a white school smock, the *guardapolvo*.

Ambrosio Ainqueó rouses himself. 'My granddaughter,' he explains, and the shadows of the past retreat a little in the presence of the smiling girl and the sunlight that streams in through the open door.

We exchange the customary kiss on the cheek. The girl – I never catch her name – stays for a bit and we chat. Ainqueó has seven children, he tells me.

And how many grandchildren?

'*Muchos*,' he says and laughs. Lots.

And then she leaves, and we go back into the past.

'School,' says Ainqueó, shaking his head. 'I went to school in Esquel. But as I told you, I had no Spanish at all. Things were different, back then. The teacher would show us pictures of animals, and ask what this one or that was called. And I would answer in *Mapudungun*, because that was all I knew. They would laugh at me, all of them. So of course I got furious, and I shouted at them in *Mapudungun*.' He laughs at the memory, at the absurdity, perhaps. 'I go into the schools now, sometimes, to talk to the children in *Mapudungun*. So that they can at least hear the language. Almost nobody speaks it anymore. It's dying out.'

I ask about his father. He was a rich merchant in Esquel, or did I misunderstand that?

'Yes. Yes, he was. He was with my mother for ten years, then they separated. Later, she had an Italian partner, and he brought me up. My own father...'

He falls silent for a long time.

'When I was in fourth grade, he came into the school. He was looking for a boy to work in his store. He picked me, and so I went to work for him. I didn't know that he was my father. He never called me his son. He never told me.'

'You didn't *know*?'

'I didn't know. I worked in his store for several years, and I had no idea. Then one day somebody came into the shop and asked me: 'Where's your Papa?' That's how I found out. And then when I looked at him, I could see the resemblance. That's how fate punished him. I looked more like him than his two legitimate sons. So his wife found out. She was a bitter woman. She gave me cold tea to drink and mouldy bread to eat. Sometimes, no food at all. That was my life.'

I daren't ask how old he was at the time. Fourteen? Fifteen?

'So I stole biscuits and cake from the shop. I ate those. One day my father caught me, he asked me what I thought I was doing. So I showed him the green bread. I told him, "I'm leaving. Unless you acknowledge me as your son."

'And when he wouldn't, I left. The only way I was going to go back was if he acknowledged me as his own flesh and blood. And when he didn't, I went away for good. I left the store, and I left Esquel. I joined the army as a musician, and I was away from

Patagonia for thirteen years. I went to the very north of Argentina, to the province of Misiones, in the subtropics. That's where I met my wife.'

Another long silence.

'I never saw my father again.'

Several Mapuche communities live in the hills and on the *altiplano* in the area around Esquel, further north towards the towns of Epuyen and El Bolsón. The majority of the community forcibly evicted from Nahuel Pan – those who had not been dumped in one of the surrounding small settlements like Ambrosio Ainqueó and his mother and sister – went to live on a territory on the shores of Lake Rosario, some 30 miles to the south. They still live there; and they are still known as the community of Nahuel Pan, decades later.

Nahuel Pan itself, in the midst in the stunning Andean landscape, is today the terminus for *La Trochita*, or *El Trencito* as they call it in Esquel: the little train, the last remainder of the Old Patagonian Express. Once, the train went all the way to Buenos Aires. These days, the small steam locomotive puffs just the 20 kilometres, 12 or so miles, from Esquel to Nahuel Pan, and back, taking tourists for a jaunt out into the country. Nahuel Pan is home, again, to a small Mapuche community. In 1943, seven years after the men with the lorries came to throw people off their land, a few hectares at Nahuel Pan were handed back to the Mapuche, and a handful of families settled there again. But the rest of the land is still under dispute.

When the tourists clamber off the Old Patagonian Express these days, they find not only a café and a small gift shop, but a museum: *Museo de Culturas Originarias Patagónicas*, the Museum of Patagonian Indigenous Cultures. Seventy years after the the authorities of the time illegally forced Ambrosio Ainqueó's community off the land, a museum is funded by public money to showcase and celebrate that community's culture.

It's something. It's a start. An acknowledgement that not all Argentine culture is European. But the problems of the displaced continue. Many Mapuche no longer live on the land. Many have migrated to the cities to look for work; others have been made to leave. They exist in the shanty towns that ring the cities, where drugs and drink and violence are rife, and escape from the downward spiral is hard.

Ambrosio Ainqueó has been working for many years with an N.G.O. to fight for the rights of indigenous people in Argentina. He used to travel to Buenos Aires frequently, to meet representatives of the government. He talks about this work with great equanimity. There was anger as well as pain in his voice earlier, when he recounted his own story. But that was directed at the individuals who caused suffering to him and his family; and at the people and the institutions of the past. He doesn't appear to be angry, now.

He moves his head back and forth when I ask him if that is the case.

'It depends,' he says finally. 'I'm always happy to talk to journalists about my work, and about the situation of the Mapuche. And when a student comes or another young person, and asks me about my life like you did, then I tell them what happened, more or less; as I have told you. But if it's an old person, I won't talk to them. I never did, in all the years since I returned to Esquel with my wife and our children. Not when it was someone old enough to know what had happened in Nahuel Pan. Someone who was around at the time. I don't know how the people of Esquel lived, knowing what was done to us. I don't know what people think they're doing, if they were around then; and now they come and ask me to tell them about my life when they could have done something to help us, and they didn't! They didn't lift a finger. I don't think I will ever lose my rage about that. It's what drives me to go on with my work. That's why I continue to fight for my people.'

There is a knock on the door.

Outside stands a somewhat dishevelled man in shabby, dusty clothes with a shock of grey hair. He asks for a coin so he can buy some bread.

Money clinks, and Ambrosio Ainqueó closes the door and comes back to sit down heavily at the table.

'He wants the money for drink,' he says, shaking his head. '*Allá en el campo, ¡es un señor!* When he's in his community, out in the country, he is a respected man. But when he comes into Esquel, he asks people for money and buys wine and gets drunk. Then he's just a wino.

'That's another thing the whites have done to my people,' Ambrosio Ainqueó tells me with a bitterness I'd not previously heard in his voice. 'The drink.'

When he says *my people*, Ambrosio Ainqueó means the

Mapuche. But there's also the other half of his life, his non-Mapuche heritage, his non-Mapuche wife. He has chosen, very consciously, to be an interpreter, a messenger who goes back and forth between two peoples, two cultures.

And two religions. Because, although he takes part in traditional Mapuche religious ceremonies, Ambrosio Ainqueó is a staunch Christian.

'To the core,' he says, tapping his chest, when he catches my surprised look. He doesn't, somehow, seem like somebody who has found Jesus. But that is exactly what he is.

'The Catholic church saved my life,' he explains. 'I went to attend mass, and they fed me, they gave me to eat and to drink. That saved me. *Yo soy un católico militante.* I'm a militant Catholic.'

But in reality, he is a very peaceful militant. He asks me whether I, too, believe in God. No, I tell him, I don't; but I do believe that there are many different paths that lead to the same place in the end. Is that a cliché? I don't care. I'm quite sure that if there should be another side, I will bump into Ambrosio Ainqueó there.

He nods and smiles; I'm not quite sure whether in agreement or indulgently at my unorthodox beliefs.

He wants to know what other parts of Argentina I have seen. Have I been to Bariloche, the famous ski resort?

Bariloche lies a few hours north of Esquel; a stone's throw by Patagonian standards. I've seen pictures of the town nestling at the foot of splendid mountains, on the shores of a huge beautiful mountain lake. It was founded by Swiss and German immigrants in the early twentieth century, and between the mountainous landscape and the architecture, it could easily be somewhere in the Alps.

I have never been to Bariloche. I've read about it: it's a place where several Nazi officials fled in the 1950s; attracted, perhaps, by the strong German presence that was already there on the ground. Throughout the 1930s and 1940s, Argentina's sizeable German community had been split down the middle. Socialists battled Fascist sympathisers with newspaper articles and pamphlets and, sometimes, fistfights. But all of that happened in the big cities, most of all in Buenos Aires. Down in the far south of both Argentina and Chile, the German community had a pronounced list to the right.

After the war, Josef Mengele and Klaus Barbie went to Bariloche on skiing holidays. In the fifties, a man named Erich

Priebke came to live there. He was a former Gestapo member who had been involved in a massacre of 335 Italian civilians outside Rome at the Fosse Ardeatine in the last days of the war.

Priebke spent over four decades living in Bariloche, openly using his real name even though the Italian police had an arrest warrant for him. They can't have looked very hard. They didn't find him until the 1990s. When he was finally about to be extradited to Italy to stand trial, the German Society of Bariloche fully intended to march on the town hall in protest. Only at the eleventh hour were they dissuaded by the mayor, who pointed out that a demonstration of sympathy for a Nazi war criminal might not generate desirable headlines for a place that makes its living mostly from tourism.[79]

It's irrational, but that, for me, is Bariloche. That's why I don't want to go there. It reminds me of the people in my childhood village who knew what was happening to me and who chose to look away. It reminds me of all that was wrong with Germany.

I feel silly trying to explain this to Ambrosio Ainqueó.

He just nods, accepting my reason.

'I ask because it's a beautiful place,' he says. 'I think you would like the land – the mountains, the lake. There's a special light in the air. My people used to live there, once.' He has a faraway look in his eyes, and there is a longing, a tenderness almost, in his voice. He makes me see Bariloche differently, adds a new dimension. There is more to the place now than ski slopes and tourists and fascists. Perhaps I will go one day to see the mountains and the lake, I tell him.

When I take my leave, with the usual kiss on the cheek, I would like to give him a proper hug. He seems very frail suddenly, after all the memories.

51

I MEET GUSTAVO MACAYO by chance in his father's bookshop. I buy books everywhere; it's a compulsion. Until now, I have been spared in Argentina simply because my Spanish wasn't up to something as complex as a novel. But now I've got to the point where I can just about read and enjoy fiction as well.

I'm looking for something local, I tell the bearded man behind the counter, who somehow looks exactly like I imagine a bookseller: learned, a bit shy, a bit stooped, and very bookish.

'Oh yes,' he says, 'we have something new, it only came out about a year ago. A history of the Mapuche of the region.'

At that I prick up my ears. We start to chat, and it turns out that Gustavo Macayo isn't a bookseller by trade. He's a lawyer who specialises in cases about disputed land rights.

'I just work in the bookshop to earn a bit of money on the side,' he explains. 'Practically all of my legal cases are *pro bono*. Most of my clients are Mapuche-Tehuelche who don't have any money, so I don't charge them. I've been working on land rights for over ten years now, and I'm still almost the only one in the region who takes on this kind of work. Most of the other lawyers don't do cases involving *Indígenas*. I don't earn much, but I'm happy doing the work I do. It's very fulfilling.'

Just then, more customers come into the shop, and Gustavo has to go back to work.

'Why don't you come round to my place tonight, then we can talk more,' he suggests. 'I'll give you my address and you can take a taxi, it's at the other end of town.'

I agree, but I feel uneasy. I'm not at all keen to meet a man I essentially don't know, in his house, at night. It's not just that I don't know him; I don't know anybody who knows him either. Dana's heard of him; she knows the bookshop, and has bought the odd book from Gustavo. But she doesn't *know* him. I'm going to meet a strange man on his own territory.

I don't know why it doesn't occur to me to suggest a café instead. Perhaps because Gustavo's pervading air of skintness has struck a cord with me. At home, I'm a bit of a Scrooge; I don't have much and I don't spend much. It's only in Argentina with its favourable exchange rate (favourable for me) that I have got into the extravagant habit of frequenting cafés with a newspaper or a book, of going out for a meal in the evening.

I don't have a phone number for Gustavo, because he doesn't have a phone. He can't afford one, he told me with engaging frankness. Also he doesn't need one. Most of his clients live in remote communities with no telephone access, and on those occasions when he has to ring someone, he can use the line in his father's bookshop. So I can't phone to cancel.

In the end, I decide to go but to take precautions. I get a taxi to the address that Gustavo has given me, and ask the driver for his mobile number. I will ring him in an hour or two from a phone box to drive me back to Dana's. And of course Dana knows where I've gone. She is bemused by my misgivings, but promises to 'send out the cavalry,' as she puts it, if I'm not back by midnight.

When I arrive at half past nine, it's already dark. Gustavo keeps the usual late Argentinian hours.

I ring the bell and explain that I have come to see Gustavo Macayo.

'*Ah, sí,*' says the woman who opened the door and smiles. '*Está en la casita en el jardín.*' He's in the little house in the garden.

She ushers me along a corridor and out of the back door. At the bottom of the garden, its lit windows radiating a warm glow in the descending evening, stands a sort of better class of garden shed. This is where Gustavo lives.

'It's cheaper than renting my own,' he explains and shrugs. 'And there's no way I could afford a mortgage to buy a house.'

It's early summer, but the night is still chilly in the shadow of the Andes. Inside, the garden house is warm and bright. We sit in a kind of combined kitchen and living room, while music drifts across from next door. Through the half-open door, I can see a sleeping bag and a boom box on the wooden floorboards. They seem to comprise the entirety of the furniture in what must be Gustavo's bedroom.

'Do you mind if I keep the music on while we talk?' says Gustavo. 'I find it calming.'

Is he as nervous about having a stranger in the house as I am about being here?

'It's my work,' he explains while he puts the kettle on to make tea for me. ('You don't drink *maté*, do you?') 'In my cases, I have had confrontations with the police, with the army, the navy, with huge multinational companies. They don't like what I'm doing.

The *estancieros* are like the mafia, they are very powerful. I have to be on my guard. I have to watch who I'm talking to in the street, who I'm seen talking to. I can't do interviews with the local media. I don't go out at night by myself because it isn't safe. I used to have a car but I sold it – I was getting too nervous about someone putting a bomb in it. Now I have a bike.'

He laughs.

'I think I must be the only cyclist in Esquel. *Nobody* here uses a bike. Everybody has a car. People think I'm mad. But it's safer, and it's also cheaper, and it keeps me fit... I have to be vigilant, all the time. I have taken on so many large corporations. I don't know what they might do.'

52

THE DRY PATAGONIAN PLAINS aren't nearly as infertile as they look. There are vast lakes in the foothills of the Andes that contain a commodity which is soon going to become more and more precious: unpolluted fresh water. Beneath the soil and the rocks lie deposits of gold and silver, copper, zinc, lead and oil. Vegetation is sparse, but as long as you allow enough space per animal, you can graze a good few cattle or sheep or horses in the steppe. Like Benetton's 300,000 merino.

Have you ever wondered where the wool for all those jumpers comes from? A good 10 per cent originate in the desert, on one million hectares of Patagonian land owned by the Benetton corporation. Benetton is the biggest single landowner in Argentina[80], and by no means the only foreign one. The financier and billionaire George Soros paid a reputed US$13 million for the largest luxury hotel of Patagonia, in Bariloche. Actors Christophe Lambert and Sylvester Stallone own vast tracts of the region, as do British billionaire Joseph Lewis and Ted Turner, the founder of news channel C.N.N.[81]

The problem is this: How do you define ownership?

The Benetton corporation owns tens of thousands of hectares of land in the region around Esquel because it bought the previous owner, the Argentine Southern Land Co., a British company originally formed in London in the 1880s. The Argentine Southern Land Co. owned large expanses of land all over Patagonia, not only in the province of Chubut, but in three of the other four provinces of Argentinian Patagonia as well.[82]

You can see where this is going. Because who had owned the land previous to the 1880s? Before the so-called 'Desert Conquest'?

The Tehuelche, Mapuche and Pampas Indians didn't have documents that proved their ownership of the land. And then they didn't own it any more, because most of them had been captured and deported or killed. Some *caciques* collaborated with the Argentine military and were given preferential treatment and lands. A number (by no means all) of the tribes who surrendered were moved to allocated reservations – although some, like the tribe of Sayhueke, had to wait for years to be given some hectares of what was left over after European immigrants had chosen the best land.

A few groups were allocated land decades after the end of the genocide: like Ambrosio Ainqueó's community in Nahuel Pan in 1908. In all of those cases, there are documents to show that the land was given them. (Which of course doesn't mean – as the case of Nahuel Pan shows – that they were always respected. In some cases, they aren't to this day.)

Soldiers who fought in the 'Desert Campaigns' were granted pieces of land in payment. Some settled on their new property, many more sold it on to property developers or companies such as the Argentine Southern Land Co. from whom, decades later, the likes of Ted Turner, Sylvester Stallone or the Benetton corporation bought it, presumably in good faith. It would be unjust to demand that those current owners now give up the land which, one could argue, morally does not belong to them. But it's just as unjust to do nothing, and continue to deprive the *Indígenas* of the land that should be theirs. Although that's exactly what is happening.

Which is why Gustavo Macayo has so many cases of disputed landownership on his hands.

'The thing is,' he says, 'the Mapuche-Tehuelche have such a radically different relationship with the land, in a way that the state, the authorities, just don't understand at all. We've made some little headway recently to make people understand that, but god, it's slow going.'

He sips *maté* and looks gloomily towards the curtained window.

'It's such an ethnocentric system in Argentina: white, western, without allowing for anything else. That goes for politics, education, law, culture – everything. That's what makes it so hard to get people to look at things differently. We have to fight prejudice every day. There is so much ignorance. People think, and say, that the Indians are lazy, they drink, they steal, they're work-shy, they're bad.'

I open my mouth to say that surely it's not that bad. Then I remember Miguel in the Gaiman museum, and close it again. Gustavo has caught the look on my face.

'Lots of people think like that,' he says and gets up to put the kettle on again. 'A lot of people think exactly that. We have a long way to go.'

He talks over his shoulder from the sink.

'We have to battle the official version of history. It's been around for a long time, it's well established, it's entrenched. In the official version, the *Indígenas* only occur in the past tense: "The Indians used to hunt, they used to live here, their culture was like this, they disappeared." The indigenous peoples of Argentina are always talked about as though they were from somewhere else, not from here, not of this place, not in this time.'

Gustavo's kitchen seems to do duty not only as living room, but as a study, too. There is a table, a couple of chairs, and another, smaller, table against the wall, covered with a profusion of papers and books and a typewriter.

Gustavo makes me another mug of tea and goes next door to nudge the music up a little. It sounds like Pete Seeger with a Latin twist: a sonorous voice accompanied by a guitar. Gustavo beams when I ask about the singer.

'Atahualpa Yupanqui. He took an Inca name to remind us Argentines of our indigenous roots. Atahualpa and Yupanqui were the names of two Inca kings. He was from the north of Argentina, from a region that had been part of the Inca empire.'

It's only by chance that I look at my watch and realise it's gone half eleven. If I'm not back at Dana's in half an hour, she might set the police on Gustavo. Actually, I don't think she will. Esquel is a small place. Things work differently here. She has bought books in Gustavo's father's bookshop; she wouldn't set the law on him. Also, the Argentine police are not the most trustworthy or best-trained in the world. It's more likely that, should she really get worried, she herself might turn up. So I'd better get a move on.

Gustavo insists on accompanying me to the phone box on the corner to ring for my taxi. But the driver's mobile is switched off. Perhaps he has gone home for the night.

Esquel at night is dominated by the vast sky, and by the mountains. They surround the city like a ring of giants holding hands, their breathing so slow it's almost imperceptible.

All of a sudden I find that I'm not the least bit afraid any more. 'Don't worry,' I say to Gustavo, 'I'll walk to the main road and pick up a cab from there.'

But he insists on walking with me. 'It's safer,' he says.

The main road is just a stone's throw away, and there's a taxi cruising down it. On the stroke of midnight, like Cinderella, I'm back in Dana's house among the soughing pine trees.

53

IN 1994, ARGENTINA PASSED an amendment to the constitution which acknowledges 'the ethnic and cultural pre-existence of the indigenous peoples of Argentina and guarantees to respect their identity and their rights to a bilingual and intercultural education... and the communal property of the land which they had traditionally occupied.'[83]

It's a wonderful law, exceeding by far the rights enjoyed by indigenous peoples in countries like Mexico, Venezuela or Chile. The problem is that it's so very rarely put into practice. Despite the right to education now enshrined in the constitution, a recent UNESCO report states that a staggering 56 per cent of Mapuche children in Argentina don't receive any schooling. At all.[84] Mapuche communities have had to take on landowners and even the armed forces to get access to schools on disputed land.

Which is something I find hard to believe when I first hear it from Mauro Millán. Mauro is the spokesman of an Esquel-based community organisation called *Organización Mapuche-Tehuelche 11 de Octubre*. The organisation owns a small plot of land a little outside the centre of Esquel, along one of the straggling gravel roads. A narrow track leads from the road through knee-high grasses and weeds to a small whitewashed house set back from the street. This is the brand new community centre of the *Organización 11 de Octubre*. The interior is lit by a naked lightbulb hanging from the ceiling. On the bare white wall hangs a flag with three horizontal stripes: blue, white and yellow; a stylised blue arrowhead in the centre. It is the same flag I saw in Oscar Payaguala's museum in Comodoro Rivadavia: the banner of the Tehuelche and Mapuche of Chubut. Next to it, a *kultrung*, the Mapuche drum. Mauro and I sit on wonky chairs that are placed against the walls of the single room. They represent the only furniture. An old plastic kettle is plugged into the wall. It's obvious that the *Organización* isn't rolling in money.

Mauro is a silversmith by profession. For centuries, the Mapuche have been well-known for their splendid silver jewellery. (All the tourist shops in Esquel sell 'Mapuche' earrings, but they are mostly cheap, factory-made copies.) Mauro occupies the bulk of his time with his unpaid work, that of spokesman for *Organización 11 de Octubre*.

Where does the name come from, I ask him. Is it the date the organisation was founded? It's the first of several gaffes I make in my conversation with Mauro.

'For us, 11 October is the last day of freedom,' he tells me. 'Not just for the Mapuche, but for the entire American continent. For us, 12 October 1492 marked not simply the arrival of another race of people, another culture, but of another ideology which has been dominating the continent to this day.'

Of course. 12 October 1492 was the day Columbus 'discovered' the Americas. It's still a national holiday in Argentina. But not for the Mapuche.

'Ten, fifteen years ago,' Mauro says, 'it was claimed in all seriousness that there were no Mapuche living in Esquel; in the entire province of Chubut even. None. When in fact there are several thousand of us. Things have changed since then. The constitution, for one. The amendment was a great triumph for us. Or so we thought at the time. But it's still a struggle, every time, to get the authorities to put it into practice. Often, the authorities are part of the problem. We face racism, discrimination. And when the perpetrator is the state, who do you turn to? I was in one of the more remote Tehuelche-Mapuche communities the other day, on the *meseta*, in the highlands to the east of Esquel. We're working to get a school and a communal wash house and toilet built there. I was there for a couple of days, and the whole time, we were followed by a police car, driving after us very slowly. They made it obvious that they were shadowing us. Just to let us know they were watching, you know? Intimidation.'

I have been brought up to look upon the police as, in the words of a German catchphrase of the 1970s, *Dein Freund und Helfer* (your friend and helper). I have since learnt about police brutality, of course, about state repression, about racist and corrupt police officers. Even so, my initial reaction is one of disbelief.

'Are you serious?' I ask Mauro.

He just looks at me. He doesn't need to say, How naïve are you?

I wish now that I hadn't told him about my interest in *Y Wladfa*, in the history of the Welsh in Patagonia. Mauro Millán is no friend of the Welsh. For which I can't blame him.

'They always go on about the great friendship between the Indians and the first Welsh settlers,' he says. 'But if they were such friends, how come that today, there aren't both Welsh and

Tehuelche-Mapuche living in the valley? Why isn't it a mixed community? Instead, the Welsh live in the most beautiful parts of the valley, and our people in the poorest neighbourhoods on the edge of the city.'

Talking to Mauro is an uncomfortable experience. I feel guilty by association somehow, even though I don't actually live here; I'm not Argentinian, I'm not even Welsh; I've never taken anybody's land away from them. I have chosen to seek out the Mapuche and Tehuelche, to hear their story.

And for the most part so far, they have welcomed me.

I've been spoilt, perhaps, by the warmth of Ambrosio Ainqueó, of Lía and Rodrigo; the friendliness of Oscar Payaguala and Gustavo Macayo. They made me feel enlightened and open-minded. Good about myself. Which is nice. But not the point.

Mauro Millán doesn't have to like me. I have come to him for information, because I wanted to learn more about today's Mapuche-Tehuelche in Patagonia, and he is happy to provide that information. So.

Numbers, I say. I've seen lots of different figures for how many Tehuelche-Mapuche there are in Patagonia today. How many are there, forty thousand, fifty, sixty? Does he know?

This question, like most of the others, doesn't have an easy answer.

'The official numbers,' says Mauro, 'are much lower than ours. I think the official number given is between fifty and seventy thousand for all of Argentina, but actually it's closer to one hundred thousand. That's because the official statistics don't include anyone of mixed heritage. They only count those who are what they call 'full-blooded'. But for us, it's not about blood, about racial purity. As far as we're concerned, if you identify as Mapuche, then you are Mapuche. In Argentina and Chile, there are three categories: *Criollos*, people of European descent, *Mestizos*, mixed-race; and 'pure' Mapuche. We don't think in those categories. We don't care if somebody is 'pure-blooded' or not. We're Mapuche. Identity, for us, is a right. Nobody has the right to decide whether someone is Mapuche or not, except for that person. That's very important. It's part of what makes us a people: that right to decide who we are. A people without a sense of identity will just fade away.'

It is deeply ironic that so much of what he is saying would be echoed, word for word, by Welsh activists in Wales. And that so many of the descendants of those Welsh who left their homeland to preserve their language, their religion and identity, these days care so little for the similar struggle of the Tehuelche-Mapuche, the people their ancestors – albeit unwittingly – helped to displace.

54

'THESE DAYS,' MAURO SAYS, 'our people are scattered; many have left their communities and gone to live in the cities. *Es como la última batalla por el pueblo Mapuche*. We're facing the last battle for the survival of the Mapuche. If we don't win now, we're lost. We will die as a people. Our culture will be lost.'

And then, from one moment to the next, he grins. 'But we won't lose,' he says. 'We know how to survive. Do you know that we beat the Spanish in pitched battles in the eighteenth century? The Mapuche were the only people in all of South America who forced Spain to acknowledge us as a sovereign nation. And now... who do you think will be better equipped to survive when the oil runs out? We, who live so close to nature? Or you city folk with your electricity and your computers, cars, skyscrapers?'

The door of the little community centre opens and somebody sticks their head into the room.

'Oh, you're busy,' says the head upon seeing us, and prepares to withdraw.

'No, no, come in,' says Mauro. And, to me, 'We're going to have a big meeting later on. We would like to set up a community radio, one that broadcasts half in Spanish and half in *Mapudungun*. We want our young people to preserve the language. It needs to be used. We need to pass on the old skills, the traditions, the knowledge of the elders. Ours is an oral culture, none of it is written down. It needs to be passed on.' He turns to me, struck by an idea. 'You don't know anyone who might be able to donate a transmitter, do you?'

Not off-hand, I say. But I'll ask around.

Mauro nods. 'We really need this radio. It would pull people in, provide a focus. The rural communities are so scattered, so isolated. Meetings like the one today are rare. Travel is expensive. But today, lots of people have come from communities outside Esquel. You can meet them and talk to them all.'

The prospect simultaneously delights and alarms me.

In all honesty, I'm more alarmed than delighted. Yes, I would love to talk to people who live out in the mountains, on the *altiplano* and the *meseta*, in those lands that I'm still hoping to explore one day. I want to hear about their lives, their background, their tales and stories perhaps. Stories, also, about their fight for survival on the land that they cannot prove is theirs. I would love to learn a few words of the Mapuche language. Perhaps getting to know the Mapuche will be a way of getting closer to the land of Patagonia, the spirit of Patagonia; that strange nameless force that has held me since my very first visit, that keeps drawing me back. But at the same time, I feel a certain apprehension at the prospect of meeting and talking to a whole lot of people. (What if they're all like Mauro?)

My Spanish is much better now than it has been, but it's still not quite fluent. I misunderstand people, I have to ask for them to repeat what they have told me. I can't always express what I want to say; I have to use crude sentences, imprecise expressions; I lack nuances, I'm all primary colours and blunt statements. I can't be eloquent in Spanish, I can't even be funny, and it makes me feel stupid and awkward.

'That's great,' I say to Mauro, and escape outside for a cigarette and a moment by myself.

Why do I get myself into these situations? Most people only dream of having adventures, they don't actually go looking for them and then dive in head first. I could have stayed at home, daydreaming and safe, and never come here. That's what I should have done, I think as I pace up and down, had I possessed any sense.

People come straggling up the track from the road in small groups; families with small children; middle-aged women and men, alone and in couples; two old, old women. The children look curiously at my green eyebrows, but everybody else nods gravely or smiles a greeting. Nobody stares. Nobody asks what I'm doing there, although one look at my face proclaims that I am *wingka*, a non-Mapuche. Maybe this isn't going to be so bad, I tell myself as I put my cigarette out and go back inside.

The room is full of people now who are all talking together. Somebody has boiled the kettle, and a *maté* gourd is circulating. *Maté* is a communal drink, originating at a time of camp fires. The first person in the round takes a sip and hands the gourd back to the person guarding the kettle, who refills it and passes it on to the second person, then the third, the fourth and so on.

I take a cautious seat on an empty chair, nervous again. They all know each other. I don't know anybody. Has Mauro told them who I am?

A small child runs into the room, clambers up onto the lap of the woman on the chair next to mine. She begins to rock it without interrupting her conversation with her neighbour on the other side. I smile at the child, who gazes at me seriously; but then the woman turns her head, catches my smile and smiles back.

'So,' she says, 'you have come to hear about us?'

I say that Mauro has been giving me a great deal of information.

'You should come and see how we live,' she tells me. 'Come to my house. I live outside Esquel, a few hours by coach, and a couple of hours' walking after that. It's quite remote. You're welcome to stay. I had a Dutch journalist staying with me a few months ago. She found it very interesting.'

I break out in a cold sweat. This is exactly what I wanted, isn't it? Get out into the country, experience how people live. But at the thought of going alone to some remote hamlet in the Andean highlands, I'm gripped by the same panic that seized me a couple of years ago on my first trip from Gaiman to Esquel when I saw the woman get off the coach and walk towards an *estancia* in the middle of nowhere in the desert.

I don't think I'm ready for this. Not yet. Not now.

I stutter something about not having time, that my visit here is almost over. (Which is true, but not so true that I wouldn't have a few days to spare.) Next time, I say. Yes, definitely next time.

I feel like St Augustine. Make me brave. But not just yet.

55

I DIDN'T RETURN TO ESQUEL for a couple of years. In the meantime – as always while I'm away – I have grown much braver, and the idea of going out into the *meseta* has taken a firm hold within me. It will be exactly what I've been dreaming of, and more. I'll have a chance, finally, to get to meet the wide open spaces of Patagonia: head on, face to face.

This time, I really will do it. I won't chicken out.

'I'll be going to stay in a remote Mapuche village,' I tell everybody. I'm almost as excited as I was the first time I travelled to Argentina, years ago, to meet those mythical beings, the Welsh of Patagonia.

I have a terrible memory for names, but I have not forgotten the name of the woman with the friendly smile who issued the invitation: Juana Luz.

But once I'm back in Patagonia, my certainty and excitement ebb.

I met Juana Luz one single time, two years ago.

She's probably forgotten all about me.

She'll certainly have forgotten the invitation.

If it was one at all.

Perhaps she was just being polite.

What will they think if I pop up again now, after all that time?

It takes me almost a month to work up the courage to ring Mauro on the number I still have for *Organisación 11 de octubre*. When I do, he answers on the first ring.

Damn.

I tell him, stuttering, about the two-year-old invitation and that I would like to accept it. I feel like an utter idiot, but I have no other way of contacting Juana Luz. I don't know where she lives. I don't even know her last name.

Why do I keep *doing* these things?

Three days later, I'm on the coach to a place called Futacura. Mauro has told me that Juana Luz – to whom I've still not spoken – will meet me there.

The coach heads out of Esquel, into the hills, turns off the tarmac road onto a *ruta de tierra*. It's even rougher than the ones I have been on before; bumpy and uneven with ruts and potholes.

The coach sways and lurches alarmingly.

The land outside is flat and brown and dry all the way to the horizon. We're travelling east, away from the Andes.

A metal grille covers the windscreen of the coach, making it look like an armoured police vehicle. I had eyed the grille askance when I clambered on board, and wondered whether the coach was a relic from the days of the military dictatorship, or perhaps a decommissioned Black Maria. Now I know: the grille is protection against flying stones. Instead of gravel, the road surface seems to be made of small boulders. They thunk against the underside of the vehicle like small explosions, hurl themselves against its sides and at the windscreen. The glass is cracked in several places despite the protective grating. Travelling on this coach is like travelling inside a hail storm; even the blaring radio can't compete with the noise of the stones.

After two hours of bone-shaking travel, we stop in a village, and the driver calls out: '¡*Futacura!*'

This is my stop. I had thought that I would be let off in the middle of nowhere, but Futacura is a good-sized village with a wide, empty main street; a few shops, a couple of bars, a cottage hospital, a hotel even. We will walk from here, no doubt.

I clamber off, apprehensive. Will I even recognise Juana Luz?

I needn't have worried. She recognises me straight away. I'm the only stranger on the coach.

And as soon as I see her face, I recognise her too.

She is smiling widely, draws me into a hug, gives me a kiss on each cheek.

'We give two kisses,' she explains when she sees my confusion. (Ordinarily, Argentines kiss once, not twice.) She laughs. 'The Mapuche are more generous.'

Behind Juana Luz lurks a small figure.

'My son Julio,' she explains.

Julio is ten years old and shy.

'He walked all this way?' I ask Juana Luz. 'And back?'

This causes some confusion. Because Juana Luz and Julio live *in* Futacura. 'Just over there,' says Juana Luz and points. 'Did you think I lived out there in the hills? No, no. *Vivimos acá en la zona urbana de Futacura*. We live in the urban zone of Futacura. I remember, last time, your Spanish wasn't so good. You must have misunderstood.'

The *zona urbana* of Futacura consists mostly of the empty gravel street. The sidewalk is gravel, too. Houses are tiny, set back from the road and hidden behind screens of shrubbery. They are built of brick or adobe, some whitewashed, others bare. All of them have corrugated zinc roofs – *chapa* – and none is above one storey in height. Every time a car passes – which isn't often – a dust cloud rises up and settles again, slowly.

A couple of horses graze in the playground. They seem to be allowed to wander about freely. A gaucho rides past; his belly as round as a watermelon inside an uncannily white shirt. His face under the black beret is tanned and weatherbeaten; except for his nose, which is an almost luminous red. (Drink? Sunburn?)

Futacura looks like the solitary villages in the desert that the coach from Gaiman to Esquel passes through. Except, of course, that it's even more isolated, because the big coach doesn't even come here. I feel a bit silly being here, a bit disappointed. This is not quite the adventure I had hoped for.

But on the other hand, it's something unexpected, and I like that. Who knows what might happen in urban Futacura?

'Let's walk down there,' says Juana Luz. 'I need to go to the baker's, we're almost out of bread.'

But the lady behind the bakery counter has no bread to sell. The baker has had an accident with his motorcycle, she explains. He broke his arm. They hope that tomorrow, his cousin will be able to come in and take over. But today, there will be no bread in Futacura.

56

TREES GROW ALL ROUND Juana Luz' garden. Once we're inside, the rest of Futacura becomes invisible. The garden is huge. Or perhaps it seems that way, because the house that stands in the centre of it is tiny. I've seen bigger garden sheds. It's got white-washed adobe walls, a door and window and a crooked *chapa* roof.

The inside is all one room, gloomy and packed. I walk straight into the stove, and only just avoid a collision with the table. My small rucksack with only the essentials for a few days suddenly seems as big and as unnecessary as a trunk.

'Have a seat,' Juana Luz says hospitably and gestures towards an antediluvian sofa. The sofa, a small wooden table (heaped high with all sorts of papers and books), a chair and a storage rack stuffed full of things in plastic bags seem to be the living room area. They're in the middle part of the house, illuminated (somewhat) by the single window. The kitchen area is by the front door: cupboard, stove, table, fridge; and an old black-and-white T.V. on a low table. Behind the sofa a curtain is strung. Behind it, Juana Luz tells me, is her bed.

As soon as we reach the house, Julio scuttled away behind the curtain. I half wish I could do the same. I'm suddenly struck by terrible self-consciousness again. Of course I had noticed, that time in the community centre of *Organisación 11 de octubre*, that the Mapuche were not rich. Most of the community – especially those who had come from outside Esquel – were dressed very simply in inexpensive clothes. I thought I'd known to expect that Juana Luz' life and house would be basic. But I wasn't quite prepared for a family of two living, cooking and sleeping essentially in one room.

I suppose I'll have to sleep on the sofa. I'm not delighted by the prospect; I had hoped to have my own space for the night. I think of Dana's beautiful, airy, light-filled house among the pine trees. Her living room with the walk-in fireplace would accommodate Juana Luz' tiny cottage more than twice over.

I'm out of my depth again, confronted with extremes of having and not-having about which I had no idea.

Juana Luz soon draws me into a conversation while she unpacks her shopping. She and Julio have been to the grocer's before they came to the bus stop. There will be what looks like a leg of mutton, pasta and assorted vegetables for dinner. No, no, she doesn't need a hand with anything. I'm to stay on the sofa and she will presently make me a cup of coffee. Meanwhile, I'm to tell her what exactly has brought me here, and what I would like to know.

While I talk, she chops onions, potatoes and a small squash.

'Vegetables for you. You don't eat meat, do you?' she says with the bemused tolerance with which most Patagonians greet my eating habits. She opens the lid of a large saucepan and, before I can say anything, adds handfuls of dry pasta shells to the already simmering mutton. 'It gives the pasta more flavour when you put it in with the meat,' she explains.

Vegetarianism is not a concept well understood in rural Patagonia. And, to be honest, I don't mind too much. I hate factory-farmed meat, but the sheep that provided the leg of mutton will have spent its whole life in the fields around Futacura, ranging freely. A good life, a quick death: that's as much as anyone can ask. My conscience will not suffer from ingesting some of this meat.

Amidst the increasingly delicious food smells comes a whiff of something sweet and flowery from beyond the curtain.

Juana Luz has noticed it too.

'It's Julio,' she says with a smile. She raises her voice. 'Have you been at my perfume again, *hijo*?' (*Hijo* means son.) 'That boy loves to put scent on himself.'

And shortly afterwards Julio sidles bashfully into the kitchen area from behind the curtain, preceded by a cloud of scent. Juana Luz smiles and tousles his hair and sends him out for water.

It's only now that I notice that there is no sink between the work surface and the cooker. Julio picks up a plastic bucket and goes outside. I hear the plashing of water, and a short time later he reappears, dragging the almost full bucket with him. Juana Luz uses a red plastic mug for ladling water from the bucket into the kettle and a plastic bowl that's used for washing.

'If you want the bathroom,' she says to me, 'it's in the garden, just beyond the turkey enclosure. Remember to take a torch, there's no electricity outside.'

Julio is now emboldened to talk to me. Juana Luz must have told him of my interest in Mapuche culture. He wants to show me his book. He's studying *Mapudungun*, the Mapuche language. Not, as I have initially assumed, in school.

'Bless you, no, they don't do *Mapudungun* classes in the school here,' says Juana Luz. (So much for the constitutional right of the Mapuche to a bilingual, bi-cultural education.)

I tell her about Lía Ñancufil Musa of the Wool Bank in Trelew, who goes into the schools there to teach traditional Mapuche crafts and some words of *Mapudungun*.

'I try to do something like that here,' Juana Luz says, 'with the crafts, but I'm afraid there's nobody to teach the language to the children.'

'I learn from the *longkos*, the elders,' Julio explains. 'When there is a *ngillatun* or a *kamarukun*, I'm a *piwichén*. We dance with the *kawell*, the horse. The *longkos* taught me that too. And I know how to play the *ñorquin*, the *trutruka* and the *pillilka*. I'm Mapuche.'

The shy child is transformed, he radiates enthusiasm and delight.

'Whoa,' I say and laugh. 'You will have to explain, I'm afraid I don't know any Mapuche words. I know what a *trutruka* is – like a big trumpet, yes?'

He nods.

'But the rest?'

Juana Luz steps in. '*Piwichén* is the sacred child. When we have a religious ceremony, a *ngillatun* or *kamarukun*, there are always two small boys and two young girls who take part in the ceremony. They're the *piwichén*.'

Julio nods energetically. He is a confident young Mapuche boy, already steeped in his culture. I think of the three generations of Mapuche-Tehuelche I have encountered so far: Ambrosio Ainqueó with his horrific first-hand experience of persecution and state repression against his people. Oscar Payaguala, Mauro Millán, who battle ignorance and discrimination. Lía Ñancufil Musa, who as a child was ashamed of her background and had to rediscover her culture as an adult. And now young Julio, who at the age of ten is studying *Mapudungun* and says proudly: 'I am Mapuche'.

As a child, I was never allowed to be myself. My parents told me that my own personality was wrong and warped and had to be corrected by blows for my own good. Julio's confidence in himself radiates out of him like rays of sunshine. I want to hug him for it, but I'm not sure what he would make of that. So I beam at him instead, and he perches on the arm of the sofa and reads me some more phrases in *Mapudungun* from his book.

57

IT'S MARCH, EARLY AUTUMN. The day has been pleasantly warm, but once the sun sets the air turns cool. After dinner Juana Luz goes outside to put the shutter – a plank of wood with a handle screwed to it – before the window and secure it with stones. Julio switches on the ancient television and expertly twiddles its knobs until he has managed to tune it to a station. (The local provincial channel, the only one available in Futacura without a satellite dish.) There is a film playing: *Fort Apache* with John Wayne.

Julio pulls a plastic stool out from under the kitchen table and sits down mere inches from the T.V., raptly following the adventures of the cowboys and Indians on the screen.

Juana Luz and I sit on the sofa with cups of tea, and talk. In many ways, Juana Luz reminds me of Dana. She is thoughtful and warm and tough; and as with Dana, I feel that even after only a few hours, a friendship, a companionship is springing up between us.

But Juana Luz has had to battle much harder odds than Dana. And she is, of necessity perhaps, much more politically and socially aware.

'I have German and Italian ancestors as well as Mapuche, but for me, my Mapuche heritage is the most important. I'm Mapuche. My grandparents still spoke the language and followed the old ways, they celebrated the *ngillatun* and the *kamarukun*. But I was brought up by *wingkas*, white people. I never learnt our language. When I was five years old, both my parents died. I was the youngest in the family. We were separated and brought up in different families. We never really came back together after that. I was five years old when *mamá* died, but even so, I was strong, because she had taught us well. I was ready to face the world. She knew she was going to die, so she prepared us as well as she could. But it was hard. *Sufrimos mucho*. We suffered much.

'I hope you don't mind me saying this – but really, the Welsh settlement is not where the history of this province begins. The history of Argentina, that's us, the *Pueblos Originarios*, the First Nations. Later, others came, some good people and others who took the land away from us, because they said that we had never worked the land, so it should be given to others who would work on it. Imagine, if I went to a European country now, they wouldn't take the land off someone who lives there and give it to me instead, would they? I don't know why it is in Argentina that what comes from abroad is valued so much more highly than what originates here.'

She shakes her head, sighs. On Julio's T.V. screen, the Apache chief delivers a noble speech and is vanquished by civilisation.

'No. The Argentinian state has to give back what it took from us,' Juana Luz continues. 'Our lands, first of all. They took our language, too. We were punished for speaking it. Our mother wanted to teach my older brothers and sisters, but there was police about, and she didn't dare. She was afraid. Her mother and grandmother were survivors of the *Conquista del Desierto*, where people were killed simply for being Mapuche. They learnt to be afraid, to be quiet. They kept their heads down. That was how the *wingka*, the whites, ruled. Communities dispersed and the language began to die. We are the fifth generation after the 'Desert Conquest'. We want our children to learn the language, to have that chance that we never had. To be able to defend themselves better than we could. They won't have it as hard as we did, because we cleared the road for them. They won't face the same obstacles that we did.'

For Juana Luz, the line from the ancestors to her descendants is unbroken: despite the genocide, despite the painful rift in her own past. She is a link in a chain that stretches back into the distant past, centuries and millennia of rootedness in these lands, in these mountains; and forward into an unknown future. It's an unfamiliar vision of the world for me. I'm the product of an individualistic society. I come from an abusive family. I have no family, now, there are no ancestors that I care to know about. I have no children, nobody who will carry my memories and teachings forward into the future. My children are my stories, and I'm happy that way. I don't regret my choices.

But now, for the first time, I see that the enmeshedness of a clan need not be suffocating, entrapping, hampering. It can be empowering. It can give one's struggles meaning. Even if Juana Luz will never see improvements in her life, she can work towards making Julio's life better. He will continue the struggle, and he will have her support, her work, her pride, to carry him forward.

In fact, he plans to continue the struggle very literally.

'He wants to be a lawyer when he grows up,' Juana Luz says with a smile. The film is over, and Julio has switched the T.V. off and gone behind the bedroom-wall curtain to read. Juana Luz looks behind the curtain and beckons for me to look too. Julio lies fast asleep, still clutching his book. She switches off the light, and we sit again and have another cup of tea.

'It won't be easy, but if he still wants to study when he's grown, then we will somehow find the money for it. In the meantime, I have him spend a couple of hours every afternoon with a car mechanic who lives in the neighbourhood. So that he'll have a trade, a way to earn money. Just in case. I want him to be prepared.'

Prepared, I think she means, in case she dies and leaves him all alone to face the world, the way she had to.

58

'HE'S NOT MY SON, YOU KNOW. I didn't give birth to him.' Juana Luz makes an expressive gesture as though she were pulling a child from between her legs. 'He's adopted. He was in a terrible state when I got him. He's fine now, but back then....' She shakes her head. 'He'd been beaten badly. He was black and blue all over.

'The doctor told me about him, he said there was this little boy whose mother beat him and wouldn't bring him into the surgery for treatment. She didn't want him, and the doctor asked me to take him in. So I thought about it, and in the end I decided to take him. He was four years old. Can you imagine? He had nightmares every night. He cried, he wet his bed. In his nightmares he was back there and they were beating him. He stole and lied. He was feral. He'd gone hungry so often. I had a little dog back then who lived in the house with us. And one day, I turned around and there was Julio at her bowl, eating the dog food. I think he must have been eating dog food, sometimes, at his mother's. They made him sleep outside. He still has a scar on his ankle from where they'd tied him up like a dog. When he cried with hunger they gave him wine to make him sleep.

'I went to the council to formalise the adoption, and do you know what they said? They told me that I couldn't, because his mother refused to give her consent, and they said they had to respect her rights. Her rights, but not those of the child! They asked me if I was related to him. It seemed more important for them that I should be a blood relative than that I had the child's interests at heart. And his family don't care about him at all. The mother has not been to see him once. Not once! In a way it's better, I think – that way he isn't reminded. He calls me Mummy now. In the beginning, I told him to call me Auntie, but a couple of years ago, he said, "I want to call you Mummy, because you are my Mummy". So that's what he calls me now. And we're on track to get the adoption formalised now. The doctor helped me.

'Children are important,' says Juana Luz. 'They're the future. And we should all remember that we were once children ourselves, however old we are now.'

I blink back tears. Meeting genuinely good people always touches me in a way that is both painful and healing. And I can never tell them, because if I tried try to express any of this, I would end up crying all over them. I'm horribly near to bursting into tears as it is. I get up and fuss with my mug of tea, rearrange the blanket, fiddle with my cigarettes. I will go outside, have a smoke, collect myself.

Outside, the sky is black and crammed with stars. I'm shivering with cold and tiredness and old, remembered pain. I can feel the loneliness of a small child for whom nobody cares; the fear, the hunger, the lack of warmth and love. Julio, so alive, so proud, so full of dreams and enthusiasm now, tied up with a cord round his ankle like a dog. Would he even be alive now, if the doctor and Juana Luz hadn't saved him?

I pull on my fleece-lined raincoat when I go back indoors. I need an extra layer not only of warmth, but of skin. Juana Luz' tale has opened old doors, old wounds.

She sees me huddling into my coat, and gets up to get me a blanket from behind the curtain.

'It gets cold here at night,' she says. 'But it's not so bad yet, when you're used to it. In winter, it's really cold; we get snow and frost. I have to have the stove on in winter, but it's expensive. You have to buy wood. There are no trees here at all, and firewood is expensive. Life here can be hard. But it's worse in the cities. Here, you have neighbours, and when times are hard, they will help you, they will give you a meal, tide you over. There is a community here. But in the city, people have no roots. No community, no help. No pride, no hope. That's why there's so much drugs, so much violence, because people lose their way. When you take the Mapuche away from the land, they're not *Mapu Che* any more, the People of the Land, are they? They become uprooted.'

Julio makes a sound behind the curtain, a snuffle, a murmur. Juana Luz gets up to make sure he's all right, then puts the kettle on for another round of tea.

'One more, eh?' she says. 'And then we go to bed. It's late.'

It's long past midnight.

'That boy,' she says, nodding towards the curtain, the sleeping Julio. 'He's as bright as a button. He's really clever! I had been afraid that the wine they'd given him might have caused brain damage, but he just zips through his schoolwork. And this year, he came home from school one day and complained about the teacher: they were doing a play for the national holiday on 12 October, and the teacher had given him the role of Columbus to play. He didn't want to do it. He didn't want to go in the next day. He was afraid the teacher would give him a bad mark if he refused. So I said, You know what, you tell them it's me. Tell them I absolutely forbid you to play Columbus.

'But in the end, he went to the teacher and he told her: "I'm Mapuche. I won't play Columbus".'

'He will start a debate like that. And the teacher accepted his reason and gave the role of Columbus to another boy! I'm very proud of him. There are lots of children in school with Mapuche surnames, but they're ashamed. They say they're Italian, Spanish, French, German, they deny that they're Mapuche.'

It's that bad, I ask, even today?

Juana Luz nods. 'Oh yes. *Fijate*, imagine, when Julio was five years old and went to school, there was this other little boy in his class, the same age; a little blond boy, the son of the mayor. They're a German family. And this boy says to Julio, 'You're not going to sit with me, you're black, you're an Indio'! Five years old, this little boy, and talks like that! He hears it at home, of course, and repeats it. It starts that early.'

59

NEXT AFTERNOON AFTER SCHOOL, Julio takes me on a walk around Futacura, and then to the top of one of the hills overlooking the village. It is stony, dry and overgrown with low prickly shrubs. Most of them look like dry straw, except for one whose leaves shine like bright silver in the sun.

From the top of the hill, Futacura doesn't look dry at all. I can see now that it lies in a river valley. Green fields line the river banks, and masses of bushy poplars obscure most of the houses. The lands beyond are dry again, dry and brown and stony like a moonscape bordered by a brown mountain ridge.

We're only really meant to come up here for the view and then go back to Juana Luz' house, but Julio has other ideas.

'Let's go fishing!' he says. 'It's not far to the river, and I can catch some fish for my dinner.'

I'm impressed by his enterprise, and agree to extend our walk. I'm rather awkward around children; I like them but I'm never quite sure what to say to them. With Julio, conversation is slow at first, but after a while we both thaw. Soon he is telling me all about his fishing technique, suggesting photo opportunities, and giving me a blow-by-blow account of the last *kamarukun* (religious ceremony) he and Juana Luz attended.

The river is wide and shallow, flowing over a bed of flat, round-edged, grey pebbles. The river banks on both sides are made up of the same pebbles. Julio casts a quick look round, then, apparently distinguishing one pebble that to me looks identical in all respects to the other pebbles, lifts it up and brings out from underneath two tin cans and a quantity of string. He digs for bait, and a few minutes later he's ready to cast.

I don't know the Spanish for fishing rod, otherwise I'd ask where he keeps his rods. This is just as well, because he hasn't got any. His 'rods' are the tin cans. He carefully winds the string around them, leaves some dangling at the end, whirls that string – with the baited hook at its end – round a few times, and when he lets go, it sails elegantly through the air and lands in the centre of the river.

In the space of ten minutes, he has expertly hooked four fish. (I avert my eyes for the *coups-de-grâce*.) He's all for staying longer, but I have remembered with a guilty start that Juana Luz is under the impression that we've only gone to the top of the hill. She will surely be wondering what has become of us.

'Come on,' I say to Julio. He's so delighted with his catch, and in basking in my admiring exclamations, that I haven't got the heart to be very stern with him. I've no idea how to deal with children except to treat them, by and large, like I treat everybody else. This works well as far as communication is concerned, but doesn't do much for me in the discipline stakes.

We amble back in the general direction of the village, with several detours because Julio has thought of some other pictur-esque spot that I really must photograph.

'*¡La placa!*' he exclaims suddenly and dashes off in a different direction, at right angles to the main path. '*¡Debes ver la placa!*'

He's going to show me a plaque out here in the middle of nowhere? I must have misunderstood him, I decide; and march after him through thigh-high, rustling stalks of grass.

'It's not far, is it? We really must go back, your *Mamá* will be waiting for us.'

Julio turns round, flashes a quick grin. 'Not far.'

We go round the side of a hill and something that's either a gigantic boulder or a small hillock. Beyond it, another valley opens up, green and level. At the foot of the hillock (or gigantic boulder) stands a slender wooden post crowned by a small metal tablet: a commemorative plaque, out here in the middle of nowhere.

'*La placa del cacique Foyel*,' explains Julio. Chief Foyel's plaque.

Which it is, in a manner of speaking.

> *Desde este lugar fuimos localizados y perseguidos por los lanceros de Foyel el 27-2-1884, percecución por la cual mis tres compañeros fueron muertos en el Valle de los Mártires el 4-3-1884. En memoria de John D. Evans, su hijo Milton Evans 27-2-1987.*

> (It was in this place that we encountered and were persecuted by the warriors of Foyel on 27-2-1884, which persecution led to the death of my three companions in the Valley of the Martyrs on 4-3-1884. In memoriam John D. Evans, put up by his son Milton Evans 27-2-1987.)

This is the first I've heard that the tribe of Foyel were the ones responsible for killing the three young gold-prospecting Welshmen. It's over 200 miles from here to Las Plumas, the 'Valley of the Martyrs'. The plaque was put up more than a century after the event, by John D. Evans' son Milton. It's possible, of course, that John D. Evans told his son details about that trip and its lethal end details that aren't known to historians. (Although on the memorial to his horse whose giant leap saved him, John D. Evans merely mentions *el atque de los indios*, the attack by the Indians, without naming any names.)

Perhaps the Evanses – father or son – felt more comfortable inhabiting stolen territories if their erstwhile owners were undeserving, bloodthirsty savages, rather than people who went about their daily lives until they were forcibly removed, persecuted and killed.

60

JUANA LUZ IS ALREADY waiting when we get back.

'In your school clothes!' she exclaims when she claps eyes on Julio. 'Your good clothes, and you've got mud and scales all over them! Now what are you going to wear tomorrow? Really, Julio....'

Julio and I assume hangdog expressions.

Julio, it transpires, only has one good suit of clothes, and now he will need to wash them so that they are clean again for tomorrow's school.

'He does all his own washing,' explains Juana Luz while Julio, chastened and sulking a little, gets water from the standpipe in the garden, fills the kettle and prepares to boil it for hot water for washing.

'I want him to be able to look after himself. He needs to understand how things work.'

I feel just as chastened as Julio. I try to explain that the trip to the river was a joint decision, but Juana Luz shakes her head. 'It's not that I mind him going fishing. It's clever of him that he caught four fish in such a short time.' A reluctant smile climbs from her lips to her eyes. 'But he should have known to change first. That's why I got cross with him.'

Soon, the clothes are clean again and fluttering on the line to dry, and Julio is in disgrace no more.

Every morning and evening, the local radio in Esquel transmits a string of personal messages. This is a service for people who live in scattered communities where many have no telephone. Juana Luz has no landline phone, but she does own a small, old-fashioned mobile. Picking up a signal in Futacura is tricky though, so she listens avidly to the radio messages every morning and evening.

'There might be something for me,' she explains. 'And it's also a way of keeping up to date with what's going on out there.'

> 'For Manuel Paredes and his sister Deborá in Costa de Lepá,' says the radio. 'You are needed in the school today at 1300 hours.
>
> 'Enrique Lincán in Piedra Parada: today at approximately 1500 hours, Mario Abillo will come and bring the thing as arranged.
>
> 'We inform Guillermo Huenchillan in Mata Grande that his

mother has arrived safely in Esquel....'

There are stories in those messages. What's the mysterious *thing* Mario Abillo arranged to take to Enrique Lincán's house? Why won't they say? Is it a surprise for someone else who might be listening – a new sofa, a fridge, a horse? Something embarrassing? Illegal? Immoral? Or are these two bored, and have hatched this mysterious message in order to get people guessing about secret *things* that are set to arrive at three o'clock this afternoon in Piedra Parada?

> 'Norma Jaramillo in Colonia Cushamen: your grandmother Isidora Jaramillo wants you to know that the package has arrived.
> 'José Paisamilla: a consignment for you will arrive this afternoon on the Don Otto coach. The sender is Floringa Longkopán...'

Then the tone changes. The announcer sits up straighter, his voice becomes more sonorous. This is now an Official Communication.

> 'The public are informed that nineteen canines have been captured on roads and public thoroughfares, in violation of public order statutes. Anybody who presumes themselves the owner of one of the said animals should come to the municipal kennels in Esquel between 0730 and 1230 hours to reclaim their dog.'

Municipal kennels. Who knew?

'Do you still want to go to a remote place on the *meseta*?' Juana Luz asks on my last evening. 'Or is Futacura remote enough for you now?'

I prick up my ears. 'Why?'

'I spoke to Mauro on the phone today. He said to tell you that there will be a ceremony held in Vuelta del Río, a *very* remote community in the hills, this weekend. You are invited to attend, if you like.'

'A *kamarukun*? Are you and Julio going as well?'

She laughs. 'No. It's a bit too remote for me, it really is in the middle of nowhere. You have to drive a couple of hours from

Esquel, and then it's another three hours on horseback.'

I used to be able to ride but I haven't so much as touched a saddle for years. I have visions of me falling off the horse in the middle of nowhere while the rest of the group disappears in a dust cloud on the horizon.

'They won't be galloping for three hours,' Juana Luz says sensibly.

I hesitate, but I don't really contemplate not going.

I will never forgive myself if I miss this chance.

If I fall off, I fall off.

Juana Luz and Julio walk me to the coach next afternoon. I feel equally sad and relieved about leaving. I have lost my heart to Julio, a little bit because he reminds me of myself; and very much because he is so fiercely and proudly and utterly himself. I have lost my heart to Juana Luz too, for much the same reasons. I will miss those two. They will be in my thoughts from now on; and while we are walking down the wide, empty, dusty gravel main street of Futacura, we are already planning my next visit.

'When you come next time...' is the start of every other sentence. We will go on excursions into the hills, Juana Luz and Julio will show me hidden beauty spots and introduce me to other members of the community.

'When you come next time...'

I'm looking forward to it already.

And at the same time, I feel relief that I'm going to go back to the world that I know. I will sleep in a bed in a room with electric light and running water tonight. I will go back to Dana's beautiful house with all its luxuries, fluffy towels and carpeted floors, a warm kitchen. I will go back to Esquel (small-town Esquel, but after Futacura, a glittering metropolis) and revel in its shops and cafés, its bright lights.

I find communal life difficult. In Futacura, I was never alone unless I declared that I intended to go for a walk by myself. And then, there was nothing to do except to walk about for a while in the fields or by the river, and then go back to the house.

And, although I do not like to admit it, I find living in straitened circumstances exhausting. I'm not much of a shopaholic; but I find the thought of possessing just two suits of clothing – one for around the house, one for school or work – unimaginable. I put on different clothes every day, and it's never crossed my mind that, really, that is a bit of a luxury. I don't *need* two dozen different tops, a dozen different pairs of jeans.

From now on, I will try to consume less, to live more consciously.

But I still look forward to returning to my own world.

I'm torn. I wish there were two of me, one to stay here, and one to go.

'You'll be back,' Juana Luz says serenely.

Julio says nothing. He gives me a very long hug at the coach stop.

I clamber onto the coach with its armoured windscreen.

'*¡Hasta la próxima!*' mouthes Juana Luz. 'See you when you come back.'

I wave until they disappear from view.

61

ON SATURDAY MORNING at nine, I'm at the community centre in Esquel. I have spoken to Mauro on the phone. He won't be there himself, but someone will give me a lift as far as the car can go. After that it's going to be horses. People know to expect me. And he'll come to Vuelta del Río later. So there'll be at least one person there that I know.

I have spent the past few days at Dana's, immersed in the urban life of Esquel and the social life of *Y Wladfa*. Last night, we went to see the concert of a visiting choir with one of Dana's Welsh-speaking neighbours. Now I'm all set to go out into the hills once more.

My lift is Catalina. She was the first person who hailed me when I got to the community centre. She's outgoing and friendly and closest to me in age. She is of Tehuelche ancestry, she tells me; and lives in Esquel, where she works for a health insurance company. But she spends most of her weekends in Nahuel Pan, the reclaimed community from which seventy years ago Ambrosio Ainqueó and his mother and sister and around three hundred other Mapuche-Tehuelche were forcibly removed. One of them was Catalina's father.

These days, a dozen or so families have gone back to live in Nahuel Pan. Catalina owns a flat in Esquel, but she has some land in the valley where she is building herself a house, and keeps a cow and chickens.

'My children think I'm mad,' she says and laughs. 'They think I should settle down in Esquel and forget all this nonsense of living off the land.'

She's dressed in jeans and a hooded sweatshirt, and I had assumed her to be about my age, in her late thirties. But she's ten years older than that, with four grown-up children. She is a widow, and although she misses her husband, she also tells me that she will never marry again.

'I love my freedom too much,' she says with a glint in her eye. 'My children think that's mad, too. Do you think I'm mad?'

I think that it's my great good fortune that I have met her.

It's a bright, breezy, sunny autumn day. The sky is blue with small puffy clouds like sheep. We zip along the tarmac road for an hour, rattle along a gravel *ruta de tierra* for another hour, and then Catalina turns off the road onto a strip of land by the river, parks the car and gets out. Shortly afterwards a battered minibus arrives, bearing a group of Tehuelche-Mapuche who have travelled from all over the western reaches of the province.

This is as far as the cars can go. Now we cross the river by a footbridge, and walk. Some horses have materialised, but not enough for all of us. Most of the occupants of the minibus seem to be *longkos*: elders. They most certainly won't be able to walk this distance.

There are also a number of rolled-up mattresses and sheets. Catalina has brought a sleeping bag. I haven't. I wonder where I will sleep. Catalina offers me the use of her camping mattress, and I hope that someone in the village will have a corner in their house where I can sleep.

The sun is warm and the wind a lovely, cooling breeze. The river curls like a huge blue snake, the steppe stretches towards the mountains.

'It's along here and then up the hill,' Catalina says, shoulders her backpack ('My children laughed when they saw me with this') and we march off, across the steppe in the sunshine and beautiful cool wind.

Catalina has a tendency to stray off the footpath. 'Lets go along here,' she keeps saying, 'it's a shortcut.' We march through knee-high clumps of dry spiky grass. The hill slowly, slowly comes closer. It's a lot further away than it looked from the river. After a while, hoofbeats behind us announce those lucky enough to snag a horse. The *longkos* ride slowly past. Among them are two old, old women with craggy and impressive faces. Even more impressive is their riding style: they sit nonchalantly on their horses' backs, with one foot in a stirrup, the other dangling free. Everyone here seems to ride like that. We get a good chance to see because they all ride past us and begin to ascend the hill while we're still toiling across the steppe.

The hoofbeats slowly fade. The wind whistles through the grass. Small grey grasshoppers jump up and sail past us with a rasping noise.

'*Langostas*,' says Catalina. This confuses me greatly, because as far as I know *langosta* means lobster, and this looks like a very unlikely place to find any of those. It finally turns out that the small grey grasshoppers are, in fact, locusts, and that they too are called *langostas*.

We reach the hill. Catalina stops to catch her breath. 'It's my asthma,' she says. 'The dust isn't helping.'

A little while later a gaucho on horseback with a second horse on a lead rein passes by at a rapid trot.

'A spare horse!' Catalina says. That glint in her eye is back. She hails the gaucho and gets him to lend her the spare horse. She offers me a lift, too, but I'm not sure if the horse, a fragile-looking creature on spindly legs, is up to carrying both of us. Also, I very much enjoy walking. All those times I travelled through the desert on the coach I wished that I could just get out and *walk*, connect with the land by touching it with every step. Now I can.

We climb the hill, Catalina and the gaucho on horseback, and me on foot. The path winds round the brow of the hill, descends into a small valley, begins to climb again. A little line of green grass indicates the place where a small stream meanders through the dusty greyness. The string of horses and riders disappears round the next bend in the road. Slowly, Catalina and the gaucho move away from me, too. I march on.

Down hill.

Up hill.

Down hill.

Up...

All I can hear is the breath of the wind, the rasping of the locusts, the sound of my own footsteps, occasional bird calls. I follow the hoofprints in the soft gravelly sand, and walk, and walk, and walk.

Until finally, the path peters out. I am standing on a rugged greyish highland. Now what?

I strain my ears to catch, perhaps, the sound of voices, or the clip-clop of hooves.

Nothing.

Wind, air, wide open spaces.

I gaze down at the ground, among the spiny bushes and rocky outcrops, trying to decipher the hoofprints. I used to be an avid reader of Wild West adventure novels when I was young, whose heroes could unfailingly read any kind of trail. I hunker down and peer at the sandy soil. There is a fairly clearly marked trail of a number of horses travelling together, all going in the direction I have been following so far.

I straighten up and walk on. Calamity Jane, watch out.

62

THE TABLELAND CONTINUES for a long time. The features of the landscape remain the same, while on the horizon, hills appear and shift and slowly disappear from view. It all looks weirdly familiar. If it was a little greener and there were a few more sheep about, it would look just like mid Wales. I peer at the openings between the far hills on the horizon, convinced that any minute now, I will see the blue of the sea.

But I am four hundred miles inland, eight thousand miles from Wales. I have not seen a human being for an hour, which isn't much time at all. But out here, in the middle of nowhere where the only sign of humanity is the occasional fence across the landscape, I feel rather small, and insignificant, and alone.

I understand a little better now that triumphant crowing of Victorian travellers about being the first to set a foot on virgin soil. I'm surrounded by a wilderness that isn't hostile, it just doesn't care. Out here, being human doesn't mean a thing. I'm no more – and no less – special than a pebble, a horse, a locust, a condor. It's as though the dimensions have been changed, and everything is the same size. All the layers that ordinarily define me have been stripped away, and I have been left with nothing but my bare self.

It's alarming. Frightening. Illuminating.

Liberating.

The hoofprints give out altogether, and for the next ten minutes I panic. It is a comfortable, luxurious kind of panic.

If I don't turn up at wherever we're going, someone will notice my absence and come and look for me. Won't they? In the worst case, I can just turn around and walk back in my own footprints, and within a couple of hours I will reach the road where I can flag down a coach or a car which will bring me back to Esquel.

I am not really lost, but even so, I catch a brief glimpse of how huge and impersonal nature is, and how small and weak and clawless I am. I think of the Welsh settlers, newly arrived in Patagonia; of David Williams who got lost in the desert and died of thirst.[85] Suddenly, I can see how easily this would have happened.

I am a stranger in these lands, on this soil. I wouldn't know which plants are edible, what to do for water. Dig? (With what – my small Swiss army knife?) Use water stored in plants? (Which plants?) Recycle my own urine? (Ick.)

I indulge in worst-case scenario fantasies for a few minutes longer, then I get up from the rock on which I have sunk down, rearrange my backpack on my shoulders, take a bearing from the hoofprints I've been following, and march off.

It is about twenty minutes later, as I am picking my way through a swampy patch along a slope, that a gaucho appears, riding a white horse.

I stop and stare.

'Along here!' he yells and gestures. He is not a vision, despite the white steed. Catalina has sent him to come looking for me. Sadly, he has not brought a spare horse for me.

'Not far now,' he says and grins encouragingly.

We descend from the tableland into another valley. The path begins to climb again. For the last part of the way, I get to ride and he gets to walk.

The top of the hill is planted all around with trees; horses stand in the shade and doze. Behind the trees, a little house. This is journey's end. There is no village.

The front door of the house stands open, smoke pours out of the chimney in the roof. There are lots of people about, children run around in the yard in which chickens scratch, geese waddle and a turkey wanders. I climb stiffly off the horse and totter indoors. I could do with a rest now. Lots of people sit on benches around a cast-iron, wood-burning stove and sip *maté*.

I find a seat on one of the benches, sink down in it gratefully, and look around. Mauro isn't here yet. I don't know a soul in this place except for Catalina. The house – an adobe hut, bigger than Juana Luz's cottage but even more basic – is almost devoid of furnishings. The kitchen has a beaten earth floor. There is no electricity. Water comes from a standpipe in the yard. Apart from the wood-burning stove and the benches, there is a calor gas cooker, a wooden table piled high with plastic bowls, plastic bags, a couple of tin mugs, packets of various dry foodstuffs, a couple of wooden boards, assorted big knives and general flotsam. A wooden crate hangs on the wall and does duty as a shelf. There is a kitchen radio on a board, an extremely rickety chair, and a plastic bucket full of water. A calendar and a couple of pictures torn out of a magazine hang on the wall; someone has sellotaped photographs of the children of the family on the back door. If you want water, you dunk a plastic cup into the bucket and drink. The kettle on the stove top is replenished by the same method. The window is covered partly with glass and partly with plastic sheeting and by no means keeps out the wind.

From the exposed beams in the roof hang large chunks of meat. (To dry? To be smoked? Is the roof the larder?) A sheep carcass hangs from the washing line outside. Next morning, I see more carcasses in the trees behind the house.

My vegetarian soul should be freaked out, but for some reason I don't really mind. Everything here is so different from what I know; the whole way of life, the poverty, the remoteness; that I half feel as though I've entered another world, another time, another reality.

63

THE KITCHEN IS WARM and smoky. The *maté* circulates. There are perhaps two dozen people in total. Some haven't seen each other for a year or more, some are here for the first time. They exchange news about friends and relatives – who got married, moved away, has found work, lost work, given birth, died since the last meeting. Children run in and out; play in the yard, clamber on laps for a cuddle and a bit of warming up, then go back outside. They don't interrupt the flow of conversation. Nobody shushes them, and they in turn don't scream or whine.

I am the only *wingka* here, but I am not made to feel like a foreigner. People ask me where I am from, how I liked the walk – with big grins; the fact that I walked all the way here becomes a running joke all through the evening – how I like the house, the place, the country. They all beam when I tell them that I'm in love with Patagonia.

When Doña Natalia, the hostess, hears that I don't drink *maté*, she looks doubtful and offers me a cup of black tea instead. There is no milk. I haven't yet broken to her the news that I am vegetarian, and won't be able to eat any of the barbecued sheep that is for supper.

Cold gusts of wind come in through the open door, make the strips of plastic sheeting in the window snap and rattle. After a while, several of the old men and women get up and leave the house, followed by Doña Natalia. I pay no heed to this until I hear a chorus of voices from outside, calling in unison. Is this the beginning of the ceremony?

I ask Catalina, but she shakes her head. 'Doña Natalia asked the *longkos* to ask the wind to calm down a bit. She gets a headache when it is blowing so strongly.'

Reality in the house on the top of the hill is a different beast from the one I know. It's as though there is no dividing line here between the mundane and the magical. I find it alarming, and enviable at the same time. The *longkos* can't really talk the wind down. Can they?

I sip my tea and offer to give Catalina a hand with making bread. I know about bread. I frequently bake my own. It's a point where this world and my own intersect.

Catalina pushes the piled-up stuff on the table aside, gives its wooden surface a brief wipe with a dishcloth, and begins to make the dough. And just as I don't have any strong feelings about the sheep carcass on the washing line, I don't mind the bread being kneaded on the not-quite-hygienic table surface. It's simply how things are done here.

I'm torn between respect for people who live such a basic, hard life, distant from the modern world; and worry on their behalf about what it must be like here in the middle of winter when the hut on the hill will be cut off by the weather, when the snow will make it impossible to leave the hill for days. What do they do when someone falls ill in the middle of the night?

'We ride to the phone box,' says Deborá and points into the hills, in the opposite direction to the one we have arrived from. Deborá is fifteen and lives here with her parents, her elder brother and a couple of younger siblings.

I envisage the phone box being a couple of hours' ride away, but it turns out that it is in fact just beyond the pass, less than ten minutes on horseback.

'If the wires aren't down,' Deborá adds. 'In winter they sometimes snap from the weight of snow, or in storms, but if they're not broken, everything's fine.'

I find the idea of a phone box in the middle of nowhere strange, but it appears that it was placed there for the use of the community of Vuelta del Río. Maybe a dozen families live scattered in these hills, and they – together with the *Organisación 11 de Octubre* – campaigned hard until the authorities agreed to provide this means of communication with the outside world. Mobile phones receive no signal up here.

'So what do you do about school?' I ask Deborá, half expecting her to say that she and her brothers and sisters don't go to school. But I am wrong.

'We ride,' she says, matter-of-factly. 'Or sometimes we walk.'

To school?

'To the road. You know, the way you came? You walked, didn't you? How long did it take you?'

'Nearly three hours.'

'Well, I can do that way in an hour,' Deborá boasts. 'I'm used to it, see.'

'And then? Where's the school?'

'In El Bolsón.'

El Bolsón is a small town maybe thirty miles away. 'Bloody hell. How long does it take you to get there?'

'We start here at five in the morning... sometimes in winter the snow is so high you can't get out of here at all. We're often really late. So we start here at five, we get a bus from the road, and then we're in school by ten.'

The school is a boarding school, and Deborá and her siblings come home every other weekend. It must be very strange to live in a town that has cars and electric light and computers and fridges as a matter of course, and then to come back home to this place in the mountains that has none of these things. Deborá shrugs. To her, that's just her life, and normal.

Just as normal, perhaps, as the fact that a little while later the strong cold wind quietens down to the merest breeze.

64

THE YOUNG MEN OF THE COMMUNITY are shy, feral people who don't mix much with other humans. They appear much more at home in each other's company and that of their dogs and horses. I don't think I've heard a single one of them say a word, with the exception of two short sentences uttered by my rescuer several hours ago. I go looking for them, and find them outside, at some distance from the house, where they have set up a big fire to prepare the *asado*, our evening meal. *Asado* means 'roast' and can be any kind of barbecued meat made on a *parrilla*, a metal grill. Or, in its original form – and the way it is being prepared here in the hills – it is half a sheep stuck on a metal spit over an open fire.

The fire sings and crackles and spits where fat from the roasting meat drips down. Then men hunker round it, some sit on chunks of wood, others squat on their haunches. They smoke and gaze into the fire and occasionally communicate in brief half sentences. They seem to inhabit a world quite separate from the domesticity of the kitchen.

I dither a while before approaching the fire, wondering whether it's some kind of sacred male space. But I don't hold with sacred male anythings; and also, I have a question for Deborá's big brother Valentín, and she has told me that this is where I can find him.

A lithe young man with a beret on his black hair uncurls himself from his crouching position when I ask for Valentín. I want to know a bit more about tomorrow's ceremony. Julio has tried to explain things to me, but he used so many Mapuche words, and talked so fast, that by the end I wasn't much wiser. Deborá has assured me that Valentín is the man to ask. So, I ask him, what is tomorrow going to be about?

'We're going to hold a religious ceremony just like our ancestors did. It's something that is slowly coming back in our community. We haven't held one here for a long time,' says Valentín. He has a tendency to look over my shoulder, towards the far horizon, even while talking to me. 'It's difficult, people have to travel, to come from other places, because there's nobody left in Vuelta del Río who knows how to conduct a *ngillatun*. Nobody in the community here speaks *Mapudungun* any more. So we're lucky that the *longkos*, the elders, have agreed to come here to teach us. It will help us to refresh our strength. We have a fight on our hands here.' He looks at me for the first time. 'Mauro told you about that, *¿no?*'

No, I say, feeling ignorant and uninformed. A fight? With whom? Against whom?

It turns out to be over land. I might have guessed.

'*Es una zona conflictiva acá,*' explains Valentín, looking sideways into the fire. There are clashes over land in this area. 'People turn up with title deeds to land inside Mapuche communities. We had that happen here, a Gringo landowner wanted this land where we live. It's been like that for a long time. Lots of things have happened here. We've been thrown out of the house, the house has been torn down, *totalmente todo*. They've done everything they could think of to get us out.'

'The house has been *torn down*? This house? What, while you were there?'

The question appears to amuse him, but it's hard to tell; Valentín's face is mostly a study in immovability.

'It used to be worse in my grandparents' time,' he says, matter-of-factly. 'And their parents' time. It was very bad for them.'

Valentín's great-grandparents would have been alive at the time of the 'Desert Conquest'. For me, that's something I have been reading about. For him, it's family history.

'Today there are the media, the radio, television, the internet; places where we can go and tell our stories. It helps. I think if it weren't for those, we maybe wouldn't be here any more. We wouldn't have been able to resist. We'd have been thrown off our land, and be living in a shanty town somewhere on the edge of a big city. *En una villa,*' he repeats, and spits into the fire.

'So this landowner came to throw you out of the house?' I repeat. I still don't know what to expect from the ceremony tomorrow. But maybe the *what* isn't as important as the *why*.

'He sent the police,' says Valentín drily. 'That was three years ago. In March, actually. Exactly three years ago.'

He lets a lungful of air out in a long breath, hunkers down again by the fireside. I sit down on a log, get out my cigarettes, take one, offer one to him. We light them from the fire.

'It was cold then, we're quite high up in the mountains here, there was lots of snow. There are all the children living here, my brothers and sisters, and some cousins, too. Luckily, on that day when the police came, they were all in school. So it was just me and my parents.' He gestures with his cigarette. 'Look where we live, so deep in the mountains, on a hill top: you wouldn't believe that a vehicle could come up here, would you? When we needed an ambulance once because my mother was ill, we rang the hospital and they told us that nothing could come up here. But the police came in a four-by-four, they came all the way up here, they threw us out of the house and started to tear the house down. They didn't care what would happen to us, that we'd be homeless.'

I think of Ambrosio Ainqueó's tale. It had seemed to belong to another era, to the bad old days when such things could happen. But three years ago, in the very place where I sit now, exactly the same thing happened to Valentín, who can't be more than twenty years old.

'So what did you do?'

He bares his teeth in what might be a grim smile or a snarl.

'We came back,' he says briefly. 'We came back and we put the roof back on, and we're going to stay here, whatever happens. We're going to continue our resistance. People helped us. The community, and other communities in the region. People showed solidarity. We have a lawyer, and some of the press wrote about us. And so...' He shrugs. 'This is our land. This is where we're from.'

'Is the *ngillatun* tomorrow going to be a thanksgiving as well, because you're still here?'

Again that brief flash of white teeth.

'We're still here, but the fight isn't over. We're going to ask for strength to continue resisting. We took the landowner to court, and we lost, but we're not accepting the verdict. We're going to appeal, so we're asking for a good outcome this time.'

65

NIGHT FALLS. DINNERTIME. There's barbecued mutton and fresh bread (tea and bread for me), and then the *maté* circulates again. Outside, the hills surrounding the hut stand black against a sky glittering with stars. Horses shift beneath the trees. A low murmur of voices drifts out from the kitchen, and the wind sighs through the branches.

It's cold now that the sun has gone in, and I am beginning to wonder where I will sleep. I had hoped that there would be space on the kitchen floor, hopefully near the stove, but the kitchen is still filled with people chatting away, and the time is coming up to eleven o'clock. I should be worried; under normal circumstances I *would* be worried, but I'm filled with a serene and completely irrational confidence that everything will work out fine.

Catalina is also tired. She sits in the warmest corner of the kitchen and tries to catch forty winks, but the bench wobbles, and when her head nods forwards, so does the entire bench, and Catalina nearly ends up with her head in the kitchen fire. She swears and laughs and gets up.

'I need to go to sleep,' she announces and buttonholes Doña Natalia, the lady of the house.

'Where can we sleep, Doña Natalia?'

There are a couple of bedrooms at the back of the house, but they have been reserved for the family, for the elders and the children.

'Haven't you brought a tent?' Doña Natalia wants to know.

Catalina and I look sheepish. Doña Natalia goes off somewhere, and we stay where we are by the side of the beautifully warm stove. I keep dozing off. Maybe, I think drowsily, I'll just stay on this bench and sleep sitting up.

It's warm, that's the most important thing. In the absence of the coddling paraphernalia of civilisation (glass windows, heating, electric light) creature comforts that I take for granted have suddenly become much more important. Nature in the shape of cold and darkness is out there, just on the other side of the window with its thin membrane of plastic sheeting. Nature is only just kept at bay by the crackling flames in the stove. I feel like a cave-dweller huddling by the fire. It's an unsettling experience. My values and my way of thinking are being shaken up again, and in the knowledge that I will soon be back in the world I know I ride the rough waves and enjoy the experience, and wonder what is really important and what is not.

Doña Natalia comes back, and with her a young woman.

'We brought a tent for two persons,' says this wonderful apparition. 'You're welcome to borrow it, we won't actually need it.'

Yet another novel experience: how to pitch a tent in the dark. Of course neither of us has brought a torch, and Catalina has never before assembled a tent. It takes us a while, and there is much rustling and giggling and stumbling under the magnificent sky.

'I can't wait to sleep,' Catalina says and yawns.

There remains the small question of what I am to sleep *on*. I haven't brought anything other than lots of layers of clothes and my waterproof coat, which Catalina has been wearing all evening because she didn't bring a coat; and the mountain night has grown autumnally chilly. Nobody has brought any extra mattresses or sleeping bags (and really, it would be a bit much to ask). Doña Natalia offers me a fleece for a mattress, and a blanket from the kitchen.

I stumble in the dark to where the men sit around the dying embers of the *asado* fire, and ask for a fleece. The fleece is exactly as it came off the sheep, rough and full of burrs and bits of dry grass, and the legs with their small, hard hooves are still dangling from it. (Happily, the head is not.) I heave it on to my shoulders (it is heavy!) and stagger back to the tent.

All I hear, after Catalina and I have finally stopped fidgeting and rustling in the tiny tent, is a faraway murmur of voices from the men by the campfire and some hardy souls who have come to stand outside to smoke. Occasionally, laughter wells up and ebbs away again, and metal clinks against metal as the *maté* is replenished from the tin kettle. My face and my hands are cold and my hair smells of woodsmoke. I feel as though I'm ten years old and have somehow strayed into the pages of an adventure novel. This is the kind of thing I've always dreamed of but never really thought would happen: I'm spending the night on a sheepskin under the starry Southern sky in the Andes, by an open fire, and tomorrow morning I'm going to experience a *ngillatun*.

66

I WAKE IN THE MIDDLE of the night, not quite sure why. It's pitch black in the tent, and quite cold. My nose is cold, my feet lumps of ice. I have no idea what the time is. I can't read my watch in the dark. I can hear a murmur of voices, and the clinking of kettle and *maté*.

Some people are still awake, and chatting, I think. We went to bed around eleven, and now it will be, what, one or two in the morning? This is going to be a long, cold night.

But just as I am about to drift off again, there is a sudden blast as of a trumpet.

Dogs begin to bark. A cockerel crows.

Another fanfare.

Catalina stirs. 'I guess they want us to get up,' she says. 'Is it five o'clock yet?'

Is it *what*?

'On days when religious ceremonies are held, we always get up at five,' she explains.

I'm glad I didn't know that last night. A moment ago, I had been worrying that there were going to be several more hours of night to come. Now, I rather wish there were. The sun won't rise until eight o'clock at this time of year. What on earth is there to get up at five for?

The trumpet sounds again, and the dogs join in with much enthusiasm. Actually, it isn't a trumpet, it's a *trutruka*.

'Come on,' says Catalina. We look for our shoes in the dark. The tent is tiny and filled to capacity with the two of us, the fleece and Catalina's camping mattress and sleeping bag; yet our shoes have found unexpected crevices in which to hide.

Shoes finally located and fumbled onto the correct feet in the dark, we unzip the tent entrance and clamber out.

It is like ink outside. A profusion of stars sparkles like diamonds in the black hair of the night sky. Even stumbling outside the enclosure for a pee on the dark hillside is a rather poetic experience.

The kitchen door stands open, bright light streams outside from the Tilley lamp, which yesterday afternoon had appeared gloomy after the brilliant sunlight. I sidle into the kitchen, a bit uneasy amongst all the people I only met yesterday. I'm beginning to feel self-conscious now that the ceremony is about to start. For one thing, I haven't a clue what's going to happen. Will it start now, soon? What will they do and where will they do it, and how long will it take? Also, I'm a stranger here, not one of them, and the act that is about to take place is not only an expression of Mapuche religion, but of Mapuche identity as well.

I don't exactly feel like a *wingka* intruder, but I do feel a bit conspicuous.

Doña Natalia sits by the stove, pouring hot water from a kettle into the *maté*. I borrow one of the mugs and some hot water and go outside to the standpipe to brush my teeth. There is no mirror that I can see, so my face will have to look after itself for today.

Teeth brushed and deodorant sprayed on, I feel much better. Even some of the awkwardness has gone.

I wash the mug under the standpipe and return it to Doña Natalia, then go back outside to join the small knot of smokers for a cigarette by way of breakfast.

The sky is coal black, and the early morning wind is cold on my face. The air smells of woodsmoke and cigarette smoke and cold earth. A horse snorts somewhere in the dark. The cockerel keeps crowing.

I am finally driven back into the kitchen by the cold. All the good seats near the stove have already been taken. Catalina sits in state in the warmest corner, wielding a kettle and *maté*. She waves and grins, and I grin back. I'm glad that I have met her.

I've been here little more than twelve hours, but somehow it already feels quite natural to go and sit in the kitchen with everybody else, near the warmth of the stove and the light of the lamp. People talk in low voices, or just sit in silence, waking slowly. The *maté* circles.

I finally find a draughty seat on a bench by the door that leads from the kitchen to the rooms at the back of the house. After a while, the door opens and a young woman comes out carrying a sleepy child. It is Victoria, our saviour who conjured up a tent out of thin air last night.

Everyone on the bench shifts a bit closer together, and she sits down and rocks the child on her lap, whispering something into its ear. The child gradually wakes up, and begins to tell her a long, involved story. She listens attentively while it searches for words, or gets tangled in the intricacies of language and the tale. Listening to children talking, I wonder sometimes if they have some native tongue of their own before they learn to speak. Their efforts to express themselves resemble so much those of a person learning a foreign language. Hearing this little one talk – he is maybe two, three years old – I get the sense that he knows quite well what he's trying to say, but just doesn't know the words.

His mother listens without appearing the least bit bored or impatient while the child talks himself awake. She smiles and nods and answers his questions as though there were nothing more interesting in the world. For all the material things this house on the top of the hill doesn't have, there is no shortage of time here. Nobody is in a hurry. Nobody is impatient.

When the child has talked himself out, Victoria lifts him from her lap and hands him over to one of the gauchos who has come in, her husband.

With her hands freed, she gets up to fill a thermos flask with hot water from the kettle on the stove. She fills her own *maté* nearly to the rim with *yerba* tea, and then adds at least three heaped spoons full of sugar. She unscrews the thermos and adds hot water. Steam curls up, and with it a strong, hot scent of herbs.

'You don't drink *maté*, do you?' she says to me as she prepares to pass the *maté* round.

The steam curls, tempting with its heat. The last time I tried *maté*, in Dudú's house in Gaiman, I found it too bitter and decided to stick with familiar tea and coffee. But now my stomach growls like a puma. I'm dying to get something warm inside me.

'Er, actually...' I say. 'I'll give it a try.'

She smiles with real pleasure as she hands me the cup. 'I think you'll like this, we make it sweet.'

The *maté* is sweet and bitter and strong and hot. It isn't heavy, like coffee or even tea; there is a herbal-ness about it that I like. Perhaps an infusion of hay (with three spoonsful of sugar) would taste like this.

'You're right,' I say to Victoria, surprised. 'I do like it.'

She refills the *maté* and hands it to the person on my right; then she turns to the woman who sits on her other side and says, 'Did you see? ¡*La señora se animó a tomar mate!*' The lady decided to try my *maté*!

67

EVERYBODY ON THE HILL is unfailingly courteous. Most people address me with the formal *usted*. Women over the age of roughly forty are addressed as *señora*; the elderly ladies as *abuela* (Grandmother) but also in the formal *usted*. Is that because manners out here are still as they were in the old days? Or is it a Mapuche custom?

Victoria is visibly pleased that is was her *maté* that tempted me to give the national beverage a try. When my turn comes again, she holds the cup up questioningly, and beams when I nod and take it for another mouthful of hot water, caffeine and sugar. I might get used to this stuff.

Slowly the night lightens to grey. I'm sliding back into sleepiness, wondering why on earth we had to get up so early just to sit about in the kitchen for hours. The *longkos* get up stiffly and make to walk outside. Nobody has said a word that I am aware of, but one after the other, everybody gets up and drifts outside.

It is light outside now, a cold, clear morning. The sky is the palest shade of blue, almost silvery white. The sun has yet to rise above the peaks.

An old, old lady is dragging a large bundle in one hand and a plastic bag the size of a bin liner in the other. She sets them down and begins to rummage, pulling out lengths of cloth: blue, yellow, red, white. From them and a handful of safety-pins, she fashions cloaks and headbands. Those the two women *longkos* put on are dark blue. Cloaks of a bright sky blue go on two teenage girls. One of them is Deborá, the daughter of the house on the hill. They are also given bright yellow headbands, and finally the *longko* pulls out a couple of silver necklaces which are braided into the girls' hair. I remember what Juana Luz told me about the *kamarukun* ceremony. The girls are one of a pair of *piwichén*, sacred children. Children and teenagers always take part in Mapuche religious ceremonies, and there is a very practical reason for that. When I ask afterwards, I am told that the girls' role was to learn, to take part; so that, when they will be grown women with children of their own one day, they will be able to pass the knowledge on to the next generation. In fact, everybody takes part at some point in the ceremony. There are no spectators.

While the *longkos* are busy with the clothes, Valentín has brought some long, thin wooden poles. They clatter together in the morning breeze. Everybody is now assembled outside, the *longkos* and the two *piwichén* girls in the front row. Almost all the women wear headscarves.

We stand and wait. I wish I knew what was going to happen. It is a little unnerving, being the only outsider here. I don't feel unwelcome or intrusive, just ignorant and rather invisible.

And cold. The effect of the *maté* has worn off. I'm wearing all the clothes I brought, but I haven't eaten anything since the bread and tea last night. I have hardly moved this morning to get my circulation going. While we wait, I dash back indoors to get the blanket I'd used last night, which I returned to the kitchen this morning. I wrap it around myself and go back outside.

Most of the men seem to have disappeared from the crowd. The rest of us get down to some more waiting.

The minutes pass. The dawn breeze touches chilly fingers to my face and my exposed hands clutching the blanket, creeps into my shoes.

Near me stands Inés. She is maybe twelve years old, and has come here in the company of a short-tempered elderly man.

'Everybody thinks I'm his grandchild but in fact, I'm his daughter,' she explained yesterday, resigned.

She doesn't speak much, and spent much of the afternoon and evening sitting quietly on a bench by herself. She's too old to play with the younger children but not old enough to be friends with teenagers like Debóra.

One of the *longkos*, an gnarled old man, has moved to stand at the front of the crowd. He is making a speech in *Mapudungun*. Inés stands near me in a hoodie and jeans, her arms wrapped around herself. Her face is pinched with cold. I struggle for a bit with my baser nature, then move closer to her and hold out the blanket, offering to share it. We huddle together and tug at the quilt until most of both of us is covered. My front is now exposed to the cold, but the rest of me is still warm, and I feel better knowing that Inés is also a little warmer. I spoke to her father yesterday, and he told me that the two of them live alone on his remote *chacra*. All his other children are grown up and left, and his wife recently died. There is something about Inés, her withdrawn air, the way her eyes look inward and don't make much contact with other people, that worries me. I used to be like that at her age: quiet, withdrawn, not making contact with anyone.

Sharing the quilt with her now, I can at least offer her some companionship.

68

THERE IS THE SOUND of hoofbeats: the men have evidently been to saddle the horses. Now, they ride in a circle around the house on top of the hill, three times. After each completed circle, they raise their fists and shout out a single word, it sounds like *Hey* or *Yay*. The women and girls and the horseless men inside the enclosure also raise their fists and shout. Perhaps this is a call to the sky, to the gods, or maybe – this is how it appears to me – it is an expression of the strength of the people, a way of saying, 'Here we still are, we are loud, we are strong, we will last.'

The two old ladies now each hold a *kultrung*, the Mapuche ritual drum. It is held in one hand and beaten with a small wooden club. As I look closer, I see that one of the *kultrungs* has been made by stretching a skin tightly over an enamel bowl.

The women *longkos* beat the *kultrungs* and chant in wavering voices, while the man *longko* makes another long speech in *Mapudungun*. The men on horseback gallop another three times round the house and the enclosure, then the crowd shows signs of dispersing. I begin to cherish hopes that this is it, and that we can go back indoors, sit by the lovely warm stove and drink more lovely hot *maté*.

I should have known, really. A fully grown *ngillatun* can go on for *five days*. Even a comparatively simple appeal ceremony like this is going to last longer than just an hour and a half.

Everybody now gathers their things together, musical instruments, the poles, various flags and a number of buckets that have appeared from somewhere, and begins to walk downhill to the valley. The bigger children lead the smaller ones by the hand, and the dogs come of their own accord.

The men on horseback are already down there, and are about to drive the poles into the ground. Once they stand securely, a flag is fastened to each: the blue, white and yellow Mapuche flag with its arrowhead in the centre, signifying the ongoing fight and resistance of the People of the Earth.

Suddenly, the place resembles a scene like ones I've seen in photos in Oscar Payaguala's museum in Comodoro Rivadavia: the flags fluttering on slender poles, ringed by a crowd of people standing in a semi-circle and a group of men on horseback. To the front of the crowd stand the *longkos*, male and female. Among the riders are two small boys, one on a brown horse, the other astride a white one. In the photos in the museum there was also one brown horse and one white. Payaguala even told me why, but I didn't understand, and didn't ask him to explain. I never thought then that I'd get to attend a *ngillatun*.

We stand here, ringed by mountains in the cool morning breeze of an autumn morning in the foothills of the Andes, and I remember my first trip to Gaiman, almost exactly five years before. How nervous I was then, how intimidated by the land, the size of it, the unfamiliarity of the landscape, the country, the continent.

And look what Patagonia has given me: new friends and adventures, horizons as endless as the sky. I'm still nervous and often timid. I probably will be for the rest of my life. But this is what Patagonia has taught me: to listen less to the voice of fear, and more to the enticing murmur of 'Why not?'

The *trutruka* sounds and the *longkos* beat a rhythm on their *kultrung*, and as many women as there are flagpoles go forward with buckets full of a mixture of what they later tell me is *chicha*, maize beer, and wheat. Each kneels down at the foot of a flagpole and ladles this mixture onto the ground. It looks like a gesture of gratitude, or perhaps a gift in exchange for the assistance they ask for. When they're done, the next half a dozen comes forward, and the next after them, while the men play a melody on *pillilkas*, little clay pipes, and the old ladies beat a rhythm on their *kultrungs*.

I get a little caught up in the spirit of it all myself. If I'm ever able to write this down and make it into a book and get it published, I decide, I will travel back to this place and bury a copy in the earth of Patagonia: as my thank you to *Madre Tierra, Ñuke Mapu*, Mother Earth, for showing me so many wonders.

The sun comes up over the mountains and floods the tableland with warmth and light; and the horsemen thunder round the circle another three times, and all the Mapuche lift up their balled fists and shout their triumph and their challenge into the light.

Afterwards, everybody takes off their ceremonial cloaks and headbands. They become ordinary pieces of cloth again and go back into the black bin liner, until the next ceremony.

Valentín and the other young men see to the horses, then light the fire again and roast the remains of last night's sheep. Doña Natalia stokes the cast-iron stove and heats water for *maté*.

Everybody has lunch – it's mid-day by now – and I eat bread and *maté*. Catalina and I strike the tent, pack our few belongings and say our good-byes to the company. An old lady, one of the *longkos*, gives us both a rib-crushing hug and a dazzling, toothless smile.

We join the steady trickle of folk making for the road, most of them on foot this time; it's an easy walk downhill. Only the *abuelos* travel on horseback again, gnarled old men and women riding nonchalantly, one foot supported by a stirrup and the other dangling free; they hold the reins loosely in one hand and with the other give us a cheery wave as they go past.

Before we know it, we're at the foot of the hill, by the bridge and Catalina's car. Standing here now, one foot still in the hills and one on the road to Esquel, it seems hard to believe that in a couple of days' time, I'll be in Buenos Aires, on my way to the airport and home.

'You'll come back,' says Catalina. It's not a question; it's a simple statement of fact.

We speed towards the mountains of Esquel, the car incredibly fast on the bumpy gravel road after a couple of days of moving at walking pace only.

It's the end of one journey.

The beginning of another.

Select Bibliography

María Teresa Boschin & Rodolfo Magin Casamiquela (eds.), *Patagonia: 13.000 años de historia*, Buenos Aires 2001

Curapil Curruhuinca & Luís Roux, *Sayhueque: el último cacique*, Buenos Aires 1986

Fundacion Ameghino (ed.), *Los Galeses en la Patagonia*, Trelew 2004

Víctor M. Gavilán Pinto, *La Nación Mapuche. Puelmapu ke gulumapu,* Santiago de Chile 2007

Olivia Hughes de Mulhall (ed.), *John Murray Thomas: pequeño hombre pero gran heroe para la historia de Chubut*, Trelew 1999

William Hughes, *A Orillas del Río Chubut*, Rawson 1993

Lewis Jones, *La Colonia Galesa*, Rawson 1993

Thomas Jones (Glan Camwy), *Historia de los Comienzos de la Colonia en la Patagonia*, Trelew 1999

Eluned Morgan, *Hacia los Andes*, Rawson 1991

George Chaworth Musters, *At Home with the Patagonians*, Stroud 2005

Lesie Ray, *Language of the Land: The Mapuche in Argentina and Chile*, Copenhagen 2007

Sergio Sepiturka & Jorge Miglioli, *Rocky Trip – La Ruta de los Galeses en la Patagonia/The Route of the Welsh in Patagonia*, Buenos Aires 2004

Cathrin Williams, *Y Wladfa yn dy Boced,* Caernarfon 2000

Glyn Williams, *The Desert and the Dream*, Cardiff 1975

Glyn Williams, 'Welsh Settlers and Native Americans in Patagonia', in *Journal of Latin American Studies* II/I 1979(b)

Notes

1. http://owain.vaughan.com/1535c26
2. quoted in Matthew Arnold, *On the Study of Celtic Literature*. Smith, Elder & Co., London, 1867, p.3
3. quoted in Rhys Mwyn', Cenedl wedi'i gorchfygu yn dioddef diffyg hyder', *Daily Post*, Liverpool 14 Feb 2007
4. R. Bryn Williams, *Y Wladfa*, Gwasg Prifysgol Cymru Caerdydd, 1962, p. 4
5. quoted in Cathrin Williams, *Y Wladfa yn dy Boced*, Caernarfon 2000, p. 35
6. quoted in R. Bryn Williams, *Y Wladfa*, p.22
7. Thomas Jones (Glan Camwy), *Historia de los Comienzos de la Colonia en la Patagonia*, Trelew 1999, p.60
8. Peter N. Williams, *A Brief History of Wales* http://waleshistoryandculture. com/wales/wales30.html
9. William Hughes, *A Orillas del Río Chubut*, Rawson, 1993, p.30
10. Jan Morris, *The Matter of Wales*, London, 1986, p.343
11. Thomas Jones, *Historia de los Comienzos de la Colonia,* Trelew, 1999, pp. 79-80
12. Glyn Williams, *The Desert and the Dream*, Cardiff, 1975, p.56
13. George Chaworth Musters, *At Home with the Patagonians*, (reprint) Stroud, 2005, p.64
14. Hughes, *A Orillas*, p.59
15. Musters, *Patagonians*, p.151
16. entry 29 Jan 1834; ed. John van Wyhe, Genesis Publications 1979. http://darwin-online.org.uk/content/frameset?viewtype=text&itemID =EHBeagleDiary&keywords=falkland&pageseq=304)
17. Curapil Curruhuinca & Luís Roux, *Sayhueque, el último cacique*, Buenos Aires, 1986, p.50
18. Víctor M. Gavilán Pinto, *La Nación Mapuche. Puelmapu ke gulumapu*, Santiago de Chile 2007, p.18
19. quoted in John Pilkington, *An Englishman in Patagonia*, London, 1991, p.1
20. Glyn Williams. 'Welsh Settlers and Native Americans in Patagonia', in: *Journal of Latin American Studies* II/I. 1979(b), p.47
21. quoted in William Casnodyn Rhys, *A Welsh Song in Patagonia – Memories of the Welsh Colonization in Patagonia*, Lulu.com 1995, p.22
22. Williams, *Settlers*, pp.46-47
23. unublished document, 'Letter from a Patagonian Cacique', Falklands Islands Archives, Inclosure 7 in No. 17
24. Williams, *Desert*, p.100
25. 'Letter from a Patagonian Cacique'
26. Geraint D. Owen, *Crisis in Chubut,* Swansea, 1977, p.17
27. Williams, *Y Wladfa*, pp.11-12
28. Williams, *Desert*, p.57

30. quoted in *Rocky Trip – La Ruta de los Galeses en la Patagonia/The Route of the Welsh in Patagonia*, Sergio Sepiturka & Jorge Miglioli, Grupo Abierto Comunicaciones, Buenos Aires, 2004, p.53
30. Williams, *Settlers*, p.57
31. *Rocky Trip*, p.51
32. Hughes, *Orillas*, p. 1
33. Stella Maris Dodd, *Gaiman – Fotográfias*, Gaiman/Buenos Aires, 1988 (no page numbers)
34. Morgan, *Andes*, , p.11
35. *ibid.*
36. Curruhuinca & Roux, *Sayhueque*, p.22
37. Williams, *Settlers*, p.47
38. quoted in José Bengoa, *Historia del pueblo mapuche*, Santiago de Chile, 2000, p.142
39. Curruhuinca & Roux, *Sayhueque*, p.64
40. Marcelo Gavirati, 'Galeses y "Tehuelches": aspectos étnicos, políticos y económicos, poco conocidos de sus relaciones' in: Fundacion Ameghino (ed.), *Los Galeses en a Patagonia*, p.80
41. quoted in Isabel Hernández, *Los Mapuches: Derechos Humanos y Aborigenes*, Buenos Aires, 2001, p.58
42. Doering, Adolfo, *Informe oficial de la Comisión científica agregada al Estado Mayor General de la Expedición al Río Negro (Patagonia), realizado en los meses de abril, mayo y junio de 1879*. Buenos Aires, 1881, p.117
43. Curruhuinca & Roux, *Sayhueque*, p. 10; Jones, *Colonia*, p.136
44. Boschin & Casamiquela, *Patagonia*, p.254
45. quoted in Williams, *Settlers*, p.59
46. *ibid.* pp.60-61
47. Boschin & Casamiquela, *Patagonia*, p.180
48. Curruhuinca & Roux, *Sayhueque*, p.147
49. Boschin & Casamiquela, *Patagonia*, p.181
50. Curruhuinca & Roux, *Sayhueque*, p.53
51. Document held in the historic archives of the Argentine military, quoted in María Teresa Boschin & Rofolfo Magin Casamiquela (eds.), *Patagonia, 13.000 años de historia*, Buenos Aires 2001, p.193
52. J.C. Walther, *La Conquista del Desierto*, Buenos Aires 1976, p.554
53. Williams. *Settlers*, p.61
54. Helmut Schindler, *Bauern und Reiterkrieger*, Munich, 1990, p.35
55. Lewis Jones, *La Colonia Galesa*, Rawson 1993, p.214
56. Jens Andermann, *The Optic of the State: Visuality and Power in Argentina and Brazil*, Pittsburgh, 2007, p.55
57. quoted in: Milciades Alejo Vignati, Iconografía Aborigen: *Los Caciques Sayeweque, Inacayal y Foyel y sus Allegados*. Revista del Museo de La Plata, 1942 vol. II, p.25

58. Lesie Ray, *Language of the Land: The Mapuche in Argentina and Chile*, Copenhagen, 2007, p.79

59. Andermann, *Optic*, p.55

60. Williams, *Desert*, p.100

61. *ibid.*, p.104

62. Eluned Morgan, *Hacia los Andes*, Rawson 1991, p.37; Hughes, *Orillas*, pp.74ff; Jones, *Colonia Galesa* p.141; *Patagonia, 13.000 años de historia*, p.218

63. Morgan, *Andes*, p.32

64. Bruce Chatwin, *In Patagonia*, London, 1977, p.36

65. John Locke Blake, *A Story of Patagonia*, Lewes, 2003, p.85

66. Erick Betanzos, 'La figura indígena en la literatura argentina', in: *Diálogo Ibero Americano* #9 May/June 1997. p.34. (http://dialogo.ugr.es/anteriores/dial09/34-9.htm); Ray, Language, p.80

67. Morgan, *Andes*, p.35

68. Williams, *Settlers*, pp.61-62

69. Olivia Hughes de Mulhall (ed.), *John Murray Thomas: pequeño hombre pero gran heroe para la historia de Chubut*, Trelew 1999, p.17

70. *ibid.* p.33

71. *ibid.* pp.78 ff

72. quoted in Federico Mihura Seeber et al., *El proceso de poblamiento de la región patagónica,* Buenos Aires, 2002, p.14

73. Sepiturka & Miglioli, *Rocky Trip*, p.148

74. Williams, *Settlers*, p.60

75. Hughes, *Orillas*, p.188

76. Morgan, *Andes*, p.52

77. Ray, *Language*, p.111

78. Decreto 105137 del 5/5/1937. IAC, Exp. 5754-1947 (781). Tercer Cuerpo, F. 361. quoted in Walter Delrio, *Mecanismos de tribalización en la patagonia. Desde la gran crisis al primer gobierno peronista, Memoria americana* #13, 2005, http://www.scielo.org.ar/scielo.php?script=sci_art text&pid=S1851-37512005000100008

79. Karin Ceballos Betancur in *Frankfurter Rundschau*, 11/04/2002

80. Pauline Bartolone, *In Sheep's Clothing*, 2004, http://www.inthesetimes.com/site/main/article/414/

81. 'Tierra de Alguien', paper published by Mesa de Trabajo de los Pueblos Indígenas de Argentina, Instituto del Tercer Mundo, Montevideo, Uruguay, 2003 http://enlinea.guiadelmundo.org.uy/informes/informe_ 39.htm

82. Ray, *Language* p.92

83. Law No. 25.607, article 75, passed 6 July 2002 http://www.iadb.org /SDS/IND/ley/leyn/topicset.cfm?country=AR&topic=8&mark=1%E2%8 C%A9=ES

84. Luiz Enrique López & Inge Sichra, *Educação em Áreas Indígenas da*

América Latina: balanços e perspectivas; in: Educação na diversidade: experiências e desafios na Educação Intercultural Bilíngüe, UNESCO report, ed. Ignácio Hernaiz, Brasilia, 2007, p. 103

85. Jones, *Comienzos*, Trelew, 1999, p. 34

The Author

Born and brought up in Germany, Imogen Herrad has also lived in London and in Argentina, and currently divides her time between Cardiff and Cologne. She writes in German and English. Her short stories and articles (in English) have been published in magazines and anthologies in Wales, Canada and the US. She is the author of *The Woman Who Loved an Octopus and other stories*, a collection of stories about female Celtic saints. Her programmes for German public radio (in German) include pieces about the Queen of Sheba, Morgan le Fay, Zora Neale Hurston, the Mapuche people of Patagonia, and the cultural histories of sheep, dragons, the apple and hermaphrodites, respectively.

Acknowledgements

Writing is not nearly as much a solitary pursuit as one might think. I could never have written this book without the assistance of more people than I can name here. First and most importantly, my heartfelt thanks to all who told me their stories, particularly those who shared difficult and sometimes painful tales.

Mis agradecimientos cariñosísimos a todos y todas que me contaron sus historias. Para su generosa hospidalidad les agradezco de mi corazón a la Familia Fermín, Rini Griffith, María Luisa y Gonzalo Huincaleo, Marli Pugh de Villoria y Rodolfo Villoria. Les agradezco por contestar a mis tantas preguntas a Ambrosio Ainqueó, Fabio Gonzalez, Rini Griffith, Vali James de Irianni, Mauro Millán y Oscar Payaguala.

I'm very grateful to Academi Gymreig/Literature Wales for selecting me for their mentoring scheme, and to Simon Rees who provided the mentoring. Without his brio, encouragement and ruthless feedback my Patagonian experiences would probably still be part untidy manuscript, part even more untidy memories in my head. Richard Davies did much to knock the result into shape, for which I owe him many thanks. I'm grateful to my publisher Mick Felton for his enthusiasm for my work and for gently ironing out the remaining bumps.

And, as ever, my thanks go to my friends for keeping the faith and for believing in me, particularly at those times when I did not. I am extremely fortunate to have all of them in my life: Donna Collier, Sandra Ebert, Judith Fessler, Alexa Lazar, Anne Massagee, Vanina Mobilia, Liz Morgan, Lindsay River, Meena Siyani, Ellis Suzanna Slack, Lola Sparkle, Penny Taylor, Lesley Trenkel and Frank Zitka.

Lastly, I cannot remember her name, but I'd like to thank whoever it was said Bydd 'na rhywun yn siarad am Batagonia yn y coleg heno all those years ago in a kitchen in Aberystwyth, for telling me about Patagonia and its Welsh inhabitants and putting the first seed of the mad idea of going there into my head.